The Manual of
Museum Learning

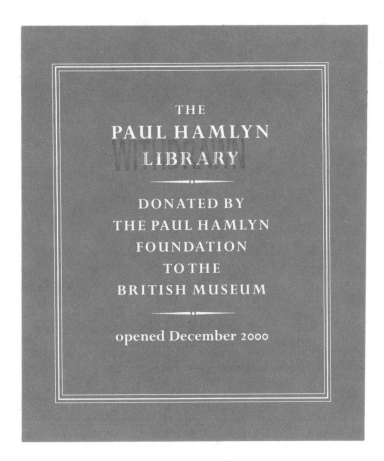

The Manual of
Museum Learning

Edited by Barry Lord

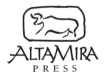

A Division of
ROWMAN & LITTLEFIELD PUBLISHERS, INC.
Lanham • New York • Toronto • Plymouth, UK

AltaMira Press
A division of Rowman & Littlefield Publishers, Inc.
A wholly owned subsidiary of The Rowman & Littlefield Publishing Group, Inc.
4501 Forbes Boulevard, Suite 200
Lanham, MD 20706
www.altamirapress.com

Estover Road
Plymouth PL6 7PY
United Kingdom

British Library Cataloguing in Publication Information Available

Library of Congress Cataloguing-in-Publication Data

The manual of museum learning / edited by Barry Lord.
    p. cm.
  ISBN-13: 978-0-7591-0970-4 (cloth : alk. paper)
  ISBN-10: 0-7591-0970-2 (cloth : alk. paper)
  ISBN-13: 978-0-7591-0971-1 (pbk. : alk. paper)
  ISBN-10: 0-7591-0971-0 (pbk. : alk. paper)
  1. Museums—Educational aspects. 2. Museums—Public relations.
 3. Museums and schools. I. Lord, Barry, 1939–
 AM7.M36 2007
 069'.15—dc22   2007003783

Printed in the United States of America

♾™ The paper used in this publication meets the minimum requirements of
American National Standard for Information Sciences—Permanence of Paper for
Printed Library Materials, ANSI/NISO Z39.48-1992.

Contents

List of Figures and Tables

FIGURES

TABLE

Preface

> "In 1949–1950, I was enrolled in the Saturday Morning Class at the Royal Ontario Museum. The kids were taken to see something—an artifact, a mummy, a dinosaur—and then we did things with paint and paper and glue and sticks and clay that were supposed to be inspired by what we'd learned. After that I was able to run all over the Museum with my pal, whose father worked there as a Greek and Roman archaeologist. It was magic! I've loved museums ever since."

This recollection by the novelist Margaret Atwood, published in the Ontario Museum Association's 2006 *Insider's Guide to Ontario Museums*, eloquently evokes the experience of museum learning. Not only did the budding writer learn about mummies, dinosaurs, and ancient archaeology but, perhaps even more important, she also imbibed a lifelong love of museums at the institution where such enjoyable learning could take place.

Heather Maximea's contribution in chapter 8 of this book sets Ms. Atwood's experience in historical perspective, as Heather recalls the struggle to establish such museum classes in Toronto's ROM through the first half of the twentieth century. Such learning experiences are the fruit of the labor of many generations of dedicated museum educators, who often had to establish our discipline in the face of indifference—or even hostility—from academics, directors, and curators.

Looking globally at learning in museums, we should not think that the struggle is by any means resolved. As Dr. Claudia Haas records in chapter 4, a positive orientation toward the visitor experience of a family with young children is of quite recent date in the museums of many countries. In too many places, it is still very common to see long lines of Chinese children being marched in two-by-two columns through museum galleries, barely able to glance at the artifacts in wall cases as they patrol the perimeter, striving to keep in step. On the other hand, there are leaders in the field in many countries, such as the brilliant children's museums in Manila and Mexico City.

Nevertheless, the voluminous literature on museum learning in the last half of the twentieth century indicates that, in general, as a global profession we have come a long way toward a more systematic—some would say scientific—

approach to learning in museums. Since there are many sources for that body of learning, the bibliography provided in this book has been deliberately limited to publications since 2000—yet even such a tentative beginning on the books and articles of this young century suggests the rich and well-informed level of research and professional practice that characterizes the field of museum learning today.

This manual, like the others in the series written or edited by my wife and partner Gail Dexter Lord and myself, and published by AltaMira, is intended as a practical guide to the provision of successful learning experiences in museums and related institutions such as public galleries, exhibition centers, science centers, zoos, botanical gardens, aquaria, and planetaria. It is based on an understanding of museum learning as an experience that occurs within a personal, social, and physical context, as masterfully analyzed by John Falk and Lynn Dierking in their book, *Learning in Museums*, also published by AltaMira (2000). Their concept of the Contextual Learning Model informs every page of this volume, which sets out to explore why, for whom, and how these contexts can be orchestrated in museum galleries with optimal results. Since Falk and Dierking's book so thoroughly presents the theoretical basis for museum learning, it is possible for this book to focus on these three fundamental questions that arise from the professional practice of museums.

Hence the three sections in which our chapters are presented:

- Part I, Why, aims to identify what museum learning is, why it matters, and its possibilities for enhancing the future of museums, and of our civilization.
- Part II, Who, explores the range of both child and adult museum learners today, probing the potential to enhance the relevance and effectiveness of the museum experience.
- Part III, How, documents the means at our disposal to achieve these results—the volunteers, professional staff, space and facilities, policies and plans, new technologies, evaluation procedures, and marketing techniques that are vital to making a museum learning program work.

The book is titled the *Manual of Museum Learning*, rather than *Museum Education*, because our focus is on the learning experience of the museum visitor or the user of our programs. The education departments of museums that provide such experiences are of course referenced on every page. But in their practice over more than a century, museum professionals have come to understand that it is the visitor, in the final analysis, bringing his or her expectations, beliefs, and values to the experiences on offer, who must be the center of our attention.

With this focus in mind, it is necessary to acknowledge—and even celebrate—the fact that many visitors come to our museums with no conscious intent to learn. Many writers on museum learning correctly stress the importance of the visitors' motivation. But what is the motivation of concertgoers? It is usually not primarily to learn about Beethoven or the Rolling Stones, but to enjoy and appreciate the music being performed. Similarly, the motivation of many museum visitors is simply to enjoy and appreciate the great works of art, the remarkable archaeological artifacts or natural history specimens, or the dazzling interactive exhibitions on view. Important learning takes place, but in a milieu that is predominantly aesthetic.

This is the joy of museums—the integration of great aesthetic and intellectual experiences with learning opportunities that can inspire us through a lifetime. Like the young Margaret Atwood, we not only learn the specific subject matter of the exhibitions, but we learn to love the experience of exploration and discovery that museums offer. This book is intended to help those who facilitate that experience to see more clearly why, for whom, and how they can best accomplish this noble enterprise.

Acknowledgments

A book on museum learning published in the early twenty-first century owes its first debt to the thousands of museum educators, both volunteer and professional, who have worked over more than a century to establish our discipline, initially in the face of resistance or at least skepticism from some academics and curators, and almost always despite constrained space, equipment, and funds. This book in particular is indebted to the volunteers and professionals with whom I have worked at museums and public galleries, originally in Canada, and more recently, around the world, in my capacity as president of Lord Cultural Resources.

Among the many distinguished participants in the worldwide process of practice and debate, I am especially grateful to those who have consented to be contributors to this volume, sharing their experience, imagination, and dedication to museum learning. Brief descriptions of each of them are provided in the "About the Editor and Contributors" section.

I am also grateful for the assistance of my current and former colleagues at Lord Cultural Resources, particularly Angela Brayham, who worked tirelessly with the contributors in the earlier stages of preparation of the manuscript, and Kristen Hawkeswood, who took over from her and also assembled the illustrations. Together with Mary Jo Megginson, Kristen is also responsible for the bibliography. Boyd Laanstra assisted with corrections to the manuscript, Laura McGowan prepared the index, and my executive assistant Mira Ovanin handled much of the correspondence with the contributors and others.

As always, our publishers have been splendidly supportive. Serena Krombach's creative approach to our publishing program has been inspirational, and I am particularly grateful to Claire Rojstaczer of Rowman & Littlefield for her patience and understanding.

Finally, I must thank my wife and partner, Gail Dexter Lord, who has been my inspiration, professionally and personally, for almost forty years. This book is dedicated to her.

About the Editor and Contributors

Dr. Michael L. Bentley retired in 2006 from the science education faculty of the University of Tennessee. His thirty-seven-year career has included teaching at the elementary, middle school, and high school levels as well as work in science museum education, school administration, and state-level curriculum supervision. His latest book is *Teaching Constructivist Science, K–8: Nurturing Natural Investigators in the Standards-Based Classroom* (2007).

Dr. Spencer R. Crew spends his life making history accessible. On November 5, 2001, he was appointed president of the National Underground Railroad Freedom Center in Cincinnati, Ohio, and has built the cultural institution from the ground up. He is the past chair of the National Council for History Education and serves on the boards of the National Trust for Historic Preservation, the American Association of Museums, and the Brown Alumni Association. He has published extensively in the areas of African American history and public history.

Maria Fernández Sabau is cofounder of Lordcultura, Spain's leading cultural planning company, with Gail Dexter Lord and Barry Lord. An economist by background, she has specialized in strategic planning for museums. She collaborates regularly with universities and speaks at conferences about the importance of understanding visitor needs and the key role of learning in the creation of successful museums and cultural developments.

Mira Goldfarb is a senior consultant with Lord Cultural Resources, and in that capacity has participated in planning for museum learning on many assignments since joining the firm in 2002. A former curator and museum educator, she previously directed the public tour program at the Whitney Museum of American Art in New York.

Barbara Gordon is the director of adult education at the Chicago Architecture Foundation, where she has been directing the docent programs and public programs since 1995. She holds a master's degree in adult education from National–Louis University, Chicago.

Elaine Heumann Gurian is the senior consultant and advisor to a number of national and international museums and visitor centers, both governmental and private, that are beginning, building, or reinventing themselves. Previously, Ms. Gurian served as the deputy director for a number of museums. In 2004, she was named recipient of the Distinguished Service to Museums Award, America's most important museum honor, presented by the American Association of Museums. In 2006, she was appointed scholar-in-residence at the University of Michigan. A collection of her essays, *Civilizing the Museum*, was published in 2006. She lectures and teaches widely, and has held many elected positions within the national and international museum community.

Dr. Claudia Haas is an authority on the planning and management of cultural facilities, and formerly a senior consultant and now a preferred partner with Lord Cultural Resources. With her Ph.D. in art history, Dr. Haas's previous experience ranges from the art world of Europe and New York to her dynamic role as founder and first director of ZOOM, Vienna's Children's Museum. Fluent in several languages, she has advised on the development of cultural and learning programs for museums in Austria, Germany, Switzerland, Italy, France, and Egypt.

Caroline Harris holds a B.A. in art history with an emphasis in medieval art from the University of Maryland, and master's and doctoral degrees from the University of Virginia. She completed her dissertation, "Le Violon de Delacroix: Musicality and Modernist Aesthetics," in 2004. She is curator of education and academic programs at the Princeton University Art Museum. Before coming to Princeton, she served as staff lecturer in charge of academic affairs at the Philadelphia Museum of Art. She has taught art history at the University of the Arts in Philadelphia and at the University of Virginia in Charlottesville. Her area of expertise is nineteenth-century painting.

Amy Kaufman is a senior consultant and director of U.S. operations at Lord Cultural Resources, specializing in business plans and strategic planning, organizational development, marketing, and operational implementation. Ms. Kaufman's recent clients include the International Center of Photography, the Orange County Museum of Art, the Denver Art Museum, the Brooklyn Museum, the Chicago Botanic Garden, and Constitution Hill in Johannesburg, where she served as project manager and acting director. She is the former director of visitor services at the Solomon R. Guggenheim Museum in New York.

Dr. Brad King is a principal at Lord Cultural Resources, combining his experience in museum collection analysis with his extensive work in market analysis and financial projections for museums. Based in Toronto, he holds a Ph.D. in history from the University of Toronto and has worked with numerous museum educators, teachers, and school district leaders across North America and in Asia, as part of the company's professional practice.

Sara Knelman is the curator of contemporary art at the Art Gallery of Hamilton in Ontario, Canada. She holds an M.A. in art history from the Courtauld Institute in London, and formerly worked as a consultant for Lord Cultural Resources in England and Canada, and with the Jane Corkin Gallery in Toronto.

Martin Lawrence is head of gallery learning at the Natural History Museum in London. He is responsible for a team of staff developing and delivering science engagement resources and programs, including Nature Live, Investigate, and Earth Lab at the NHM.

Barry Lord, with his wife and partner Gail Dexter Lord, is cofounder and copresident of Lord Cultural Resources, the world's largest firm specializing in the planning of museums and related cultural institutions, dedicated to creating cultural capital worldwide. The Lords coauthored *The Manual of Museum Management* (1997), and coedited *The Manual of Museum Planning* (2nd ed. 1999) and *The Manual of Museum Exhibitions* (2002), all published by AltaMira Press. Mr. Lord has directed hundreds of museum planning and management assignments in North America, Asia, Africa, and Europe, including his recent work for the Louvre in Paris. Before the foundation of the company in 1981, he was well known in Canada as a curator and art critic, and in 1970–1972 served as the head of education services for the National Gallery of Canada in Ottawa.

Gail Dexter Lord is copresident (with Barry Lord) of Lord Cultural Resources. She coauthored *The Manual of Museum Management* (1997), and coedited *The Manual of Museum Planning* (2nd ed. 1999) and *The Manual of Museum Exhibitions* (2002). Her most recent publication, coauthored with Kate Markert, is *The Manual of Strategic Planning for Museums* (2007), also published by AltaMira Press. Ms. Lord has conducted museum planning and management assignments across North America and Europe, including assisting in the development of new cultural institutions like the Lowry in Salford, England, The Museum of the African Diaspora in San Francisco, and the Canadian Museum for Human Rights in Winnipeg which are dedicated to lifelong learning. Before founding the company Gail was an art critic, cultural animator, and college lecturer; today she is in demand as an inspiring speaker on cultural planning subjects around the world.

Heather Maximea is a senior consultant specializing in facility planning with Lord Cultural Resources. Based in White Rock near Vancouver, B.C., she wrote the chapters on facilities planning for *The Manual of Museum Planning* (2nd ed. 1999), and *The Manual of Museum Exhibitions* (2002), both published by AltaMira Press. Ms. Maximea was formerly a registrar and documentation specialist at the Royal Ontario Museum in Toronto, and holds degrees in anthropology and museum studies, as well as certificates in interior design and archives management.

Danielle Melville, as a political science and law graduate, has a firm grounding in South Africa's political, social, and economic environment. She began her professional career in communications and public relations in Cape Town with a focus on new empowerment business initiatives and related corporate citizenship projects across diverse sectors including the arts, property, and mining. At Constitution Hill in Johannesburg, she was in charge of public program development, which included strategic content development, the establishment of public/private partnerships, relationship management, and fundraising. She currently works as an account director at a global communications firm focusing on travel, tourism, and telecommunications.

Dr. Elisabeth Menasse-Wiesbauer holds a Ph.D. from the University of Vienna; her research there focused on the history of childhood and history of science. On behalf of the Austrian Federal Ministry of Science and Education she was responsible for the organization of the research program Xenophobia. Dr. Menasse-Wiesbauer has been the director of ZOOM Children's Museum in Vienna since 2003.

Toni Parker is the Reaching Out, Drawing In project manager at the National Portrait Gallery, London. She is currently on leave.

Keri Ryan is a senior program manager at the Art Gallery of Ontario, and is currently involved in managing the installation of a suite of galleries in the new AGO designed by the leading Canadian-born architect Frank Gehry. She was formerly a consultant with Lord Cultural Resources, in which capacity she managed the production of the Trinidad and Tobago version of the Go Creative exhibition, among many other assignments. She previously worked on the interpretative and educational aspects of exhibitions at museums in Canada and New Zealand.

Dr. Barbara J. Soren is an educator who has been working with museums and science centers, performing arts organizations, community organizations, health care facilities, and schools since the mid-1970s. Her consulting work, research, and teaching have focused on lifelong learning and human development, understanding experiences that individuals have in museums, arts, and community organizations, and evaluating quality online museum user experiences. Dr. Soren currently is program coordinator of the museum studies program at the University of Toronto and teaches a course there called Museums and their Publics.

Hugh A. D. Spencer was a senior principal at Lord Cultural Resources from 1987 to 2007, focused on interpretative planning for museums. He has written the chapters on interpretative planning for exhibitions for *The Manual of Museum Planning* (2nd ed. 1999) and *The Manual of Exhibition Planning* (2002), both published by AltaMira Press. As a writer of fiction and radio drama, he has had original work published and produced both in print and electronic media.

Susan M. Taylor has been director of the Princeton University Art Museum since 2000. Since that time, she has reinstalled the museum's galleries of Western art and significantly strengthened the museum's permanent collection. In addition, she founded the museum's first department of education. She is a member of the advisory committee for the Center for Arts and Cultural Policy Studies, the President's Advisory Committee on Architecture, and she recently served on the President's Task Force on the Creative and Performing Arts. Ms. Taylor holds degrees from Vassar College and the Institute of Fine Arts at New York University

Charlie Walter joined the Fort Worth Museum of Science and History in 1986 as the museum's first visitor services manager. He currently is chief operating officer of the museum, where he fosters systems thinking and a learning culture in the museum's operations. He has a B.Sc. in wildlife and fisheries science with an emphasis on museum science from Texas A&M University, and an MBA from the University of North Texas. He is currently chair of the Association of Science and Technology Centres' Annual Conference Program Planning Committee, a board member of the Association of Children's Museums, an American Association of Museums Accreditation Visiting Committee member, and an advisor for the National Center for Informal Learning and Schools.

PART I:
WHY
The Rationale for Museum Learning

Introduction

BARRY LORD

Why does museum learning matter? Learning in museums or from museums might be regarded as a pleasant but relatively marginal activity, akin to working crossword puzzles or a passion for Scrabble. This book suggests a much more significant role for museum learning, an activity that is at the heart of building the kind of world we can and indeed must have in the twenty-first century. Museum learning is a vital component of the lifelong learning that we now perceive as essential to the development of both the individual and his or her society.

Gail Dexter Lord's opening chapter accordingly situates lifelong learning in the context of the creation and maintenance of a civil society. Gail identifies museums as successful participants in the past century's communications revolution, describing them as institutions whose unique medium of communication is the display of objects in three-dimensional space. Yet as Gail observes, museums have also been in the forefront of utilizing all other media of the communications revolution to enhance their own unique capacities, particularly in the interpretation of the meanings of these objects.

Because they are the communications medium that is most deeply immersed in the three-dimensional world around them, Gail suggests that museums can be crucial in helping to establish an environment of lifelong learning as the basis for a creative community. Such a community can become what is now called a "creative city," a thriving center of the knowledge economy that is today the social and economic motor of public life all over the world. Thus it is no accident that as Gulf States cities such as Dubai, Abu Dhabi, and Doha have determined to play a greater role in the global knowledge economy, they have each embarked on museum-building programs, just as Singapore did in the 1990s.

Gail further suggests that through their provision of lifelong learning, museums can become "cultural accelerators." In this role they can be at the center of the ongoing endeavor to create a civil society—one based on tolerance, respect for human rights, and on open discourse rather than repressive control.

In this context my own chapter 2 sets out to define what museum-based learning is. Some examples of museum learning are cited—how museums have influenced artists or scientists, and how museums can serve the communities of origin of their collections. Yet most important for our purposes is to understand museum-based learning for the rest of us, an informal, voluntary, mostly nonacademic activity focused on the evidence that objects—artifacts, specimens, archives, and works of art—present to our eyes and minds. Interpretation of those objects and the information technology that increasingly delivers that interpretation are important contributors to the learning experience, but at the basis of the experience, at least for all collecting institutions, are the objects in the museum collection. These objects may be presented didactically—as evidence of a thesis—or simply for themselves, to be enjoyed, understood, and appreciated for their inherent meanings as perceived by the museum visitor or user.

In chapter 3, the distinguished museum theorist Elaine Heumann Gurian goes beyond what museum learning is today to project its potential as the twenty-first century continues to unfold. Elaine sketches the possibilities of an even greater role for museum learning, so that museums might become what she calls "essential," rather than merely important, institutions. On the model of the public library—and with a nod to the publicly open character of the shopping mall as another example of public accessibility—Elaine points to the far greater potential of transforming the museum into an essential public institution of everyday reference and relevance. She particularly suggests that smaller local or regional museums may be in the best position to accomplish this transformation. In his case study in chapter 3, Martin Lawrence describes a challenging step in this direction that has been taken by a very large institution, Britain's Natural History Museum, in its exciting new Darwin Centre.

By defining museum learning in large or small institutions as instrumental to the building of civil society in the twenty-first century, with the prospect of making museums even more essential in future, the initial section of this book sets the parameters within which the participants in the learning process (part 2, WHO) and the ways in which museum learning happens (part 3, HOW) can be best understood. Our hope is that museums, and the learning that happens in them, can become ever more central to our lives and times.

CHAPTER 1

Museums, Lifelong Learning, and Civil Society

GAIL DEXTER LORD

Museums are huge success stories. The museum is a communication medium that has been functioning continuously for more than two hundred years. As technological change has transformed communication industries from print to radio to television and the Internet, museums have absorbed the technology into their exhibition and work processes, from IMAX to Web sites to podcasting. Museums have been among the early adopters of new communication technologies. What's most amazing is that museums seem to absorb these technologies without fundamentally changing—whether you date museums from the cathedral vault or the princely schatzkammer or the great eighteenth- and nineteenth-century universal collections, they remain powerful public spaces of representation of the leading ideas of their time—based on the study of the objects that they collect and preserve.

The ideas represented aren't always good ideas; sometimes they have been very bad ideas such as eugenics and imperialism, but museums are places where ideas are presented and contested—and have been for hundreds of years. Today, for example, there are at least fifteen initiatives throughout the world to create museums and galleries of immigration or migration to address one of the most pervasive and contested ideas of our time—the free movement of people throughout the world.

Museums are *cultural accelerators*—a term borrowed from communications theorist Derek de Kherkove.[1] Just as the car's accelerator speeds up the vehicle, museums actually intensify our awareness of technological and social change. Museums accelerate our cultural awareness in three ways:

1. by collecting objects that demonstrate change—for example, displaying three hundred years of transportation objects from the oxcart to the jet in a few hundred square meters, intensifying our awareness of change;
2. by interpreting change in ways that help us understand it;

3. by exhibiting works of art—since artists express change in advance of its full impact on the rest of us—so that these works are appreciated as cultural accelerators, celebrating, warning, or deploring the changes around us.

Curiously, museums that are still seen by many as static are just the opposite. They are one of our society's main adaptive strategies for managing change. We see this in some countries in Africa and Asia that are undergoing massive change and that are simultaneously building new museums at an incredible rate. The apprehension of change creates the need for museums not only to preserve the past but to help people adapt to the present and future.

This theme leads to some of the questions affecting the potential of museums for lifelong learning:

- Why do people still think of museums as static places?
- Is it an image or marketing problem?
- Is it that too many museums still operate in a static mold?
- Why don't museums develop a vocabulary of relevance?

1.1 THREE-DIMENSIONAL SPACE

Museums are a unique communication medium because three-dimensional space is their defining characteristic. That place and space matter was brought to my attention in an unlikely location, the monotonous Microsoft campus near Seattle. I was conducting a workshop with some of the workers to get their views on how they might use a new art museum being planned for a nearby community. One of the participants said:

"I spend all day working with a two-dimensional screen. When I get home, I relax in front of another screen. And for entertainment, I watch a bigger screen. For me, three-dimensional space is where I can be creative."

On average, people in technologically advanced societies are spending six hours a day in front of some type of screen, including messaging via cell phone screens.

This goes a long way toward explaining why museum space matters so much to so many today. Museum space is emphatically three-dimensional, punctuated by three-dimensional objects. It is a kinesthetic experience, during which our mere movement seems to change the space, and the place somehow changes us. We wander, we gaze, we browse. Because this is an interpreted space—a place with assigned meanings—we may also be challenged to see things in a new way: to find our own way, at least figuratively.

It is not only the prevalence of the screen that makes us appreciate museum space; it's also the increasing privatization of the public realm through advertising, shopping malls, and corporate office towers that dominate and direct not just our footsteps, but our hearts and minds. We see everywhere the encroachment of the two-dimensional world of billboards, posters, and giant TV screens. The same shops, brand names, logos, and images punctuate urban space the world over. Derelict buildings, historic sites, and contested places have become increasingly important because here, at least, meanings and emotions have not been predetermined by the force of global economics. Does this very spatial quality pose insurmountable challenges for those who are fearful of new and unfamiliar places? The evidence seems to be that magnificent new spaces from the Staatgalerie in Stuttgart to the Museo Guggenheim in Bilbao are capturing the attention of a greater public. But there are still many who are intimidated by these spaces.

And why hasn't the education room made it out of the museum basement? I know of several major art museums undergoing huge expansions—but leaving the education department completely out of the project. Does learning not need beautiful spaces? Do museum educators think in terms of space?

1.2   THE CREATIVE ECONOMY

Museums' employment of three-dimensional space as a medium for lifelong learning is important because museums are a critical success factor in what is referred to as the creative economy. The creative economy (sometimes also called the knowledge economy) consists of science, engineering, research and development (R & D), technology-based industries, arts, music, culture, design, and the knowledge-based professions of healthcare, finance, and law. One hundred years ago, during the era of the industrial economy, less than 10 percent of the population was employed in this way. Today it is 25 to 30 percent of employment in advanced industrial nations. It may account for 50 percent of wages and salaries. This is as huge an economic transformation as we had when moving from an agricultural to an industrial society.

Economist Richard Florida has persuasively argued that creative workers gravitate to certain urban environments because the creative economy depends on access to people and ideas, not to land or natural resources or raw materials. Creative workers can and do move from place to place in pursuit of the best environments in which to work. Richard Florida identifies the characteristics of cities that support the creative economy as "the Three Ts"[2]—talent, tolerance, and technology. He has developed measures for these qualities so that cities and countries can be compared, and these measures bear an interesting correlation to museums:

- *Talent* is measured in terms of the percentage of the population with a B.A. or B.Sc. degree or more, and the number of research scientists per one thousand workers.
- *Tolerance* is evaluated in terms of the openness of a community and the degree to which it has modern values, welcomes gays, diversity, and self-expression.
- *Technology* is measured in terms of the research and development expenditure as a percentage of gross domestic product (GDP), and the number of high tech patents achieved.

Museums are typically employers of highly educated people, and attract visitors from the ranks of the most highly educated. In this sense they can be seen as a talent magnet for the creative economy. Museums can also represent openness to diversity and self-expression. (On the other hand, museums can also represent closed and static ways of thinking.) Museums can be hubs for the creative economy as cultural accelerators, forums for debate, places for the display and creation of new ideas. However, this implies some changes in the ways that museums operate: for example, they need to be dialogic not monologic, and truly open to diversity and interdisciplinary approaches.

It needs to be said that in this new approach to museums there is great potential for conflict, especially where there are more conservative governments, boards, and patrons. As a result, some museums will benefit profoundly from the creative economy, but others will not be part of this new creative economy, except perhaps through cultural tourism. This is a strategic choice that museums need to make now.

Some people think that this notion of the creative economy applies only to a small percentage of the population, say 30 percent in cities, and, therefore, a museum's decision to change in the direction of openness, dialogue, and interdisciplinary activity impacts only an elite group. That would miss a very important point: all human beings are creative—whether or not they work in or earn their living through the creative economy. Lifelong learning is thus for everyone—and museums, because they are open to all, no matter what their level of academic or economic achievement, can be places of lifelong learning for everyone. Maria Fernández Sabau's case study in this chapter of the Laboratorio de las Artes' intergenerational program at the CaixaForum in Barcelona illustrates how artifacts and works of art can be utilized to stimulate ongoing learning among children, adolescents, and adults of all social classes.

To bring forth human creativity requires confidence building, skills training, human networks, civic participation, risk taking, and intercultural understanding. The museum experience and museum learning activities have great potential in each of these areas. Sociologist Robert Putnam[3] has demonstrated that participation in cultural activities is one of the most effective means of creating civil society—by which is meant a society in which people work together to solve problems and create knowledge. An open civil society is the necessary foundation for the creative economy. There is indeed an important link between the creative economy, civil society, and lifelong learning.

This brings us back to museums' defining characteristic—three-dimensional space. Civil society happens in real places—not on television, nor the Internet. These are just some of the tools. The museum occupies a central role in civil society because it is a real place that can influence meaningful change to an even greater depth in the creative economy of the future. To accomplish this objective, the museum must give priority in the use of its spaces—its galleries, classrooms, and auditorium—to achieving lifelong learning for everyone. This is a challenging but attainable goal for museums of the twenty-first century.

NOTES

1. Derek De Kherkove, *The Skin of Culture: Investigating the New Electronic Reality* (Toronto: Somerville House, 1995).

2. Richard Florida and Irene Tinagli, *Europe in the Creative Age*, Carnegie Mellon Software Industry Center and DEMOS (February 2004).

3. Robert Putnam, *Bowling Alone* (Toronto: Simon & Schuster, 2000).

ARTS LAB, CAIXAFORUM BARCELONA
María Fernández Sabau

Cultural inspiration starts with experimentation at the Laboratorio de las Artes (Arts Lab), the learning department of CaixaForum Barcelona. At the Arts Lab each visitor is seen as centrally positioned in the relationship between the work of art and his or her contemporary individual circumstances. Each person's perception of art is different and contemporary to its time. Arts Lab animators use their knowledge of the arts to help visitors organize their own knowledge and understanding of modern and contemporary art through deconstructive exercises. The Arts Lab is a mediator between the audience and the arts; the objective is to experiment with new ideas about art, music, and literature. The essence of the Arts Lab is, as they call it, the "contemporaneity of vision."

At the core of the department is a spirit of change to adapt to new, contemporary realities in which the arts are created and taught. This orientation started with the aim of making contemporary art accessible to new audiences. In doing so, animators discovered the need that audiences have to build relationships with every form of art, so the concept of the artifact was introduced to the Arts Lab activities—artifacts in the Arts Lab are objects of human creation that speak to the public of all times, no matter whether they were created during the third or the twenty-first century.

The Arts Lab, started in 1987, has changed as contemporary times have evolved, and now includes in its program dialogs with the contemporary art collection of La Caixa Foundation as well as with the temporary exhibitions of more traditional or classical art at CaixaForum and other La Caixa Foundation centers. The lab operates on the premise that it is important to learn from our experience of the past, present, and future.

Arts Lab work is based on the fact that every visitor has a personal view, a contemporary vision, on the basis of which he or she dialogs with the objects. Curiosity and respect for each individual are key lab values, in order to integrate what each visitor has to say about his or her personal experience, of each artifact—from an ancient Greek vase to a video installation by Bill Viola—through inspirational activities and workshops.

The Arts Lab works in coordination with other departments of CaixaForum Barcelona, such as Plastic Arts, Music, and Humanities. The program developed by the Arts Lab includes more than six hundred annual activities organized by age, area of interest (plastic and visual arts, music, architecture, or literature), and by exhibition. Its main aims and objectives are to:

- stimulate active audiences who enjoy thinking, watching, and listening
- facilitate an open dialogue and exchange of ideas, especially among younger age groups, as it is fundamental to create connections between each individual's personal experience and the arts
- contribute to the generation of knowledge, providing references and asking questions rather than giving answers
- think about art education in the context of existing school programs, and develop new tools and methodologies to stimulate the formal education sector.

Understanding the relationship and connections between works of art and visitors' contemporary views is fundamental to the planning and development work that the Arts Lab carries out for all its activities. The starting point is always the questioning and reaction that an artifact provokes in people who don't usually have a background or understanding of art. CaixaForum acts as cultural inspiration in the broadest possible sense: it aims to open people's minds to the contemporary reality that surrounds them so that they start asking questions—whether young or old.

The Arts Lab has acquired a high level of knowledge about how visitors' views originate, thanks to several years of experimental work with school children. The lab has developed a very successful and interesting relationship with schools and teachers in the area. In these schools children of different ages are shown four images every week during the course and are asked to talk about what they see in them. The images represent all sorts of artifacts, and there is no right or wrong answer, every comment is useful to the Arts Lab's staff who collect them. This experiment is carried out only with school children, but the Arts Lab finds the responses useful to develop activities for all of its audiences.

The Arts Lab develops active audiences who derive inspiration from the arts to live their daily lives. The workshops promote creative thinking and contacts with reality through which participants get in touch with the arts, the artists, and forms of expression, as well as with new social realities and people of different ages, beyond traditional stereotypes.

Projects like *Distrito 3* (District 3) and its most recent version *Miradas Cruzadas* (Dual Visions) are the Arts Lab flagships. Participants are invited to observe the reality that surrounds them through a walk in the neighborhood or a visit to one of the exhibitions at CaixaForum. In several of its editions *Distrito 3* invited teenagers to think about their lives, district, and perceptions of everyday activities. In a second phase they were asked to select a theme and write, record, or photograph words that linked their themes with the neighborhood. The next stage were workshops at CaixaForum where they experimented with the possibilities offered by the spoken and written word, with the help of adults. In its last edition participants learned how to create and edit videos, and the final results were exhibited at CaixaForum.

Miradas Cruzadas goes beyond geographic boundaries and age, inviting audiences to observe how different generations look at each other in an effort to improve mutual understanding. Portraits of teenagers by the Dutch photographer Reinike Dijkstra started the discussion process that ended with an exhibition of portraits of adults by local youngsters and a Web site where older and younger participants shared their visions of youth and adulthood, discovering that their contemporary visions of life are not so different.

The Arts Lab is a successful example of how learning at museums can go beyond museum boundaries and traditional forms of art to become a source of inspiration for ordinary people who break stereotypes and intellectual barriers to enjoy the arts and experiment with creativity.

CHAPTER 2

What is Museum-Based Learning?

Barry Lord

On at least one occasion, probably more, during the first decade of the twentieth century, Pablo Picasso went into the basement of what was then the Musée de Trocadero in Paris. What he learned there about the art of Africa changed the course of art history.

What did Picasso learn, and how did he learn it? We can probably never say definitively, since much of his experience was necessarily subjective, but certainly we know enough to be able to identify his learning in objective art historical terms. Picasso saw how the bold forms of carved wood in the African statues and masks represented the structure of the figure or face more expressively and more tellingly than the academic principles of representation that he had learned as a student but had already surpassed. He also liked the African artists' forthright use of mixed materials. He perceived that the power of these forms realized something he had been reaching for in his own art. He was able to integrate this insight with his own practice of art to develop what we now recognize as the founding principles of Cubism, from which sprang so many subsequent forms of modern art history.

These principles included a structural revelation of the subject through interlocking planes comparable to the African artists' bold forms, and a direct use of collage to achieve a two- or three-dimensional image with an inspired mix of materials, similar to the African artists' combinations. Nevertheless, what Picasso did with these ideas was indisputably his own, because he was able to integrate these influences with the direction that his own work was already taking. He might have arrived at the threshold of Cubism without this experience, but probably not with the same clarity, freshness, power, and insight as we can observe in *Les Demoiselles d'Avignon* and subsequent works.

Picasso's learning was made possible and was conditioned by two factors:

1. The museum's display of African carvings, which were actually presented as ethnographic artifacts.
2. Picasso's own interests arising from his work at that time.

So we are reminded that we can only learn from museums what we are ready to learn. Friedrich Wilhelm Nietzsche observed that one learns from books only what one already knows. This is not quite true of learning in museums, because there is always the spark of something new—yet it is true in the sense that we can only recognize and respond to that spark if we are ready for it because of the ideas, interests, attitudes, and concerns that we take to the museum.

And we may be impressed by the fact that the museum's interpretation of its collections—in this case as ethnographic artifacts—need not limit the learning that visitors take from them. Even when curators establish a highly structured context for the interpretation of the collections on display, visitors remain stubbornly free to take from the exhibit what they choose. This degree of freedom is one of the attractive features of museum learning for many visitors, making museum learning a creative and rewarding experience.

The art history of the past few centuries abounds in examples of learning from museums: students went to museums to learn artistic technique, composition, and the like by copying the works of the masters. In the early seventeenth century, Peter-Paul Rubens had to go to Italian churches or be admitted to the Vatican chambers in order to study and sketch the work of the masters of the Renaissance. But by the eighteenth century the Royal Academy in France expected artists like Jacques-Louis David to begin their careers by copying great paintings in the Louvre. This tradition of learning by copying has continued to the present day at the Louvre, the Prado, and many other great museums with masterworks permanently displayed on their walls.

In the twentieth century the Futurists were among the first of many artists who have learned from museums in the opposite sense, striving to develop art forms that went beyond, or even repudiated, the art they saw in museums. Dada was the most absolute expression of that desire—which of course has not prevented the formation of major museum collections of Dada and shows, such as the definitive Dada exhibition at the Centre Pompidou in Paris in 2005. Learning in museums can sometimes be—perhaps often must be—learning to reject or surpass what they have to offer. Yet if this apparently negative learning is deep and subtle enough, it can lead to substantial advances in the life's work of the learners.

The late Stephen Jay Gould has written evocatively of the influence that early visits to the American Museum of Natural History had on his development as a scientist. As artists may learn positively or negatively from art museums, so young scientists may be inspired or challenged by what they see in natural history museums, zoos, botanical gardens, or science centers, with future ethnographers, archaeologists, or anthropologists being similarly stimulated by what they find in ethnographic, archaeological, or anthropological museums. Aspiring historians or even politicians may be inspired by what they see in history museums. But the question of learning in museums extends also to those of us whose life's work is not related to what is on display: What is museum learning for the rest of us? How do we learn in museums?

An important group of potential learners at many museums or exhibitions is any community directly related to the objects on display—a group whom we may refer to as the *community of origin*, in the sense that they or their ancestors originated either the objects themselves, or at least the context in which these objects have or had meaning. Native Americans in the United States, First Nations people in Canada, or Aborigines in Australia, for instance, may learn from exhibitions of their respective cultures much that has been lost from their oral or performed traditions. Often hostile to the museum as an agency that has removed ritual or other objects from their original living functions, they may nevertheless seize the opportunity presented by a museum exhibition or collection to study and learn more about their cultures than was previously available to them. Many Canadian Northwest Coast artists, for example, have begun their own work after a careful study of the totems and other carvings and textiles preserved in museums. Museum learning in these instances consists of learning more about one's own ethnic or cultural identity. In Washington, D.C., the Smithsonian Institution's National Museum of the American Indian has devoted its entire collection storage building, the Cultural Resource Center, to this kind of learning.

In a broader sense, every group of museum objects of human material culture has a community of origin, the people who have been involved in the initial creation of those objects or the meanings that make them significant. This may be an individual artist, a group of collectors or dealers, an international community of scientists, or the people who have lived in and built the nation, state, or city whose story a history museum is telling. For all such people, museum learning is a matter of reinforcing their own cultural identity, looking in a mirror and learning from the accuracy—or lack of it—in the reflection.

Yet for all of us who are neither occupationally related nor members of the community of origin of the objects on display, museum learning is still possible, and can be a powerful experience. What is this kind of learning, and how does it happen?

In attempting to define what museum learning is, it is helpful first to identify what it is not. It is not the kind of learning that takes place in schools or universities. At such formal places of learning, one is required—or one chooses—to take a collection of classes or lectures in which teachers more or less successfully explicate the subject in context, so that after having supplemented the courses by reading a textbook and/or working through set problems, exercises, or experiments, one may attain a certain mastery of the subject matter. Although some museums are part of universities, and may form part of the students' educational experience, museum learning as such is not formal or academic in this sense.

Nor is museum learning the kind of learning one undertakes when enrolling in a class to learn a trade, to lose weight, or to acquire a new dance step. Here one follows the example and advice of a trainer until attaining the ability to replicate the process or the movements with comparable results. Although some museums may offer courses of this kind, it is *not* the type of learning experience that is on offer in their exhibition galleries.

Closer to museum learning, but still very different, is the kind of learning that takes place in a library. This is somewhat similar because it is usually voluntary and relatively informal, as the student looks up data or interpretations of data in print material. Here the learning is the cognitive assimilation of what has been recorded or observed about the subject. The library reader comes away better informed about what people past or present have written about the subject.

Of course today the visitor to a library may not even see a printed page, but may be engaged entirely in a search for intelligence about a subject through a study of databases or surfing on the Web. Learning from information technology is comparable to museum learning in its informal, self-motivated character—but like learning from print material it ultimately consists in learning what others are saying or have said about the subject.

From these brief contrasts we may begin to see what museum learning is:

- Museum learning is *informal*, as distinguished from formal academic courses.
- Museum learning is *voluntary*, selected by the learner (or perhaps by the leader of a school or tour group of which he or she is a member).
- Although museum learning is always partially cognitive, it is primarily *affective* learning, distinguishing it from the type of learning that takes place by studying print sources in a library or searching on the Internet.

Learning is primarily *affective* when it is focused on our *feelings* about things—when it affects our attitudes, interests, appreciation, beliefs, or values. Of course, cognition of data accompanies this affective experience—even the transformative experience of an original contemporary work of art in a museum context usually drives us immediately to want to find out who the artist is, the title of the work, its date and medium, and the circumstances of its creation. However, the essential museum learning experience is the change in our feelings, interests, attitudes, or appreciation of the subject matter due to the museum display. Because this involves a change in these attitudes or interests, it is correct to refer to a successful museum learning experience as a transformative one.

Museum learning is a transformative, affective experience in which we develop new attitudes, interests, appreciation, beliefs, or values in an informal, voluntary context.

This statement has important implications for our evaluation of museum learning. The exiting visitor's retention of any specific data or even of the curatorial interpretation of the subject is not the critical factor to be evaluated. What matters is whether the exiting visitor takes away a new interest in or attitude toward the subject. A successful museum exhibition is one that offers a transformative learning experience, sparking a new interest or appreciation that was not there before.

Yet there is something more. *Collections* are at the heart of museums. As books are to libraries, as plays are to theaters, so objects are to museums. Although text is obviously important, and interactive experiences aided by information technology may be helpful, the affective learning experience that takes place in most museums must be stimulated by museum objects—archival documents, artifacts, specimens, or works of art. Science centers, children's museums, or visitors' centers that are noncollecting institutions are interesting exceptions, but the learning experience at most museums, zoos, and botanical gardens consists in learning from what's on display.

What and how can we learn from objects? In the nineteenth century, museum professionals put their confidence in the organized presentation of specimens—and by extension of works of art or artifacts—hoping that the visitor would learn by associating those objects placed together in sequence. In the first half of the twentieth century, art museums especially put far more emphasis on the display of individual works of art, confident that they could communicate directly on their own—or if not, they were simply not effective as works of art. Later in the last century museum educators taught the truism that objects cannot speak for themselves, so museum "interpretation" and departments of communication became important.

When the exhibition galleries of the National Museum of the American Indian opened in Washington, D.C., early in the twenty-first century, one wall of over a hundred artifacts was presented as evidence of the cultures that existed prior to the arrival of Columbus in the western hemisphere. These powerful objects evinced not just the existence of these cultures, but also their sophistication, their complexity, and their contribution to the human story. So one important way in which we learn from objects is that they constitute *evidence* of the story the museum is telling. We believe the story because we see the evidence, and so we learn to transform our opinions, our attitudes, and our appreciation around the evidence we have seen.

The same may be said of natural history specimens. Natural history museums present the evidence for evolution, for instance, in their displays of fossil specimens or casts. A health museum may transform the beliefs of a smoker with a display of a lifelong smoker's lung alongside one of a nonsmoker. In the Jardin des Plantes in Paris, Le Muséum National d'histoire naturelle presents the evidence for biodiversity with its dazzling *troupeau* (a fanciful herd never found in nature) of the great variety of taxidermic specimens in its collection, arranged as if trekking across the floor of the main central gallery of the building.

History museums are obsessed with evidence. The U.S. Holocaust Memorial Museum in Washington, D.C., is an outstanding example, where the objects are so powerfully moving, even for visitors who have read many history books and articles about the subject. A comparably revelatory object at what began as the National D-Day Museum in New Orleans (now called the National Museum of World War II) is the archival fragment on which General Eisenhower had drafted his alternative communication to the world if the Normandy invasion had been repulsed: it is all the evidence one needs of the drama of the historical moment, when despite the extensive preparation and training all depended on the unknown outcome.

Social history museums present the objects of everyday life as evidence of the economic, political, and social conditions of the time and place represented. Industrial museums and historic sites present the evidence of how tasks were performed, or how certain social classes lived. Archaeological and ethnographic museums present the evidence for their and our imaginative reconstruction of the past.

Even science centers without object collections present evidence such as DNA analyses, weather maps, and star charts. Those children's museums that operate without collections use replicas as objects for the role-playing learning activities of their young visitors. What these institutions have in common is an emphasis on learning by doing, which requires touching and therefore generates a need for replicas or models rather than original objects.

In recent years we have seen the emergence of "idea museums" aimed at communicating a thesis or a lesson about history or humankind. The Museum of Tolerance in Los Angeles, Mémorial: le Musée pour le Paix at Caen, and the planned Canadian Museum of Human Rights in Winnipeg are examples. These institutions are much more consciously didactic, focused on our learning of their subjects more than on preservation of a heritage or culture. Nevertheless, they are keen to acquire and display evidence wherever it is available—such as the exciting archival film footage of the Normandy landings taken from film archives of both sides in the Musée pour le Paix, or a cabin used in the slave trade at the National Underground Railroad Freedom Center in Cincinnati.

Art museums may be seen as presenting the evidence for art history. This is a valid description of part of their function, especially for those with art historical collections and exhibitions. Yet for them, especially for contemporary art museums, the main purpose is not evidential, but in order to provide a direct experience and appreciation of the work of art in and of itself. Unlike artifacts or specimens, an object that is intended as a work of art should be able to communicate directly to the visitor, whose response is one of appreciation rather than merely recognition of the object as evidence.

A fine art museum may therefore combine exhibits of both kinds—not only in different galleries, but also in each and every gallery. We can approach art history galleries as evidence of the values, technology, and accomplishments of various cultures and periods, yet at the same time we can appreciate the works in and of themselves. In Berlin, for example, crowds understand the bust of Nefertiti as evidence of the sophisticated culture of the Egypt of her time—yet they also appreciate the statue directly as a profoundly moving masterpiece that speaks to us directly about women, beauty, mortality, and power.

In a contemporary art museum there may be little or no evidentiary role for the latest installation by a local artist, but it is available for direct appreciation (or not) by visitors who share the current culture from which it comes. Remembering the example of Picasso, of course, visitors can only respond to what their life and work pattern allows them to appreciate. If not much museum learning takes place, it may be a deficiency of the piece, or it may simply be the case that most of its viewers are not yet consciously sharing the affective space of the artist, so that very little affective learning can occur. Over time, if the artist is in touch with emerging new realities, this may change.

In summary therefore, we may conclude:

Museum learning is a transformative experience in which we develop new attitudes, interests, appreciation, beliefs, or values in an informal, voluntary context focused on museum objects. Museum learning may be aided by interpretative text, hands-on activities, and interactive information technology, but for all collecting institutions learning will be focused on the objects in the museum's collection that are presented either for appreciation in themselves and/or as evidence of a larger subject.

CHAPTER 3

The Potential of Museum Learning
The Essential Museum

ELAINE HEUMANN GURIAN

> "Ethnologists, anthropologists, folklorists, economists, engineers, consumers and users never see objects. They see only plans, actions, behaviours, arrangements, habits, heuristics, abilities, collections of practices of which certain portions seem a little more durable and others a little more transient, though one can never say which one, steel or memory, things or words, stones or laws, guarantees the longer duration."[1]

What if our profession created a museum in which visitors could comfortably search for answers to their own questions regardless of the importance placed on such questions by others? This chapter explores the philosophy behind and the ingredients and procedures necessary to produce such a museum. This new type of museum I wish to characterize as "essential." (This may be wishful thinking. We may, in the end, have to settle for "useful.")

I contend that most museums are "important" but not "essential" establishments. I acknowledge that the customary museum continues to be valuable for some, beloved by its adherents, and defended against transformation by those who understand and celebrate its value. Nevertheless, I propose that there is room for another kind of museum, one that arises not from organized presentations by those in control, but one that puts control into the hands of the user.

"People are somewhat exhausted after 25 years of blockbuster exhibits being served up with these heavy tomes and yammering 'acoustiguides' and all the learned labels. These days, they want the opportunity to escape that kind of directed discovery."[2]

I suggest that while some useful experimenting with such control shifts within museums is already afoot, most especially in resource centers and study storage embedded within galleries, there is no current category of museum in which the visitor is intended to be the prime assembler of content, based on his or her own need.

I am interested in transforming how users think of museum visits—from an "occasional day out" to a "drop-in service." I believe small, local museums are the best candidates for enabling this transformation because they can program more nimbly and with less fuss than can highly visited, larger establishments. If and when these small neighborhood museums come to be regarded as a useful stop in the ordinary day of the local citizen, I believe that, like the library in that very same community, the museum will have become essential.

In this new museum, the staff's role will be changed. Their current responsibility as the controlling authority determining the choice of displayed objects, interpretation, and expressed viewpoint will be diminished and their role as facilitator will be expanded. We know that many potential visitors have not felt interested, welcome, or included by traditional museums, and have demonstrated their indifference by not attending. I believe there is a correlation between the intellectual control by staff and the lack of relevance seen by many of our citizens.

The essential museum would begin with four assumptions:

1. All people have questions, curiosity, and insights about a variety of matters large and small.
2. Satisfaction of internalized questions is linked to more than fact acquisition and can include aesthetic pleasure, social interaction, and personal validation (recognition and memory).
3. A museum could be a useful place to explore these.
4. Visitors can turn their interest into satisfied discovery if the appropriate tools are present and easy to use.

Unfettered browsing of objects will be the main organizing motif in this museum, and to facilitate such visual access, the majority of the museum's objects will be on view. The technique of visible storage installation will be expanded and take on renewed importance.

Attendant information, broadly collected, will be considered almost as important as the objects themselves, and thus a database with a branching program of multiple topics will be available within easy reach. To access the database, a technological finding aid will be on hand so that the visitor can successfully sort through the multiplicity of available data. Visitors in this new museum, once satisfied with their own search, can offer the results of their investigation or their queries to subsequent users. Everyone who enters has the possibility of becoming both investigator and facilitator.

Once the mission of such a museum is established, the staff will concentrate on acquiring and researching relevant objects, locating, collecting and collating associated information from a broad and unexpected array of sources, and facilitating the public's access to same. While this sounds like the standard curatorial job, the basic mediating role of the curator will have changed. The curator will not limit the objects for view, nor determine the only topics available. Instead almost all information and objects will be made available and the user will mentally combine them as he or she sees fit. The museum will become a visual nonjudgmental repository in which many intellectual directions are possible. Within reason, no topic will be off limits and no idea will be rejected by the staff as unworthy. The museum will grow with the input of its users.

Before the reader finds this model too radical, consider that this is not dissimilar from the way shopping malls, the Internet, or public libraries currently operate. I wish to align the essential museum with these models.

Why create a new kind of museum? In part because surveys have continued to show that museum visitors remain a narrow segment of our society. Try as we do to broaden the user group through many different strategies, we have, by and large, failed to make an appreciable dent. Museum visitors remain predominantly well educated and relatively affluent, while the majority of our citizens remain outside our doors. So I began to consider how else museums might operate if they really wanted to broaden their audiences; that is, if they wanted the profile of visitors to include more people from the lower, middle, and working class, and more users who fit in minority, immigrant, adolescent, high school-credentialed, and dropout groups than is currently the case. If the rhetoric about museums continues to suggest that museums are inherently important civic spaces, then we must propose new strategies that would involve more of the citizenry.

In the last half century, curators, who are generally steeped in museum traditions, have seen their role criticized, and in response they have generally changed their voice and intention from that of a benevolent but authoritarian leader into that of a benign and helpful teacher. They have incorporated new strategies of exhibition technique and given credence to the theories involving various learning modalities.[3]

Overall, the traditional museum has generally become less "stuffy" with added visitor amenities that encourage sitting, eating, researching, shopping, and socializing. These changes have helped most museums evolve from being formal "temples" of contemplation into more inviting gathering places. The iconic museum has begun to look different from its turn-of-the-century forebear.

To enlarge the audience from the continuing relatively static profile, many have previously encouraged additional approaches:

- Expanding collections to include works created by underrepresented peoples.

- Adding exhibition subject matter to appeal to specific disenfranchised audiences.
- Utilizing exhibition techniques that appeal to many ages, interests, and learning styles.
- Fostering mixed-use spaces in response to theories of city planners (especially those of Jane Jacobs).[4]

I have suggested that museums should combine these steps with continued thoroughgoing community liaison work. Most recently I have advocated free admission as an important audience building strategy.[5]

Reluctantly, I now concede that these measures, while good, will not permanently expand the audience very much. I am newly convinced that the potential for broadening the profile of the attendees visiting the traditional museum is limited. Instead, museums of inclusion may be possible only if the object-focused mission is separated from the equally traditional but less well understood intellectual control by staff, and a new mission is substituted that satisfies a range of personal motivation by facilitating individual inquiry. In short, while I am not advocating that all museums need to change in this way, I am saying that the role, potential relevance, and impact of the traditional museum, while useful, is more limited than I had formerly believed.

I concede that the public wants, and may even need, these time-honored, often iconic, museums. I remain a member of that public. However, the history of these museums is intertwined with the history of social and economic power. Described by Carol Duncan and Alan Wallach as the "Universal Survey Museum," (one which operates as a ritual experience intended to transmit the notions of cultural excellence), they state:

> The museum's primary function is ideological. It is meant to impress upon those who use or pass through it society's most revered beliefs and values. . . . Even in their smallest details . . . museums reveal their real function, which is to reinforce among some people the feeling of belonging and among others, the feeling of exclusion.[6]

Even if this view by Duncan and Wallach is only partially correct, then it is not just object choice or intimidating architecture that is keeping the majority of the public from feeling welcomed in museums, it is the nexus between those objects, what is said about them, and by whom.

3.1   COMPARE LIBRARIES

Have you ever wondered why some contemporary collecting institutions, such as public libraries, serve an audience both larger and more diverse than museums, while others—for example archives—do not? I believe that the library's easy access and intention to provide nonprescriptive service for its users are differences that deserve to be explored and emulated. I suggest that the perception of the library as a helping rather than teaching institution interests a broader array of users. I propose that there is a link between the public's greater use and appreciation of libraries and the fact that they are funded as a matter of course (rather than exception) by politicians. As a side benefit, changing museums so that they too serve a broader audience may result in enhanced funding opportunities.

The process for acquiring library materials uses a system equivalent to museums—but unlike museums, each item once accessioned is treated and presented in much the same way one to another. Except for occasional holdings of rare books, there is no value-laden hierarchy imposed on the collection or access thereto. Most important for purposes of this chapter, within a broad array of possibilities *the determination of the topic for research is in the mind of the user rather than preselected by the librarian.*

Most library filing and access systems are ubiquitous. When visiting a new library, most patrons having made use of another library can easily find their way and for those not completely acclimated, there is the help desk where a librarian is available if needed, but unobtrusive if not.

In order to facilitate queries, libraries use knowledge locator systems—that is, catalogs—that, once understood, allow users to find information they seek, in a manner and time that fits within their ordinary day. Additionally, there are helping aids embedded in the catalog (such as key words) that allow the inexperienced user to succeed in his or her search. So, unlike museum visits where the unfamiliar attendee tries to see everything, library patrons can, if they wish, drop in casually, focused on an errand that can be completed quickly. And because the library is free and is usually close by, this pattern can be repeated often.

In their past histories, both libraries and museums were seen as august, quiet, imposing places. Why has the library democratized more than the museum, and why do both the citizen user and the politician funder feel that the library is more essential and worthy of more sustained support than the museum?

"A central feature of public librarianship in the United States is that librarians have worked to develop a climate of openness by defining library policies to create an institution where all are welcome. In 1990 the American Library Association adopted the policy, 'Library Services for the Poor,' in which it is stated, 'it is crucial that libraries recognize their role in enabling poor people to participate fully in a democratic society, by utilizing a wide variety of available resources and strategies.' (*ALA Handbook of Organization*, 1999–2000, policy 61). This policy was adopted because there had been a shifting level of emphasis in the interpretation of 'openness' since the establishment of the public library. Open doors are very different from proactive service."[7]

While museum and library rhetoric relating to public access written post–World War II might have sounded the same, libraries took on the process of transforming themselves much more seriously and continuously. Libraries "examined how the set of techniques developed and promoted by the Public Library Association allowed public librarians to engage in user-oriented planning, community-specific role setting, and self-evaluation."[8] Perhaps museum personnel are also ready to turn the museum writings of the past into a set of actions that will produce the same inclusive outcomes.

3.2   COMPARE SHOPPING MALLS

Moving on to another example, shopping malls display materials chosen by others and placed in a visually pleasing and stimulating environment. Like the contemporary museum, the mall incorporates additional amenities that facilitate browsing, strolling, and eating, and offers ancillary activities such as performances and social and civic events. The mall and the museum are both mixed-use spaces. Yet in the aggregate, mall users are of a much broader demographic than even the patrons of libraries.

While specific marketplace ambiances differ worldwide, almost all people, no matter what class or culture, are experienced shoppers and browsers. It is a skill almost everyone has learned from infancy. By extension, early training in museum use, as espoused by many, may continue to have relevance in audience development. However, except for an occasional school class visit, most young museum visitors are the children of the current users. Aligning museum going with known elements of shopping practice might expand that.

Two avenues to explore more fully may be the study of shoppers' behavior (motivational theory) and scrutinizing the mall's systems created to satisfy that need. In reviewing papers on consumer motivation, there appears to be a predictable sequence. The shopper decides that he or she needs something and determines the possible location to fulfill that need. That need leads to intention—the planning to go to that location—and then action. Once the shopper arrives, he or she begins a search, which involves locating, browsing, and comparing. The material is laid out to be visually inspected, and often touched; shoppers process their experience, combining and recombining what they are seeing until they make a self-directed decision: to buy or not to buy.

The system is codified and relatively easy to learn. The grouping of merchandise is often repeated shop to shop (for example by size, by types, or by price.) The purchase system is well marked, easy to find, and often separated from the inspection of merchandise. The wayfinding system is replicated in many locations. And there are browsing aids and amenities to be found in convenient places.

One can argue that the placement of articles in shops is as carefully controlled as the exhibitions presented in museums. I would not contest that claim, given many marketing studies that substantiate that position. Yet I would point out that people comfortable in their role as experienced shoppers feel empowered to bypass the shop-initiated preferred outcome and operate instead on their own. Those shops that wish to have more restricted clientele intentionally impose barriers to free exploration, much like traditional museums.

As unrelated as we might wish these activities to be, I am suggesting that the shopping and library experience have some important elements in common with each other and that these might usefully become embedded in the new type of museum I am proposing—that is, ubiquitous systems, free exploration, and a large volume of visual material on view. Most important, the decision to frequent a library or a mall originates from an internalized impulse, question, or need (a quest, if you will) that is sufficient to lead to action.

I understand that associating museums with shopping may offend some, and that there are important differences as well. Nevertheless, I expect that when consumer motivation theory is better understood and the physical facility of the museum adjusted to satisfy the individual's broader needs, the public will change the way they think about the usefulness of museums.

3.3   THE ROLE OF COLLECTIONS: THE POTENTIAL OF VISIBLE STORAGE

After this encomium to other venues, what is the special reason one would go to a museum at all, you might ask. The museum's comparative advantage remains the visual, and sometimes tactile, access to special physical things (some of them natural, some unique and original, some examples of a class of objects, and some purpose-built environments). The museum remains one of the few places where one can come face-to-face with hard-to-find, sometimes beautiful, and potentially intriguing stuff. It is the physicality of realia that makes museums special.

While current technology makes it possible to see almost any item on a computer screen, the computer cannot accurately reproduce the nuances, especially of scale and texture, that individuals absorb in the actual presence of the objects. It is the evidence in its tangible form that the public values.

If the public wants access to things, then it stands to reason that museums should provide access to lots of things. In fact, why not set up visual investigation of all, or almost all, of what the museum holds? The exhibition method currently in use that attempts to do that is a technique called study, open, or visible storage, and there are contemporary examples in many places.

However, the scale of these vis-à-vis the square footage allocated to prepared or curated exhibitions is small. In this model, I am suggesting that the amount of visible storage will be substantial.

I understand that when browsing amidst organized displays in today's typical museum, the visitor is already participating in a limited "free choice learning" space.[9] Most exhibitions are currently organized to allow visitors to wander at their own speed, and in their own pattern. I am also aware that some organizing structure is a comfort for the novice user, so I am not suggesting random placement of objects. In the essential museum there would be "light arrangement"—a framework—which might generally mimic the museum's own collections storage strategy, that is, by topic, by material, by culture, or by artist. Further, I am suggesting that in current installations containing a substantial amount of collections material on view we begin the process of enriching these exhibitions with an overlay of substantial and diverse information.

Some portion of the collection and display square footage could be reserved for changing installations responsive to a timely idea. As an analogy, we have all visited libraries that shelve detective novels together alphabetically by author, yet some books from that section are removed to appear, for example, in a shelf of new acquisitions, in the librarians choice of "good reads," or picks related to a current movie or holiday.

The Museum of Anthropology (MoA) at the University of British Columbia in Vancouver, which piloted open storage in the 1970s, currently has 13,000 objects on view. The MoA works with students to produce small occasional exhibitions within this visible storage. This experiment started a trend. Among large institutions, the Darwin Centre at the Natural History Museum in London and the Hermitage in Leningrad have relatively new installations. Martin Lawrence's case study in this chapter describes the Darwin Centre in more detail.

Augmenting visible storage with ancillary information was the logical next step. As an example, in 2001, the New York Historical Society opened a whole floor devoted to open storage, with additional information available on computers embedded in the space and downloadable onto handheld personal digital assistants (PDAs).

DARWIN CENTRE—A CASE STUDY
Martin Lawrence

Figure 3.1. Scientists and Visitors Meet in the Daily Program Nature Live

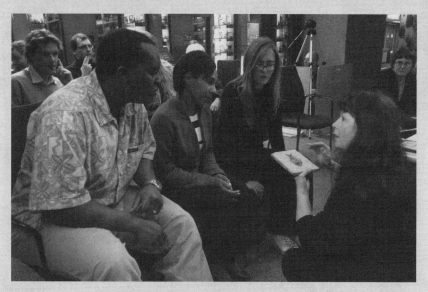

COURTESY OF THE NATURAL HISTORY MUSEUM, LONDON.

The Natural History Museum, London, is the United Kingdom's national museum of life and earth sciences. It holds collections of over 70 million natural history objects, which it uses as the basis for scientific research and extensive public engagement programs. It is one of those rare institutions with the capacity both to do science and to communicate with the public about science.

The opening of the Darwin Centre in 2002 was a dramatic change for the public engagement program at the museum. The success of the Darwin Centre depends upon a new kind of partnership between science and public engagement staff. In a significant change to their job descriptions, the museum's 300-plus science staff made a commitment to support a daily program of "meet-the-scientist" sessions: *Darwin Centre Live* (or *Nature Live* as it is now called).

Various sources, including the House of Lords,[1] have called for a different approach to public science communication, centered more firmly on dialog, discussion, and debate between scientists and public audiences. The

Figure 3.2. The Natural History Museum, London

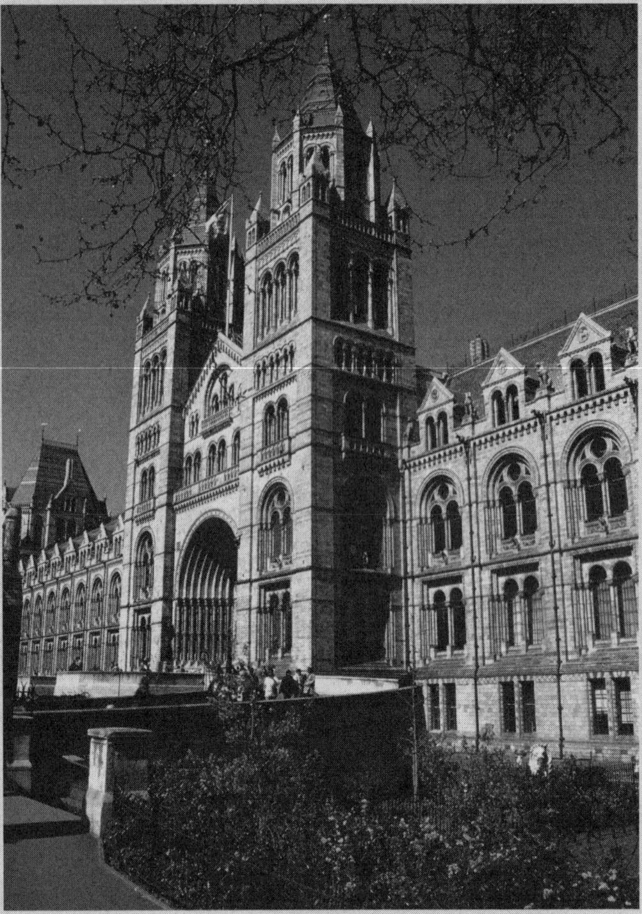

COURTESY OF THE NATURAL HISTORY MUSEUM, LONDON.

Darwin Centre can be seen as a response to this policy direction, and is reflected in the intended visitor outcomes for the *Live* program:

- increased confidence and ability to engage with scientific issues
- feeling inspired and enthused to find out more about the natural world
- deepening understanding of the processes of scientific enquiry
- becoming more aware of the type and range of museum research projects.

The *Live* program is aimed at adults, families with older children, and formal learners aged 16 to 18. Hosted by a team of science communicators, it provides opportunities for visitors to find out about the latest research activities of museum staff, engage in discussion about topical issues relating to the natural world, and question staff about what it is like to be a scientist.

Many of these sessions are Web cast via the museum's Web site (www.nhm.ac.uk), and virtual visitors are given the opportunity to make comments or raise questions by e-mail. Sessions are then archived onto the Nature Online section of the Web site. In that sense, visitors' contributions to the discussions are recorded and publicly represented.

Visitors to the Darwin Centre also have the opportunity to take a behind-the-scenes tour into the spirit collections of the zoology department. On the *Explore* tours they can view impressive specimens such as

Figure 3.3. Scientists and Visitors in the Darwin Centre

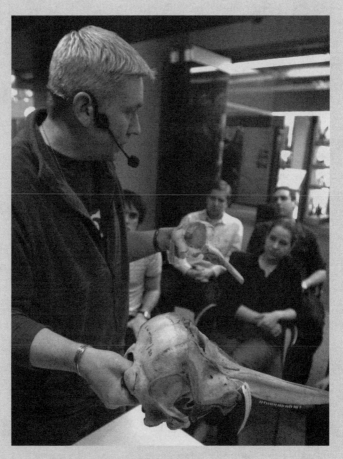

COURTESY OF THE NATURAL HISTORY MUSEUM, LONDON.

the giant squid, find out how the collections are managed, and view some of the labs where research work is undertaken.

In order to facilitate these tours, a new kind of position was created. The *Explore* tour guides have an unusual job description. They are both curators and communicators, working 25 percent of their time on the collections and 75 percent as tour guides. This mixed role has several advantages. As curators they are part of the zoology department, and can speak confidently about the collections they manage. Having access to the latest information about the collections and research activities enables them to engage in wide-ranging discussions with visitors of hugely varied knowledge and experience. The zoology department is more confident about allowing public visitors into the collections, knowing that the guides are zoology staff. Additionally, the learning and zoology departments have forged a much stronger relationship through their joint responsibility for these staff.

The Natural History Museum opened to the public in 1881, and from the beginning has been concerned with both scientific research and learning. Richard Owen, its first director, firmly believed that the galleries "should accurately reflect the natural world itself, and that specimens of every known animal, mineral and vegetable should be freely available for the public to see."[2] The exhibitions were "open" displays of the collections. Early visitors would have seen row upon row of specimens arranged in taxonomic order, displayed with minimal interpretative information, and saying little about the biology of the organisms. In 1912, in response to calls for more interpretation of the collections, John Leonard was appointed as the first Guide Lecturer, giving two one-hour tours each weekday.

In 1977, the opening of the *Human Biology* exhibition marked a significant departure from traditional models of museum exhibitions. It was not concerned with objects (with very few specimens on display) but with biological concepts, and explored in detail several areas of human biology. It also had very little connection to the research of the science staff at the museum. Later exhibitions, such as *Dinosaurs* and *Power Within*, were more closely related to museum research and collections, and explored aspects of the nature of science. Current NHM exhibitions portray scientists at work, highlight the social nature of science, and explore—to a limited extent—the role of doubt, debate, and controversy in establishing scientific knowledge.

The opening of the Darwin Centre was an important event for The Natural History Museum, and has wider implications for all scientific institutions and their relationships with public audiences. J. Gregory and S. Miller observe that there has been a shift in emphasis in the museum community, "from simply conserving culture to also communicating it; from advocating science to debating it; from the museum as a bank vault of the history of science to the museum as a living treasure trove of the scientific culture in which all can share."[3]

With the Darwin Centre, once again visitors to The Natural History Museum have access to large areas of the collection, and unprecedented opportunities to meet the Museum's science staff. Web casting and archiving of the *Nature Live* sessions enables a wide range of actual and virtual visitors to contribute to discussions and have their inputs recorded and published on the Web site. In the future, we plan to explore new ways of enhancing the visitor voice in our public engagement activities, for example through the use of blogs. We want our visitors to value the museum as a place that generates scientific knowledge and provides opportunities for discussion about issues relating to the natural world.

NOTES

1. House of Lords, *Science and Society* (London: HMSO Books, 2000).

2. J. Thackray and B. Press, *The Natural History Museum: Nature's Treasure House* (London: The Natural History Museum, 2001).

3. J. Gregory and S. Miller, *Science in Public: Communication, Culture and Credibility* (London: Plenum Trade, 1998).

This chapter, in some ways, extols a return to a very old-fashioned role for museums—publicly available visible storage. It is ironic that after a quarter-century of narrative exhibition development, museums, to follow this line of reasoning, would have to focus again on the *non-narrative* aspect of their collections and pay renewed attention to collections care and collections management systems.

Prior to the advent of modern exhibition techniques in the 1950s, museums often had much of their collections on view with very little interpretation. Some visitors found that boring; others, bewildering. So why return to it now? What would be different from and better than those previous static displays?

To confess, I never found those installations tiresome. I have found that even without any of the associated information available, those old-fashioned visual storage installations were often the source of magic and wonder. Wandering in the aisles of the Museum of Comparative Zoology in the mid-1960s with my own then small children was a delight. Their interest roving between cases and their associated flights of fancy remain indelible experiences for this museum writer.

But I am in the minority. For most people, uninterpreted collections were mystifying. This new proposal adds a critical ingredient: *information*—lots of it, connected to the objects on view.

3.4   THE INFORMATION AND REFERENCE SYSTEM

In the past, most object-centered museums contained only terse labels using highly refined and often technical words. There was no accompanying easy-to-understand omnibus system that held both information about the objects and cross-disciplinary references. By contrast, techniques such as user-friendly finding-aid systems existed in libraries, as card catalogs with key words.

Comparable systems continue to be only rarely available to museum visitors. While the technology needed to create a fully responsive system for museum use is not yet fully developed, there are experimental prototypes in various facilities that museums could employ to start down this road.[10] The Institute of Museum and Library Services (IMLS) conferences called *Webwise* have listed topics on organized metadata and public access to cross-platform archival records, for example, asking such questions as, "What approaches do cultural heritage institutions use to support collection discovery? How can cultural heritage institutions learn from one another and adapt behaviors of the different curatorial traditions to improve discovery and open up our collections?"

I am proposing coupling the power of the object's physical presence with the speed of the Internet and am suggesting that the result would encourage the visitor to find out more than just the information the museum has about a subject of interest. I am eager that the proprietary information held within individual museums be combined with related information from many other sources for the public to use. It is the availability of linked, unexpected, and even "stream-of-consciousness" information connected to the physical objects and made readily available on the spot through an electronic search engine that might make the museum fully interesting to the visitor.

The fundamental difference between what I am now recommending and what has been tried in the past is a freer relationship between the object and its many possible spokespersons. I am interested in making museum collections, and *all* associated information, accessible in ways that are analogous to browsing in library stacks. Further I am interested in expanding our information system to become like the online Wikipedia (with all its faults)—a collection of accumulated explorations.

The object becomes the fulcrum around which all kinds of information are arrayed for an individual's exploration with the potential for cross-disciplinary connections like those referred to by Ian Wedde as "discourse spillage," in which he whimsically suggests we could go to "an exhibition about war for information about bicycles."[11]

Originally, museums held collections records that were hand-written and contained only a small amount of information—that is, the name of the object, the history of ownership, the dimensions and material, and some attribution as to the maker. But what of the stories? Stories (as in oral histories), even when fondly appreciated by curators or registrars, did not seem appropriate to record at the time, and many were lost. That is changing in some quarters. Information now linked to cultural artifacts of indigenous people often contains associated stories. I am suggesting that the essential museum, in order to be encyclopedic, should gather and include such stories. Janet Hoskins in her book *Biographical Objects* has said, "What I discovered, quite to my surprise, was that I could not collect the histories of objects and the life histories of persons separately. People and the things they valued were so complexly intertwined they could not be disentangled."[12]

In collecting stories as relevant and useful data, the museum would have to become comfortable with transcribing seemingly antagonistic, competing, or overlapping knowledge systems often described as "differing world-views," commonly polarized between science and myth. The Internet, as an example, contains "accurate," personal, and potentially faulty information. The Internet makes opinion blogs, factual reporting, and skewed viewpoints all available at the same time. It is up to users to decide what they wish to see and how to regard it. Accordingly, users sometimes go to their choice of "reliable" third parties to differentiate between and choose among the information gathered. That is why some people use Consumer Reports when deciding on the right dishwasher to purchase. In the essential museum, the curator would be one of several "reliable" commentators whose views would always be available as part of the record.

There is a vigorous discussion among those who favor a fully open Internet, trying to find the best path between inaccurate, offensive, and slanderous material on the one hand, and censorship that impedes individual freedoms on the other. The museum interested in such an allied information system would have to wade into that murky stream and get wet. I do not find such a prospect sufficiently threatening to deny the public such broader information. It is the mixing of unique proprietary information and the associated rumination by others that would make visiting a museum a new and intriguing experience. One of the quickest and cheapest ways to begin this process would be to have the Internet itself easily available in the exhibition space.

What I am proposing is the creation of a visual and technological support system that allows individuals to delight in the adventure of making individualized connections amidst real things. I am interested in supporting the visitor whose quest may be information gathering but equally others who come with more subjective goals. "While studies show that some visitors may seek and experience relaxation, social bonding, self-identity, self-esteem, and other outcomes from the museum experience, it is still relatively rare that museums choose to focus explicitly on facilitating outcomes other than cognitive gain. What museums can uniquely offer is an opportunity for individuals to encounter collections of evocative artifacts, and a laboratory for understanding the powerful connections between people and things."[13]

I am suggesting that this become a two-way street with these self-same visitors leaving some imprint behind that allows others to enjoy and participate in their new discovery. Technology makes that possible. As an example, young people are creating and downloading personalized tours of museums on their iPods and giving them to friends.

To fulfill the need as I describe it, the essential museum will have to create an understandable reference aid that is replicated, at least in general outlines, in many other museums. Like the Dewey Decimal System for libraries, imperfect as it may be, there are a number of such models or analogous systems. The phone book is available in most households to be consulted when needed. The Internet utilized by the computer-literate is currently even more convenient, and is used often to find answers to questions in a timely manner. On the Internet, Google's search engine is not much different from Yahoo's. Every railroad has a timetable quite like each other's, and every newspaper reader can find a set of useful and timely information (such as the weather forecast or the starting times of movies) within every issue. Individual members of the public having learned how to use finding aids in one context can assume that they will be available in other related venues.

Museums would have to invent and then generally adopt such a transferable system. Some within our profession have been working on collections management systems based on agreed taxonomies, and these might prove useful. In effect, the system may already partially exist. However, regardless of the current state of these electronic finding-aids, they are not widely available. In the essential museum they would be. I am suggesting that the lack of transferability of the individual museum's collections record system is working against public familiarity.

3.5 COLLECTIONS CARE AND THE ROLE OF THE CURATOR IN THE ESSENTIAL MUSEUM

A renewed focus on visible storage could be useful at this time in our history. A 2005 report on the state of American collections concludes that they are in substantial disrepair.[14] Much of the museum community has not adequately financed the care of their collections because, compared to other activities, collection care has not risen to a high priority. This lack of funds may be exacerbated because grant funders, politicians, and the public do not currently see a connection between collections care and public service. Funders are right to believe that once collections are conserved they will most likely be locked away again, awaiting some uncertain rebirth in an exhibition in the unknown future. Addressing collections care for its own sake has not made for a compelling case.

Further, there has been a cycle of unfocused collecting in some museums that is followed by deaccessioning decisions that can provoke public controversy. So in addition to substantial collections care, the system I am proposing requires a focused mission with rigorous decision making about which collections to retain. In this transformed museum where the objects fit within the mission, where most objects are visible (and perhaps sometimes touched) and where abundant attendant information is available, collections care would rise to higher funding priority.

To transform the museum, those in leadership positions will have to take delight in helping patrons learn what they wish. This will require staff to rethink their role, their passion, and their skill set. I am respectful of the scholarship curators have amassed and do not suggest that they discard it, but I am recommending a change in their role from teacher and transmitter to facilitator and assistant.

"Clearly, in this kind of contestable, unstable and multi-user knowledge domain, the museum-based researcher needs disenchantment as well as sympathy, intellectual rigor as well as relativist flexibility, in order to find and disseminate the narratives about collections that will entertain and inform audiences, and add to the nation's useful store of scholarship."[15]

The new type of position described by Martin Lawrence in the case study on the Darwin Centre in this chapter—guides who are scientists with

25 percent of their time curatorial, 75 percent spent on tours—is an interesting example of this evolving new kind of museum staff. Exhibitions other than visible storage should be continued, but these exhibitions should occupy a smaller percentage of the available area than currently allocated, and their content and installation design should be adapted to allow for frequent change. Rather than exhibitions that take years to develop, cost a great deal of money and remain unchanging for decades, I am suggesting that the developer's identity be revealed in smaller exhibitions that are more personalized, timely, and involve open and evolving dialogue with the public.

Having struggled for decades to get museums to see education as a priority, I am now suggesting that the word needs a changed definition—from one that implies the interrelationship between teacher and student to one that clearly denotes the facilitation of individual inquiry. In the essential museum, fostering individualized learning will be listed first in the mission preceding the usual "collecting, preserving, exhibiting, and researching" menu.

To help create prepared staff who embrace this new concept, museum trainers will have to rethink their course offerings, elevating customer-focused assistance to a valued endeavor. Students would study such topics as motivation theory, inquiry-based technology, and oral history in addition to their subject matter scholarship.

3.6   IMPLICATIONS FOR MUSEUM DESIGN

To be welcoming, this new visible storage and knowledge system will need to be coupled with responsive space design. Attention will be paid to creating comfortable physical amenities including access to terminals, research tables, and implements for close looking that fit the needs of visitors. These will be combined with platforms for storytellers or performers, and added interactive elements of interest to families.

The shopping mall and the library have space elements worth emulating. Their designs intentionally allow patrons to enter anonymously, and to sit and stroll without committing to organized activity. These amenities allow "lurkers"—unfamiliar users—to figure out the services and customs required without drawing attention to themselves. Access to facilities such as toilets is available without entrance fees, and malls (and increasingly libraries) offer opportunities to socialize while eating.

In a paper titled "Free at Last" I wrote, "I have reluctantly but unequivocally come to the conclusion that the first encounter with the ticket taker may be the single greatest impediment to making our museums fully accessible.[16] I believe that the essential museum, like the library and the mall, must be free to enter."

Library designs include other special elements that also fit within this new model. They include:

- Spaces both for small group interaction and for private contemplation that don't interfere with each other.
- Help desks that are in a physical location that can be easily seen, but do not require the visitor to interact.
- Front doors that are convenient to public transportation and foot traffic as well as parking for the automobile.
- Hours of operation that suit neighborhood users.
- Acceptance of behavior, clothing choice, sound level, and styles of interaction that are consistent with norms of courtesy within the individuals' community.
- Unobtrusive security systems.

3.7   RELEVANCE TO SMALLER MUSEUMS

I believe that the museums most receptive to this transformation will be the smaller natural history, cultural, and local history museums. It is these rather unprepossessing and certainly underfunded places that hold the most promise for me. Many of the great national omnibus encyclopedic museums should continue on their valued way. Even there, the open storage that many are installing can become more fulsome by adding the kind of information overlay and finding aids suggested in this chapter.

In the small museum the audiences, current and potential, are local, and can get to the museum easily and often. The collection has local relevance but is usually neither rare nor valuable enough to need excessively intrusive security. The associated stories are easier to find because they often reside in local memory. And these institutions have particular importance to local schools. These local museums have the advantage of being "below the radar screen" and thus can experiment with less risk.

Over the last century there have been many examples of smaller museums that have experimented. They often had charismatic directors with vision and talented, devoted staff. These institutions became the incubators of new ideas that were later emulated when deemed to be safe and no longer novel.

Ron Chew, the director of the Wing Luke Asian Museum in Seattle, has written, "At the small museum, there are no inflated expectations, no pretension, and no awful waits. The exhibitions may be small and somewhat idiosyncratic, but they mirror the small, somewhat idiosyncratic world we know, close to home."[17]

It is my hope that with this important transformation, local governmental agencies will begin to see that these newly dynamic institutions right in their own backyard are serving a real public need and should be supported. They will see the essential local museum as a service that is as relevant and constant as the local library.

And as this new form emerges, it is my hope that the museum community will begin to value the unique position of these small local museums, create a separate niche that has criteria all its own, and develop a rhetoric that no longer compares them with the much larger iconic museums.

3.8   SUMMARY

In summary, to create more inclusive museums I believe that we must change our basic mindset and emulate aspects of those institutions deemed essential by a large cross-section of our citizenry. These include libraries and shopping malls. In order to be regarded as essential, museums would have to understand, respect, and facilitate each visitor's individual quest and accommodate a broad motivation for entering.

In order to become essential, the museum will provide visible access to its holdings in a lightly organized manner, concentrating on access to information systems that are easy to understand, repeatable, and transferable. In addition to making the object and the associated proprietary information available, the museum will accumulate and merge information that resides elsewhere—in books, records, movies, slides, and the like—so that each object becomes the impetus for unexpected exploration. Further, museums would have to include ways for the public to add information to the system and respond to the information left by others. Physical layouts and concomitant training will be needed to ensure visitors' ease upon entry, welcoming attitudes among staff, help available only when needed, and clear ways to learn how to use the system by simply watching.

This proposal turns museums upside down, transferring authority to the visitor and transforming the staff, who have been knowledge accumulators, preservers, and translators into knowledge brokers and sharers. Some museums have experimented with bits and pieces of this in the past. I am certain that this new system could—and should—be created, wholesale, in the future. Envisaging it helps us to appreciate the full potential of museum learning.

NOTES

1. B. Latour, "The Berlin Key or How to do Words with Things," in *Matter, Materiality and Modern Culture,* ed. P. M. Graves-Brown (London and New York: Routledge, 2000), 10.

2. J. Ramirez, "New York Museum Opens Vaults to Public," in *Associated Press* (23 January 2001).

3. H. Gardner, *Frames of Mind: The Theory of Multiple Intelligences* (New York: Basic Books, 1983); G. E. Hein, *Learning in the Museum* (New York: Routledge, 1998).

4. J. Jacobs, *The Death and Life of Great American Cities* (New York: Random House, 1961).

5. E. H. Gurian, "Function Follows Form: How Mixed-Used Spaces in Museums Build Community," *Curator* 44, no. 1 (2001): 87–113; E. H. Gurian, "Threshold Fear," in *Reshaping Museum Space: Architecture, Design, Exhibitions*, ed. S. MacLeod (London: Routledge, 2005).

6. C. Duncan and A. Wallach, "The Universal Survey Museum," in *Museum Studies: An Anthology of Contexts*, ed. B. M. Carbonell (Maldern, MA: Blackwell Publishing, Ltd., 2004), 52, 54, 62.

7. K. De La Pena McCook, " Poverty, Democracy and Public Libraries, " in *Libraries & Democracy: The Cornerstones of Liberty*, ed. N. Kranich (Washington, D.C.: American Library Association, 2001): 28.

8. Ibid., 34.

9. J. H. Falk and L. D. Dierking, *Learning from Museums: Visitor Experiences and the Making of Meaning* (Walnut Creek, CA: Alta Mira Press, 2000).

10. NISO Framework Advisory Group, *A Framework of Guidance for Building Good Digital Collections*, 2nd ed. (Bethesda, MD: National Information Standards Organization, 2004), http://www.niso.org/framework/framework2.pdf

11. I. Wedde, *Making Ends Meet: Essays and Talks 1992–2004* (Wellington, NZ: Victoria University Press, 2005), 286.

12. J. Hoskins, *Biographical Objects: How Things Tell the Stories of People's Lives* (New York and London: Routledge, 1988), 2.

13. L. H. Silverman, "The Therapeutic Potential of Museums as Pathways to Inclusion," in *Museums, Society, Inequality*, ed. R. Sandell (London and New York: Routledge, 2002), 75, 77.

14. Heritage Preservation, *A Public Trust at Risk: The Heritage Health Index Report on the State of America's Collections* (Washington, D.C.: Heritage Preservation and the Institute of Museum and Library Services, 2005).

15. Wedde, *Making Ends Meet*, 287.

16. E. H. Gurian, "Free at Last: A Case for Eliminating Admission Charges in Museums," *Museum News* (September/October 2005): 33–35, 61–66.

17. R. Chew, "In Praise of the Small Museums," *Museum News* (March/April 2002): 36–41.

PART II:

WHO
Participants in
Museum Learning

Introduction

Barry Lord

It was over forty years ago that the Art Gallery of Toronto (as it then was, now the Art Gallery of Ontario) hosted a seminar on the future of art museums and public galleries. One of the speakers was a wealthy investor who was also a prominent collector and one of the key donors to the gallery's collection. Not surprisingly, he spoke eloquently of the benefits of the institution to society, as well as for him personally.

Another participant—it was the 1960s—was the business director of a trade union. He also enjoyed the gallery's exhibitions personally, but advised that in his judgment relatively few of his union's members would be likely to attend. Looking around at the exhibition of nonrepresentational paintings and sculpture in the gallery where the seminar was held, he observed that, quite aside from whatever specific schools or techniques were represented, the overall spirit of the works of art on display was one of individualistic creativity—an ethos that his union's members might or might not admire, but which in any case they could not live their lives by. He contrasted their life experiences with those of the investor seated beside him, who could be much more responsive to works of art that evoked such a lifestyle.

Forty years later, with Tate Modern setting attendance records, and the Museo Guggenheim Bilbao transforming the local economy of a postindustrial city, the distinction drawn by the union executive appears to be less and less significant. Contemporary art has become mainstream for very large numbers of people. When the appeal of blockbuster art historical exhibitions is added into the account, the future of art museums and public galleries—despite funding challenges—seems to be assured. With their dinosaurs and Egyptian, Chinese, or other archaeological artifacts, science, natural history, and human history museums appear to be equally assured of a mass audience.

Nevertheless, for those of us involved with the learning process in our museums, the trade union executive's point remains a concern. What is the relevance of our exhibitions and other public programs to those who attend—

and perhaps even more important, to those who do not come through our doors? Who are the actual participants in museum learning, and what of those who are not? Can the content and presentation of our museums be made more accessible and more pertinent to an even wider audience?

As several contributors in this section observe, these are questions that have become more urgent as government funding sources have become more interested in accountability and getting value for the public money invested in many museums. Especially under the Labor government in the United Kingdom there has been a strong emphasis on public access, and increasing the proportion of those from economically disadvantaged and ethnic or racial minority groups in attendance. Similar concerns have been raised in the United States and elsewhere.

Dr. Claudia Haas begins this section in chapter 4 by reminding us that the learning that was formerly available in most museums was originally intended primarily for the cognoscenti—those who already knew enough to appreciate the terse labels on works of art or the sequence in which fossils were laid out in display cases. In the United States, that attitude began to change as early as the late nineteenth century in some places, and in Britain by about the end of the third quarter of the twentieth, but as Claudia and her case study contributor Dr. Elisabeth Menasse-Wiesbauer agree, it persisted in Vienna and elsewhere in continental Europe as late as 1990.

Those two contributors have been instrumental in transforming museology in Austria, as Dr. Haas conceived, developed, and initially directed Zoom, Vienna's Children's Museum, of which Dr. Menasse-Wiesbauer is the present director. Claudia's chapter draws the lessons from her experience, underlining the sea change in organizational priorities that must accompany a genuine reorientation of our institutions to serve families with children.

Toni Parker's case study, also in chapter 4, of the National Portrait Gallery's Reaching Out Drawing In program, provides just one example of the many undertakings launched by British museums and galleries in order to address the challenge, not merely of fitting programs to the interests and needs of families with children, but specifically of reaching out to involve families from economically or socially disadvantaged, minority, and immigrant communities. Most interesting is the facilitation of the involvement of these families themselves in helping to determine the shape and content of an NPG exhibition and activities. Toni also emphasizes the importance of the host institution itself reaching out to form partnerships with other organizations in the target community.

The importance of appropriate partnerships as a means of providing access to learning participants is also very much the subject of Dr. Brad King's chapter 5 on changes in the relationships between museums and schools—institutions of informal and formal learning, respectively. Brad documents the effect on museums of the past decade's heightened emphasis on grades and a strictly defined curriculum in schools, especially but certainly not exclusively in North America. By making school tours harder to justify, and forcing museums to prove curriculum relevance, Brad observes, this change has actually resulted in more effective museum learning programs in many instances.

Another imaginative response that Brad documents, and Dr. Michael Bentley illustrates in his case study in chapter 5 of a museum high school in Roanoke, Virginia, is the development of the museum school. This is clearly a promising new institutional type that is currently still evolving, primarily in the United States, as the list included with Michael's case study indicates. It will be interesting to see if museum schools become an integral part of museum learning programs worldwide over the coming decades.

Still another locus of change is the university museum. The case study in chapter 5 by Susan Taylor and Dr. Caroline Harris of Princeton University Art Museum exemplifies the current trends toward involving a wider range of the faculty in a multidisciplinary approach to exhibitions and other programs, getting students to participate in the development and delivery of programs, and reaching out to the wider community beyond the campus.

In chapter 6, Dr. Spencer Crew takes the discussion still wider, including adult education in his scope, and returns us to the original question of participation in and relevance to a broader audience. Like Dr. Haas, but working in the much more intense American context of the demand for proportional inclusion of racial and ethnic minorities and disadvantaged groups among museum visitors, users, staff, and board members, Spencer establishes a recent historical context for the emergence of institutions that not only involve members of the community in the development of their programs, but also consciously adopt prescriptive mission statements addressed to social issues so that they have been termed "museums of conscience." He himself provides an excellent example in his case study of the Dialogue Zone at the National Underground Railroad Freedom Center in Cincinnati (of which he is the director), while Danielle Melville offers another inspiring instance in her case study in this chapter on Constitution Hill in Johannesburg, South Africa. Situated in the historic prisons in the heart of Johannesburg, where both Mahatma Ghandi and Nelson Mandela were incarcerated at different times, but adjacent to the new Constitutional Court building that is dedicated to protecting the rights and freedom won in the struggles that swept around those prisons, Constitution Hill has responded imaginatively to the challenge of involving its complex communities, locally, nationwide, and globally.

Like museum schools, museums of conscience are a twenty-first century response to the issues of inclusion and relevance that have characterized museums from their beginnings. This section describes the present state of responsiveness to these challenges and identifies the actual and potential communities who can participate in museum learning, in the context of the rationale for it that was established in part I. It shows that to work meaningfully in museum learning programs today, anywhere in the world, is to be on the front lines of a transformative practice that has exciting and highly relevant implications for all of our lives in this new century.

CHAPTER 4

Families and Children Challenging Museums

Claudia Haas

Children very rarely come to museums by themselves—they come either with a family member or with their school class. Children visiting museums with their families or in school groups are nowadays a common sight in museums all over the world. Nobody questions any more the right of children to be welcomed as individual visitors with special needs and expectations. Indeed, museums depend heavily on family and school audiences in order to achieve high visitor numbers.

Psychologists, early learning experts, and teachers, as well as museum educators, agree that museums offer children important learning experiences. Some experts even declare learning in museums as more effective for children than learning in schools.[1]

To validate this assumption, extensive research and case studies have been undertaken showing that museum visits from an early age have a positive impact on lifelong learning, social intelligence, and creative thinking. Based on this recognition a new priority on education has been set in museums by founding or enlarging educational departments and expanding programs targeted on children and grown-up visitors, developing concepts of how to better interpret objects and make them more intellectually and physically accessible. Scientific learning theories serve museum educators as a reference base in helping to develop learning strategies and create tools to address young learners more effectively.

There was a time when children did not even appear in visitor statistics of some museums. They entered museums as a nonpaying escort of their parents, enduring the next hours by quietly looking at objects placed so high above them that they could hardly observe them. The objects had no meaning for them. Knowledgeable parents familiar with the codes of museums, the artwork or historic material displayed, were the only interpreters between objects and children. This limited the family visit to the very few highly educated parents who were also willing to slip into the role of educator and interpreter.

During the author's schooldays in Austria, school classes were not accustomed to using museums as learning spaces. Museums were visited perhaps once a year when pupils participated in a general guided tour that had not been specially developed for a school audience. Learning at that time mainly took place in schools within a formal structure defined by the state curriculum. The attraction of the museum visit for school children was simply not to be in school.

At first glance this seems contradictory to the origin of museums. Museums from their earliest times have seen their role—in addition to their responsibility as collectors and preservers of material culture—as educators. They were places for research and study wherein a dialogue with objects' meanings was created, but with one essential difference to the present: museums previously served the "knowledgeable" by extending their knowledge.

The repositioning of museums as powerful learning centers for a wider audience including children has been accomplished throughout the twentieth century. The change was accelerated as museums became more accessible and client centered. American museums, followed by British museums, were in the forefront of opening their institutions to children coming with their families and in school groups. In the 1990s, continental European museums slowly started to consider families and schools more consciously as potential audiences. This delay can be explained by the different museum traditions and the place of children within continental European society.

At the beginning of our new century children and families are seen as one of the most important audience groups in museums all over the world. New museum projects in Europe, America, Asia, Africa, and Arab countries plan, build, and program for family audiences and school groups. Interestingly, family-friendly museums that offer vast learning opportunities such as children's museums and science centers are especially prospering in countries that do not rely on a long museum tradition.

But is this positive attitude toward the very demanding children's audience true throughout the museum? A closer look often shows that the responsibility for effective knowledge transfer remains primarily with education departments, and rarely has an effect on the whole museum. Education departments are often isolated, do not have high esteem in the museum hierarchy, and lead a frustrating battle for the rights of their visitors. *In order to change the museum from a research and discovery place for the very knowledgeable to an open learning environment addressing wider audiences, a process of change that involves the whole institution is necessary.*

This means not only reaching out for new audiences and inviting children and families into the building, but making the "riches" of the collections intellectually accessible by offering learning experiences according to the needs and expectations of each individual visitor. The whole museum organization has to identify itself with this objective, which must involve the whole staff, from curator to education officer, to guards and cashiers. This commitment has an impact on the building and its facilities, and the museum's organization, programming, exhibition design, and staffing.

4.1 PUTTING LEARNING ON THE MUSEUM AGENDA

What has been responsible for the opening up of museums to invite children and their families to learn and gain experience from the objects on exhibit? Two main factors—social change and economic pressure on museums—are identified as having the greatest impact on the process of change in museums.

4.1.1 Social Change

We may identify at least six aspects of social change that have affected and are still affecting museums:

1. Social change in the second half of the twentieth century had a significant impact on families. The higher percentage of women working outside the home has completely rearranged family life. Families spend less time together. Children's daily routine is arranged around school time—a formal learning environment—and organized leisure time, which also very often requires formal learning. There is very little time for unorganized free play.
2. Leisure time in the family is spent very differently from thirty years ago, and is no longer focused on shared meals where so-called "kitchen table learning" took place. There is less time for communication between parents and children. In times of high divorce rates, parents are often looking for spaces where they can spend "quality time" with their children on weekends.
3. The leisure industry offers a variety of possibilities for family entertainment, all competing with each other. Their selling point is in offering a combination of entertainment and education, and therefore they are advertising, "Here you can have fun with your children, and by the way they will also learn something."
4. Museums have not been seen by all members of a family as fun places to spend free time. Although parents may be more convinced that their children will learn in museums, many children still have to be persuaded that they will have fun.
5. Cultural tourism has been one of the strongest growing economic sectors of the last twenty-five years. Children are no longer left with grandparents

while their mothers and fathers explore museums all over the world. Families are experiencing new countries, visiting the cultural highlights, and hoping to learn in museums about the countries' material culture. The great collections worldwide, therefore, have a high percentage of family visitors with small children—although they are often not well prepared for family visits.

6. In a knowledge-based society, economic growth will be generated by values created, applied, or extracted from information that is individually transformed into knowledge. Lifelong learning therefore has become one of the main career factors. The twentieth century was the age of formal education in the classroom; the twenty-first century is the age of personal learning at every stage in life. Learning is no longer limited to the classroom, but takes place not only in educational institutions but also in cultural institutions such as museums.

4.1.2 Political, Economic, and Financial Pressure on Museums

Along with social change the political, economic, and financial situation in many countries of the western hemisphere has changed in the last fifteen years. Countries and communities are facing economic crises that have led to falling income in the public sector.

Especially in European countries that are traditionally highly funded by the public purse, museums have been losing government support. On the other hand, the private sector is not supporting museums in the way it used to in flourishing economic times. Funding is very often for a one-time capital investment, leading to shortages in the operational budget. This results in the following changes:

1. Museums are strongly reliant on self-generated revenue. This implies the need to win and build audiences. Schools and families—whether local or as tourists—are an important visitor potential for museums.
2. More and more governments are expecting museums to expand their audiences. They want to see tax money well invested, and not serving only an exclusive group of people. They want a greater number of citizens to profit from learning possibilities in museums.
3. Governments, especially in Britain, have linked funding with obligations to reach out for new audiences, particularly children, families, and minorities. The Campaign for Learning, which started in Britain in 2001, set a new standard for learning in museums, archives, and libraries.
4. The Programme for International Student Assessment (PISA) showed high deficits in public school education, primarily in continental European coun-

tries such as Germany and Austria, which had been proud of their educational systems. Governments reacted by putting more priority on education and called for a common effort among all public cultural and educational institutions to overcome this deficit.

4.1.3   Museum Responses to These Changes

Some museums responded quickly to these social, economic, and political changes. Fortunately, models and good examples of how to establish museums as learning spaces for families could be found within the worldwide museum landscape. Forerunners were those museums already serving as informal learning environments: children's museums, which from their beginning defined themselves by their audiences, and science centers, which from their origin understood themselves as places where learners could generate knowledge about science. Both museum types were immensely successful, and showed traditional museums how to open up for new audiences. The case study in this chapter on ZOOM, Vienna's children's museum that the author developed and first directed, provides a good example.

ZOOM CHILDREN'S MUSEUM—THE FIRST HANDS-ON MUSEUM FOR CHILDREN AND FAMILIES IN VIENNA

Elisabeth Menasse-Wiesbauer

As Dr. Claudia Haas points out in this chapter, the situation of children in Vienna has changed dramatically over the last fifteen years. When my daughter was born in 1990 there were almost no restaurants or coffee-houses that accepted babies. Even on public playgrounds you could not leave your child playing and exploring the surroundings; you had to defend your child's space against dogs and to take care that he or she did not run or fall into dog excrement. And if you entered one of the beautiful Viennese museums with a child under 10 years of age, the guards looked at you with an irritated expression to let you know that in these holy halls children should not move and would have to keep quiet.

In today's Vienna children are likely to be seen everywhere in public space: restaurants and coffeehouses have babyseats and toys, dog owners have to keep parks and streets clean. And the museums, offering special programs for school classes and families, are full of children. Museums in Vienna have discovered children as a main target group, primarily because they increase the numbers of visitors rapidly.

What happened during these last fifteen to twenty years? What was the trigger for this change? Of course there was a change in mentality. Children became a relatively rare value. Many young couples are childless, and the one-child family became the norm for those who do give birth. Social conditions have improved, and middle-class families nowadays treat their children as very special persons with very special interests and needs that have also been discovered by the economy.

But in the Viennese situation there was also something else. There was one new institution that really cared for the cultural interests and needs of children and families, and led the way to all these positive developments: ZOOM Children's Museum. This was the first public place in the city where intergenerational play could take place in a friendly child-caring environ-ment, where children were not only endured but warmly welcomed and allowed to touch and explore the exhibitions and objects.

A SHORT HISTORY OF ZOOM

ZOOM started in 1993 as a private initiative. At this time, the idea of build-ing a children's museum was met with reservation and a lack of understanding, especially by politicians and the city administration. Nobody had any idea what a children's museum was supposed to be. Traditional museums also reacted to the idea with disapproval and distrust. At that time, museums generally were not recognized as places for families to spend leisure time. Children usually had to enter museums holding their parents' hands and look at objects that were placed far too high for them to observe.

The first step of the founding initiative was to commission a feasibility study by Lord Cultural Resources that included a market survey of potential visitors. The study clearly proved that there was a strong need among schools and young Viennese families for cultural programs for children, and that an institution such as a children's museum was missing.

But another important step had still to be taken: to explain to future audiences how a children's museum works and what it can provide. Therefore it was decided to start off with interactive exhibitions for children. With a minimum of public funding but a lot of courage and the pioneering spirit of the founding director Dr. Claudia Haas, the first exhibition was organized. A tried and tested children's exhibition was taken over from Le Musée en Herbe in Paris. Although there was no money to spare for marketing, school classes and families stormed the exhibition.

The Children's Museum continued to operate for the next seven years on temporary premises. But while money was still very tight and the location lacked the appropriate infrastructure, there was plenty of time to experiment with various methods of exhibition design and the presentation of different themes and topics. Most important, the project promoters gained in-depth knowledge of the needs and requirements of visitors and target groups.

In this pioneer period ZOOM showed more than fourteen interactive exhibitions on different themes, introducing hands-on museum experience to Austria.

The enormous public success—more than 280,000 visitors saw the exhibitions of the original ZOOM—convinced the city and the Austrian government to fund the building of a children's museum in the refurbished complex of the Museums Quartier, the renovated former Imperial Stables in the heart of Vienna.

THE NEW ZOOM ... ALL SENSES COME INTO PLAY

The new ZOOM opened in 2001. It is the product of many years of experience as well as exchange with international museum experts, scientists,

Figure 4.1. Young Visitors at the ZOOM Children's Museum

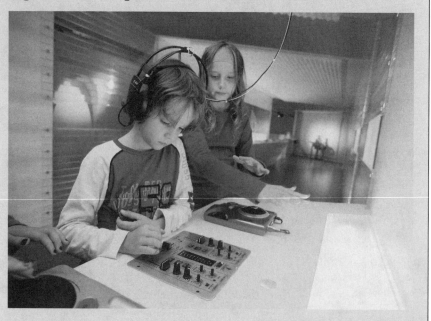

COURTESY OF ZOOM KINDERMUSEUM.

and artists. Its special position within an outstanding cultural district, surrounded by the Museum of Modern Art, the Leopold Museum, the Kunsthalle, and the Architekturzentrum, has had a major influence on ZOOM's orientation: more focused on the arts than many other children's museums, ZOOM has become a center of interaction between children and artists. Artists from various disciplines work with the children on topics relating to science, everyday culture, sociology, philosophy, and, of course, the arts. Artists and scientists collaborate in the development of the programs offered by ZOOM. And it is visual artists and committed young architects who create a large part of ZOOM's objects and installations. Experts of the senses, they manage to keep surprising us with original and playful ideas.

"Hands on, minds on, hearts on!" is the motto of this now internationally recognized museum. At ZOOM, children are welcome to ask questions, to touch and to feel, to examine and to explore the world with all their senses, in their own individual way. They zoom in on objects and situations and by doing so find out about themselves and discover their own skills and abilities. In ZOOM's exhibitions and workshops the children playfully gather sensory impressions and emotive experiences, which set learning processes into motion and allow them to acquire new knowledge.

The way children acquire knowledge is quite different from that of adults. The exhibitions and workshops at ZOOM take children's special

Figure 4.2. Young Visitors at the ZOOM Children's Museum

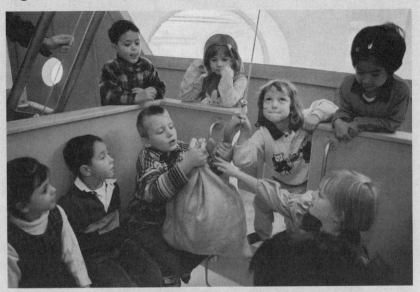

COURTESY OF ZOOM KINDERMUSEUM.

requirements into account, both in terms of their design and thematic focus. On a floor space of 1,600 square meters (17,222 sq. ft.), ZOOM Children's Museum now offers four distinct areas for different target age groups.

A Changing Exhibition Space of 600 Square Meters (6,460 sq. ft.) for Children from 6 to 12 Years Old

ZOOM presents two exhibitions per year on various themes that are determined by the interests of children. Most exhibitions are interdisciplinary and are always thoroughly curated by experts, like any "grown-up" exhibition. To illustrate the variety of themes: the new ZOOM started with an exhibition on space and how to feel space by using different senses, followed by exhibitions on design, on music and mathematics, archaeology, sculpture, and science fiction.

A 2006 exhibition on Mozart—*Wolfgang Amadéus: A Perfectly Normal Wunderkind*—encouraged children to relate to the boy Mozart, to identify with him, and to compare themselves to him. "What was Mozart actually like as a kid? What kind of music did he write when he was my age? How often did he wash and brush his teeth? What games did he play?" And last but not least: "What are my own talents and abilities?" In addition to biographical

Figure 4.3. Young Visitors at the ZOOM Children's Museum

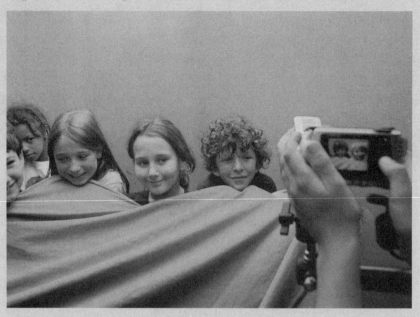

COURTESY OF ZOOM KINDERMUSEUM.

facts, the exhibition also focused on the history of everyday life in the eighteenth century, vividly illustrating the differences between life in the past and today for a number of different areas: traveling, fashion and beauty ideals, games, hygiene and medicine, aesthetics, role models, and feelings.

From 2006 onward, ZOOM plans exhibitions on sustainability, ancient Greece, and football (soccer), among other subjects.

An Artist's Studio of 100 Square Meters (1,076 sq. ft.) for Children from 3 to 12 Years Old

ZOOM Studio is situated in a glass cube offering lots of light. In this beautiful atmosphere children are accompanied and motivated by visual artists and experts to approach different artistic media and ideas playfully. In ZOOM studio, kids are free to be creative, to examine, test, construct, sculpt, draw, and paint. They can experiment freely with the materials provided to give form to their ideas on a set topic. Experimenting with different techniques and materials helps them to realize and build up confidence in their own abilities. The themes of the workshops often correspond to the main theme of the changing exhibition. In this way the studio is deepening the content of the changing exhibitions.

A Young Children's Area for Kids from 0 to 6 Years Old

Right next to the studio is ZOOM Ocean, ZOOM's toddlers' and young children's area. The objects and playing facilities of ZOOM Ocean are designed by artists. They address and stimulate the children's senses and thus foster the development of their motor and language skills. Taking the various stages of child development into account, different thematic areas have been planned for.

At the foot of the lighthouse, ZOOM Ocean's youngest visitors are invited for a dive into a mysterious underwater world. Among sea anemones and beds of seaweed a wonderful world waits to be discovered: Baby Island for the very young to practice their motor skills; caves for young explorers; the sea anemone glove theater and a coral reef, complete with plants, animals, and other objects that can be touched or heard, searched for and collected, studied and closely examined. From this colorful underwater world, a ramp leads upwards gradually turning into the deck of a ship. Up here, there's plenty of space to climb and romp around. Young sailors are invited to catch fish, throw anchors, and untie knots. The ship's engine room and a captain's cabin complete with navigational instruments offer further attractions. This early childhood area is one of the most successful spaces of ZOOM where young parents can relax and watch their children explore themselves and their abilities.

The ZOOM Lab for Kids from 8 to 14 Years Old is the Multimedia Laboratory of ZOOM

Children spend a lot of their leisure time in front of the television, playing with computer games, and surfing the Internet. Their media experience is mainly passive because they deal with preset contents and rules that they cannot change. This is exactly the starting point of ZOOM Lab. Its goal is to give children the experience of an active and creative use of media and new technologies. They can discover that new technologies can be used as tools, just like a pencil or a brush, in order to express their own ideas and visions. In doing this, they become media literate and learn a lot about interfaces of the real and digital worlds. For this purpose ZOOM developed a special new soft- and hardware program that allows kids to create animated films, 3D animations, sound collages, and pop songs. In the media lab children and teenagers take the roles of scriptwriters, cinematographers, photographers, and sound engineers. All works created at ZOOM Lab are published on the ZOOM Web site, where individual productions can be called up. ZOOM Lab is undoubtedly the most innovative part of ZOOM.

ZOOM also offers interesting special programs all year round. There are lectures, book readings, and discussions between adults and children. One of the most successful programs is the series called Viennese Children's Lectures, in which internationally known scientists explain their research fields to children and answer their questions. The titles of these lectures include: "What do human beings have in common with flies?" "Would you like to have a clone?" and "Why are parents so difficult?" These lectures make it clear that to be curious and to ask questions is extremely valuable, and is actually the essence of science.

Another series aims at informing children about different professions. People with different occupations, such as a bishop, a social worker, or a manager, are asked to talk about their work and give kids the opportunity to learn more of the grown-up world. The first lecture in this series was given by the current president of the Republic of Austria. (The lecture series by the way is also very interesting for adults.)

The story of ZOOM is a perfect success story. Coming up as a small private initiative in the 1990s it became a wonderful children's museum, perhaps one of the most beautiful worldwide. ZOOM is also acknowledged as one of the most important and prestigious cultural institutions in Vienna. Nearly everyone has forgotten that the rationale for this institution was

Figure 4.4. Young Visitors at the ZOOM Children's Museum

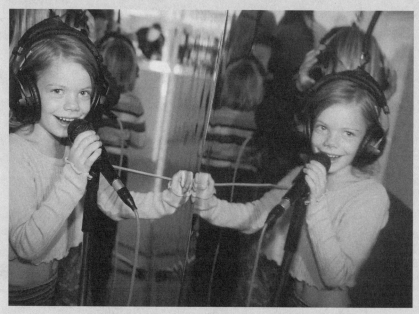

COURTESY OF ZOOM KINDERMUSEUM.

initially questioned. As the first hands-on institution in Vienna, ZOOM has also influenced all other museums in the city, so that now they offer lots of children's initiatives and programs.

More than 100,000 children visit ZOOM every year. ZOOM has become part of their lives. They have their first museum experiences here, and realize that visiting a museum can be something exciting and joyful. They comment "ZOOM is cool" and "I love ZOOM" in our guestbook. That is our real satisfaction.

Traditional museums, partly impressed by the success of these museum competitors and partly under the pressure to win new audiences, started to follow their examples. In consequence, museums established or enlarged educational departments to improve intellectual accessibility. Unfortunately these departments often had a difficult position within the museum. Educators responsible for programs for children and families sometimes were not employed directly by the museums, but worked on a contract or volunteer basis. Curatorial departments did not consider it within their scope to ask for the expertise of the educational staff in developing family-friendly exhibitions. On the contrary, most of the time educational departments were confronted with exhibitions overwhelming the visitor with too many objects. They served as troubleshooters who, at the very last moment, had to create information paths for visitors without having had any influence on the whole exhibition concept. They had to develop a storyline supplementary to the exhibition in order to inspire the visitor and arouse his or her interest. But exhibitions themselves are means of communication. Educators and curators have to agree on what kind of messages they want to send. Otherwise, contradictory information paths are developed—one of the exhibition itself, which communicates a message for the knowledgeable visitor, and the other the story of the educators told to families and children, which may differ from the original message of the curator. Hence the priority became to develop a more integrated approach of how to establish museums as learning environments for families and children by involving all museum departments in order to better serve children and families.

4.2   CHANGING MUSEUMS INTO FRIENDLY FAMILY LEARNING SPACES

Here are seven steps aimed at helping museums develop into more friendly family learning institutions.

1.   Institutional Change: A Learning Strategy

The first step toward change is the explicit will of the whole institution to define itself as a learning environment and resource center targeted at families and children. This has to be inscribed in the mission and vision of the institution. It may not be the whole mission of the museum, but certainly this commitment must be a vital part of the museum's mission or vision statement.

A written Learning Strategy should be developed explaining how the museum wants to address these audiences and what it will offer to them. Objectives and goals have to be specified, standards have to be set. The strategy should be read and signed by the entire staff. The Victoria and Albert

Museum (V&A) in London provides an excellent example of how to establish the museum as a learning space in a change management process including the whole staff. The learning strategy of the V&A can serve as a model for museums in how to fulfill this task successfully.[2] The museum has to constantly research the needs and expectations of these audiences and has to plan accordingly. The museum has to happily embrace and welcome families and school groups. In the case study of London's National Portrait Gallery in this chapter, the first step in launching the new *Reaching Out Drawing In* strategy was the identification of families as a priority audience in the NPG's Forward Plan 2005–2008.

REACHING OUT DRAWING IN: DEVELOPING FAMILY AUDIENCES AT THE NATIONAL PORTRAIT GALLERY

Toni Parker

Over the two years 2004–2006, the National Portrait Gallery in London explored new approaches to audience development with an innovative project titled *Reaching Out Drawing In*. Supported by the Heritage Lottery Fund, this project consisted of a series of temporary exhibitions that aimed to engage nontraditional audiences by combining works from the collection with work and interpretation produced by community groups and educational organizations. Each exhibition focused on a particular set of visitors who are underrepresented in the gallery's audiences, including people with disabilities, families, young people, and black and minority ethnic visitors. Within these groups, the project targeted young people outside formal education, young people at risk of offending, refugee families, blind and partially sighted visitors, the Chinese community, and black and Asian audiences.

The project straddled the spheres of education and exhibitions, and was run by a project manager based in the Learning and Access Department. It relied on close collaboration between the gallery and participant groups. Each group worked with an artist and the project manager, first in selecting works from the collection, and then on linked outreach activities and workshops in which they created new work. The project also involved developing alternative types of interpretation, including labels written by participants and a variety of interactive methods of engaging with the displays. A key priority was to present each exhibition as part of the gallery's overall program, so they were held in the Studio Gallery, which is accessible to all National Portrait Gallery visitors. Feedback and evaluation also provided opportunities to examine public responses to the shows, and to explore new audiences' attitudes to the gallery as a whole.

Family Faces took place in the summer of 2005 and was the second of the exhibitions in the *Reaching Out Drawing In* program. The target audience was families living in Haringey, a culturally diverse but socially disadvantaged borough in North London. The gallery had previously identified families as a priority audience in its Forward Plan 2005–2008 and was looking for ways to extend the traditional profile of this group. *Family Faces* provided an opportunity to work with asylum seekers and refugee families, so that 60 percent of the project participants were drawn from these groups, including a high proportion from the Somali, Turkish, and Kurdish communities. One hundred eighty-seven people took part, including parents, children, caregivers, siblings, grandparents, and stepfamilies. The youngest participant was two years old and the oldest was seventy-three.

Participants were approached through seven Family Learning Groups affiliated with the Education and Social Services Department of Haringey Council. Partnerships of this kind represent an important part of the *Reaching Out Drawing In* project methodology. They enable the gallery to identify target groups and build relationships more effectively, first by drawing on specialist advice and expertise, and second by enabling us to link up with existing organizations and groups. Partnerships also help us to remain in contact with participants after their project has ended and to sustain their interest in the gallery and other cultural organizations. The involvement of Haringey's Family Learning Services was vital to the success of *Family Faces* in facilitating access to participants, supporting learning objectives, and providing additional local marketing and publicity for the show.

Once they had agreed to take part, groups of parents and children worked with the ceramicist, Matt Sherratt, to create clay sculptures that explored their individual and cultural identities. The groups visited the gallery and made sketches of works on display. They also discussed how families were represented in portraiture of different periods and how elements such as pose, expression, and setting can affect the appearance and meaning of an image. After their visits, the families designed and made their own family portraits inspired by work they had seen at the gallery. The themes they chose were diverse and often quite personal. They included family celebrations, family meals, emotions, holidays, their homes (both in London and in their country of origin), and particular family members.

The exhibition featured ninety portrait sculptures. It also included twenty-five works representing families from the gallery's collection, ranging from recent photographs and drawings to historic oil paintings. The participants selected these works, often for their relevance to their own lives or histories. *The Shudi Family* by Marcus Tuscher, for example, was chosen partly because the Shudis were an eighteenth-century immigrant family who had risen to the top of their profession and had become renowned for their skills as piano makers.

The families also wrote the labels interpreting their work. These focused on the meaning behind their sculptures, and many alluded to personal and moving stories. Additional interpretation included jigsaws of works in the collection, costume and mirrors enabling children to dress up and pose as figures in the paintings, and drawing and writing activities. Visitors described the labels and activities as particularly engaging elements of the exhibition. They liked the personal insights provided by participants' accounts of their work and felt that the activities—used by young and older children and some adults—were both enjoyable and educational, encouraging discussion and closer attention to the works on display.

Family Faces opened on February 14, 2005 and ran until September 4, 2005. During that time the exhibition received 53,285 visitors as well as 19,462 virtual visitors to the Web site. It was also used as a resource within the regular family program. After the exhibition closed, the family sculptures were displayed at Bruce Castle Museum, which was local for the majority of the participants.

So, what did this exhibition achieve and what lessons can be learned from the project? From the participants' perspective, the experience was unequivocally positive. In feedback they described their satisfaction in developing creative skills and an increased awareness of art. They also expressed their appreciation of the opportunities that the project afforded to explore their identities, and to think about themselves, their family units, and their relationships. Even more significantly, they felt that they had gained in confidence and self-esteem, and that their language and communication skills had improved through teamwork and expressing their emotions. "I am so proud of my family," observed a mother who took part in the exhibition. "I never thought I could learn these skills, and thought 'I can't do this' at the beginning. Now I feel much more confident, and it has been such a wonderful experience."

For the parents, especially, the exhibition gave them a chance to work together and support each others' learning as well as increasing their ability to support their children's school and home-based learning. Several of the schools involved reported feeling confident and inspired enough to deliver comparable activities themselves. They have engaged an artist to deliver workshops involving groups of parents and children along similar lines to those used in *Family Faces*.

The National Portrait Gallery's experience of the project was equally favorable. The exhibition more than fulfilled its aims of attracting new audiences. From questionnaires, interviews, and focus groups, we found that 63 percent of visitors were new to the gallery, 41 percent of visitors were families, and 27 percent were from black or minority ethnic communities. This compares with 26 percent first-time visitors, 4 percent child visitors, and 6 percent black or minority ethnic visitors recorded in surveys for the same period in the previous year.

The exhibition also enabled us to develop partnerships with new groups and communities in areas of social and economic deprivation. We have worked with Haringey and its Family Learning Services Department on several subsequent projects. Furthermore, there is evidence to show that exhibition participants have continued to visit the National Portrait Gallery and other galleries. One participant declared: "Before doing this I didn't go to galleries at all. But now I have taken my children to a few galleries and museums and have learned so much. The children are very keen to visit. They see things in pictures that tell stories. I will definitely continue to visit either with or without my children."

Finally, the exhibition seems to have had wider social and cultural benefits. Comments in the visitors' book reported that the sculpture in *Family Faces* made visitors more understanding of other communities and encouraged them to think about their own families.

Some of the remarks recorded during the focus groups were also interesting. The people who took part had visited the exhibition and all ranked their experience as either excellent or good. They were particularly enthusiastic about the interactive and participatory nature of the show. However, their reactions to the gallery as a whole were more reserved. They were disappointed not to find similar types of interpretation in the permanent collection galleries and felt that the building and the displays were not as family-friendly as they could be. Most felt that although they would definitely return to the gallery, they would limit their visits to a time when they knew that there were exhibitions or events designed specifically with families in mind. These responses are not especially surprising. Museums and galleries know that new audiences need to be nurtured with ongoing programs of activities and displays that are relevant to their interests. Experience has also shown that families, in particular, prefer to visit galleries where parts of the interpretation are aimed at children and include participative elements.

Nevertheless, the *Reaching Out Drawing In* project has encouraged the National Portrait Gallery to reconsider its approach to exhibitions and displays in the light of their appeal to different audiences. This approach has driven the gallery's new interpretative portrait display which opened in July 2006 at Beningborough Hall in Yorkshire. The process of developing and sustaining new family audiences continues.

2. Establish the Museum as a Family-Friendly Space

Museums can be an adventurous learning experience for families and children. Yet some of the great museums are among the most challenging and foreboding for families and children. Children and families should be welcomed in all kinds of museums. Nonetheless, some museums whose collections are targeted at expert audiences are less appealing to family audiences. It can also happen that museums that normally offer programs for families from time to time show special exhibitions for specialist audiences that are less suitable for families.

Museums that want to create a family-friendly image should consider the following requisites:

- Clear communication

Museums that are targeting families should first of all communicate that they are destinations for children and families, and that they offer excellent learning environments. This should be made clear in all communication material, starting with a statement on the Web site as well as on brochures and other informational publications.

- Family friendly pricing policy

The pricing policy of the museum should reflect the financial difficulties that most families are facing. Many museums offer family tickets that are defined as tickets for parents and two children. This definition may cause problems: in times of patchwork families, families come in diverse formations. Mothers arrive with children and their friends, grandparents with several grandchildren, nannies with more than one child. This often causes difficult situations for cashiers who have to defend strict museum pricing policies to angry visitors. As families are more and more under financial pressure a more permissive ticket policy will help to establish a family-friendly image.

By offering family tickets museums also acknowledge families as clients. This raises expectations on the part of the family, which then anticipates special treatment and service. Consequently it also means that grown-ups and children are expecting experiences to learn and explore according to their needs and intellectual capacity.

- Offering free entrance on special days

In order to reach out to new communities museums may offer special days to families free of charge. Some cities subsidize family days in their city museums and help with marketing and promotion of these events. It is advisable to offer special family learning programs on these days.

- Making it an enjoyable experience

It is essential to know that reaching out and inviting families is not enough. They have to enjoy and value their visit in order to come again and motivate others to come. It has to be a satisfying experience for all members of the family.

3. Motivating Museum Staff

Apart from the educators it is the staff on the floor at the entrance hall who have the first and most direct contact with family audiences. Unfortunately, these museum employees may be the least willing to deal with this specific audience group unless they have been trained and motivated for this task. For them families are hard work and cause stress—they are demanding, loud, disturb the other visitors, and are often seen as safety risks for the objects. Often guards and staff working in visitor services do not get any help, support, or training from museum management in how to deal with families. Clear rules on visitor behavior and security should be provided in writing so that staff can refer to them. It should be explained that parents are responsible for their children. Staff should get training in how to address parents and children. It is of great importance for the museum to create an atmosphere where families feel included. Effective learning and social exchange can take place only when children and parents feel comfortable and get adequate help when needed.

4. Knowing Your Visitors: Reaching Out to Families

Museums have to know whom they are inviting through their doors! Families have certain characteristics in common that museums should take into account:

- They consist of different generations
  Families are a group of individuals belonging to different generations. Whether it is a two-generation difference (parents/children) or whether they are divided by three generations (grandparents/children), each of the individuals is building knowledge on a different experience base.
- Different learning styles between grown-ups and children
  Children learn differently from grown-ups. They have to explore and discover by using more than their visual sense. Tactile experiences are very important, especially for younger children.
- Different learners
  Each family, like any other group, consists of individuals with different learning abilities. Some are analytical learners, others need to discover and experiment, still others prefer to discuss and reflect with a companion.
- Different concentration span
  Children need attention and motivation to focus on exploring and discovering. Their curiosity has to be aroused in order to keep them interested.
- Families differ from each other
  Each family differs from one another due to their social, cultural, and educational background, their learning experiences and their common values.

5. Inviting Families to Come

Families have to be invited and motivated to come. Museums are often not their first choice. Families can choose among a wide variety of leisure time opportunities. In order to compete, museums have to define their strengths and values. In order to distinguish themselves from other leisure offerings, museums have to promote and communicate why families should enter through their doors.

As museums do not have large marketing budgets like commercial leisure institutions it is essential that museums invest in networking and building relationships in order to reach out to family audiences. This needs extensive study of the community in which the museum is located, knowing about local family structures, school practices, local commonly held learning theories, family norms and values, and cultural norms. Museums have to be aware of the demographic structure of their visitors and nonvisitors. Constant research enables museums to react quickly to changes within the demographic structure of visitors and nonvisitors—such as a decline of family income or a rise in the divorce rate.

Most important are strong connections with other institutions that serve families and children. Such links offer the possibility to exchange audiences and to invite new families through museum doors. An excellent example is the *Family Faces* exhibition that was part of the *Reaching Out Drawing In* program at London's National Portrait Gallery that is described in the NPG case study in this chapter.

6. Helping Parents to Prepare for the Museum Visit

Taking your family to a museum is sometimes hard work. Traveling with children in cities on public transit can be quite exhausting. If families then finally arrive and are confronted with sold-out family programs they will be extremely annoyed and will probably never come back. It is therefore extremely important to help families to organize their visit well in advance. Exact descriptions of the programs should be provided on the Web site, via telephone, and on information material. Often museums forget to give important information on:

- whether families are specially welcomed
- if a family discount on the entrance fee can be expected
- if prebooking is necessary
- what kind of programs are offered for families with children and for what age
- what kind of educational value can be expected—what can be learned
- the length of the program
- what kind of role the grown-ups play in this educational program: whether the parent is directly involved in the learning process as an interpreter,

explorer, playmate, or is just accompanying the child to a special workshop program or gallery activity.

Sometimes families ignore prebooking and improvise a museum visit at the very last moment. If in any case families have to be turned down because a program is fully booked, there should be a way to compensate their effort of coming to the museum by giving them preferential treatment for the next visit in order not to lose them as customers, or by proposing alternative programs such as a family gallery visit at a reduced rate.

7. Learning From Your Family Visitors

In order to serve special audiences museums need to start a dialogue with their clients.

Asking people's opinion is a very effective way to learn about their needs: a simple method is to motivate visitors to write about their learning experience in a visitor book, leave a message on a bulletin board, or send an e-mail through the Web site.

It is important for museums to react to visitor remarks and to answer them personally. Observations of visitors and visitor behaviors might clarify obstacles, hindrances, and difficulties in physical, emotional, and intellectual access. Children's museums and science centers have developed a system of trying out installations and exhibits before final installation. They are also more willing to change exhibits if observation clearly indicates that visitors show no interest or engagement.

Finally it is important that museums periodically evaluate the learning experiences of families with children in their galleries. In part III of this book Dr. Soren addresses the challenge of evaluation.

4.3   PROGRAMMING FOR FAMILIES

Programming for families includes the whole museum staff. When planning a new exhibition it has to be clear from the very beginning of creating a concept how this exhibition will target a family audience. The early involvement of the educational department is essential. Curators and designers have to agree to listen to the suggestions of the educational experts and plan accordingly.

4.3.1   Spaces for Family Learning in Exhibitions

Creating an exhibition for families has an influence on:

- exhibition design
- graphic design

- display of the objects, height of showcases, labels, hanging of objects
- quality and sturdiness of installations.

Science centers and children's museums were pioneers in inventing different types of exhibits that lead to social interaction between visitors and can engage families with children, offering hands-on experiences, exploration, and discovery with all senses. Traditional museums can follow these examples by integrating hands-on areas in exhibitions targeted at younger children. Here children can dress up or solve a puzzle, or play with replicas of toys from different times. A very good example are the hands-on areas in the British galleries of the Victoria and Albert Museum, placed as separate spaces within the exhibition galleries. Here families can peacefully play together and are secluded from the display areas of the exhibition.

Some museums offer research labs allowing direct contact with specimens and artifacts in a separated area. Here children with their caretakers can use microscopes or do simple experiments. These places allow exploratory learning and facilitate child-parent communication.

Other museums have objects displayed within the exhibition that can be better observed from a child's perspective, whereas a grown-up has to kneel down in order to observe. In this way the child's curiosity is aroused because she or he is directly addressed as a visitor, bringing the different viewpoints of grown-up and child into perspective. In this case the best learning happens when children and parents exchange their points of view.

4.3.2 Intergenerational Learning

Museums should offer diverse kinds of family learning possibilities according to the content of the specific museum. Science centers, natural history museums, and children's museums will offer more hands-on learning possibilities and discovery opportunities. Art museums should find ways to address generations differently by offering diverse information paths and special guided tours for families, encouraging family members to start a dialogue about their different perceptions. Family learning will be most effective if a dialogue between generations is encouraged, and knowledge and meaning is created in the exchange between generations. This deepens understanding and tolerance among different points of view and perceptions.

Learning can be an interaction between family members in various forms, depending on whether parents serve as teaching authority, or if the museum is the ultimate authority, providing children and parents with interpretation and intellectual help. The museum should foresee diverse possibilities in planning exhibitions where intergenerational learning can take place.

4.3.3 Parents and Children Having a Common Experience

Families can follow different programs in museums. One main difference between these programs is whether the parents act as the educator and tell the story, or whether both generations learn with the help of the museum on a more equal basis. This leads to the question of who tells the story—who is the resource of information?

The very traditional form is the one in which the caregiver selects and interprets artifacts—he or she serves as the ultimate authority who educates children in the museum. This can work very well in history museums or cultural heritage museums where parents or grandparents use artifacts to tell stories about their own past. In this way museum objects are familiarized to the child in an engaging mode of expression.

In art museums or science centers often only the very well-educated parent can fulfill the role of interpreter and educator. That is why these museums often assist the parents, providing them with information that can be transferred to the children. In this way the museum takes the role of the educator and serves as an intermediary between parents and children. The museum acts as the knowledge authority that tells the story, assisting parents in transferring the museum's narrative to the children. This can be done in different ways:

- Creating an information path for parents explaining how to interpret objects to their children.

  Parents are informed via information sheets or special labels regarding what they can explain to their children and what children can learn from this artifact or installation. Science centers and children's museums are successfully using this method. They help to start the dialogue between children and parents. Parents are still the narrator, but can rely on information provided by the museum.

- Activity sheets for parents and children for experiencing an exhibition together.

  By answering questions or solving a riddle, parents and children are invited to look closer, start a dialogue, and compare different points of view. These kinds of activities are introduced in art museums to help arouse the interest of children and to interpret difficult content. Here parents and children learn on an equal basis, since both are addressed as learners. Some museums offer activity sheets for parents and caregivers to take home and continue the learning process. The Science Museum in London offers this service, with learning material also available over the Internet.

- Hands-on environments and installations that can be operated by children and parents.

  These can be open learning spaces—as in science centers and children's museums—inviting parents and children to play together. These exhibits invite families to experiment freely without an intended outcome—the creative approach depends very much on the learner and on social interaction between learners. Answers are not prefabricated but depend individually on the learner. This means that caregivers and children may pose different questions and find different answers. Here again children and parents are addressed equally as they learn from a different knowledge base.

- Discovery installations that formally lead to a certain predisposed answer.

  With this approach learners can experience scientific phenomena or laws. Installations that need more than one person to be activated invite social interaction between generations. In this way parents and children are invited to learn and work together.

- Workshops for children and parents.

  Many museums have started to invite caregivers and children to create works of art or do scientific experiments in a workshop setting. Most of these workshops are facilitated by educators who serve as intermediaries between parents and children.

4.3.4 Children Having Their Own Experience

Here children follow special programs. The parents fulfill the role of children's escort while the children follow a guided tour for their age group or attend a workshop where children create and work with the help of educators or artists. Parents are invited as observers and can observe their children in a new environment and admire the children's creation after the workshops. Some of these programs give parents the opportunity to visit the gallery or exhibition while children are taken care of in their special program.

4.3.5 Children and Parents Having Separate Experiences

Still another possibility enables children and parents to walk through an exhibition individually. Museums can offer audioguides for children or activity sheets that enable children to find their way through an exhibition by themselves. Parents meanwhile are able to choose their own path. This type of program attracts more experienced museum visitors and older children who feel confident to walk by themselves. It also requires parents who are willing to talk and reflect with their children after their museum visit about their specific experiences, and answer questions that have arisen during their gallery walks.

4.4   CONCLUSION

Families are discovering more and more that museums are places for joint learning experiences. But not all museums—especially the museums with grand collections—are fully prepared to best serve these audiences.

Families are one of the most challenging visitor groups, as they consist of individuals belonging to different generations and have diverse personal needs, learning experiences, personal histories, learning needs, and knowledge levels. It requires the effort, creativity, and involvement of the whole museum organization to approach these audiences, welcome them, and offer them intellectual and physical comfort, and help them in their learning process.

> By changing museums into learning spaces for families, museums contribute to fulfilling an urgent need in postmodern society:
>
> - To promote learning.
> - To newly connect parents and children and activate the dialogue between different generations.
> - To help parents and children construct knowledge out of common experience, through language and social interaction.
> - To create and construct identity.

In contrast to other leisure offerings for families, museums at their best allow multiple views on content. They help to construct meanings and provoke questions without giving simple answers. Therefore, parents using museums to teach but also to learn with their children wisely contribute to preparing them for a future where creative thinking will be needed more and more. Museums should acknowledge the important role that they are playing in family learning, and offer the best possible environments for children and caregivers.

NOTES

1. Howard Gardner, *The Unschooled Mind: How Children Think and How Schools Should Teach* (New York: Basic Books, 1991), 202.
2. *Creative Networks: Knowledge and Inspiration: The Victoria and Albert Museum's Strategy for Learning* (London: Victoria and Albert Museum, 2001).

CHAPTER 5

New Relationships with the Formal Education Sector

Brad King

The relationship between formal and informal learning institutions[1] has changed considerably in recent decades in response to two major trends. The first and perhaps primary development may be termed *marketization*, discussed in section 5.1, whereby museums and schools are increasingly relating to one another in terms of service provider and consumer.[2] This marketization has led to a number of new initiatives and partnerships between museums and the formal education sector, as explored in section 5.2.

The second major trend, which is closely related to the first, is *increasing formalization* of pedagogy in the formal learning sector. While formalization has also been a contributing factor to the marketization of museum-school relationships, it has produced effects of its own. From a pedagogical point of view, the trend to increasing formalization in public school teaching has the most potential for innovative structural changes in museum-based education. As Barry Lord reminds us in chapter 2 of this book, the learning that takes place in museums "is *not* the kind of learning that takes place in schools or universities" but is in fact informal, self-motivated, and affective. Thus, the informal learning that happens in museums can act as a counterbalance to the heightened formality so prevalent today in North American school districts and elsewhere.

In fact, the evolving balance between formal and informal learning is a theme that runs throughout this chapter's discussion of changing museum-school relationships. While it is true that museums offer a somewhat different learning experience for their school visitors than for their casual visitors—for one thing, a schoolchild's attendance on a scheduled museum field trip is usually not voluntary at all, and the experience is not always as self-directed as is the case for other visitors—the learning that occurs remains qualitatively informal in terms of the process. More important, informal learning is being valued to a greater extent by educators in response to a number of significant academic, socioeconomic, and political changes—and perhaps also in recognition of evidence suggesting that up to 80 percent of *all* learning happens informally.[3] Thus, section 5.3 reflects educational reform efforts that are based on informal learning rather than the opposite, as well as the evolving balance between the two. The focus here is on the "museum school"—which in its most developed incarnation is a new institutional partnership between museums and schools that could craft a creative pedagogy specifically suited to twenty-first century needs.

5.1 THE MARKETIZATION OF MUSEUM-SCHOOL RELATIONSHIPS

Marketization here refers to a growing client–service provider relationship between schools and museums, insofar as the rules of the marketplace now apply to the informal-formal education relationship to a greater extent than ever before. There are several key trends behind this development.

The first and perhaps preeminent factor has to do with pedagogy in the formal learning sector, which has become even more formal in recent decades due to a shift in the broader political culture.[4] In the United States in particular, there has been much distress over a perceived decline in student achievement and school performance since the 1970s, which is correlated to (although not necessarily caused by) an increasing level of informality in teaching styles that began in the 1960s. The solution for many politicians and school reformers in North America—a return to the so-called "3 Rs" (writing, reading, and arithmetic) and standardized testing—has produced a narrower and more incentives-based pedagogy in North American public schools.

There is no doubt that the increasing formalization of learning in the formal education sector has generated some difficulties for museum-school relationships. Museum educators have expressed concern about the impact of such standards and philosophies on museum education programs, particularly on field trips. For example, museum staff in some jurisdictions report that many teachers see museum visits as "frills" that do little to boost standardized test scores. Others have even reported difficulties in merely initiating or maintaining contact with school districts, especially if they work in institutions that teachers see as offering little to improve such scores (art museums, for example). This is important because the opinion of teachers remains crucial; according to a 2002 survey by the U.S. Institute for Museum and Library Services, "respondents continue to report that teachers most influence a school's decision to use museum resources."[5] Museums are therefore obliged to see teachers as key "target markets" who must be carefully cultivated and wooed in order to maintain existing levels of school group visitation.

Another factor in the marketization of the museum-school relationship has been the combined effect of a dramatic increase in the number of museums over the past fifteen years, combined with chronic financial shortfalls within school district budgets in many jurisdictions (which often means decreased school participation in museum programs). A surfeit of museum options has in effect increased competition among museums for school visitors, and when school district budgetary problems are added to the mix, the result is a buyer's market. Under these conditions, the impact of increasing formalization is magnified, leading to a growing chasm between have and have-not museums—those perceived to offer the best potential for direct curriculum-linked outputs, and those perceived to be lacking.

Finally, museums themselves have become more market-oriented in a general sense due to much larger museological trends, as well as for financial reasons. As museums shift from an earlier emphasis on functions like collections preservation and documentation to a greater focus on public service and accessibility, they have found value in tasks such as audience research and exhibition evaluation, designed to ensure that the museum's exhibitions and programs correspond with the needs and desires of their markets. With regard to finances, an increasing need to justify public operating subsidies in a long period of government cutbacks and financial restraint has forced museums to demonstrate clearly the public benefit that results from their existence—part of which includes attendance. Hence there is a strong incentive to focus on markets as well as the museum's mission. Marketization, then, is a phenomenon in museums that extends well beyond the museum-school relationship. Nevertheless, it shapes that relationship profoundly.

5.2   THE MUSEUM RESPONSE

Like private sector firms forced to innovate constantly to remain competitive, museums have responded to marketization in various ways:

Higher Expenditures on School Programming: Museums are focusing more of their internal resources on program development. According to the 2002 survey of the U.S. Institute of Museum and Library Services, the percentage of American museums' median annual operating budgets spent on school programming in 2000–2001 increased fourfold from that reported in 1995.[6] While firmly in line with the general tendency toward enhanced public education in museums since the 1960s and 1970s, this is a dramatic increase in a relatively short period of time. Given the trends outlined above it is not surprising that museums are spending far more resources on school programs in recent years, at least in part to maintain an expected share of the school market.

Curriculum-Linked Programming: Although museum educational programs have long been developed with reference to school curricula, one of the obvious results of marketization has been a reconsideration of educational programs so that they show a clear curriculum-related output, so that in turn teachers may justify participation to their principals—and indeed, show a direct improvement in standardized test scores. Given the increasing difficulty in attracting school groups, general tours of the galleries are rarely sufficient in and of themselves to attract large numbers of students—of course these are still offered by most museums, but more museums are now offering curriculum-linked programs designed to help teachers raise test scores. Such programs respond to the reality that teachers must now "teach to the test" (i.e., focus their teaching on standardized test subjects in order to ensure that their schools achieve the mandated results). In any case, virtually all museum educators view curriculum-linked programming as nothing less than a necessity, for market-related as well as mission-related reasons.

The Museum as Programmatic Partner: Recognizing that the one-time field trip may not satisfy a school's requirements in terms of curriculum outputs, some museums have tried to position themselves as ongoing year-round resources for teachers—in effect, the museum becomes a partner with the school in longer-term projects. Part of the challenge inherent in this approach is to move teachers away from the traditional end-of-year field trip toward a more sustained relationship. While this is a worthy goal, in practice it has proven difficult, with most museums in the northern hemisphere still reporting the traditional mainstays of April, May, and June as the highest-attendance months for school groups. Part of the reason why longer-range programming with schools has proven to be so difficult may be because it requires fundamental institutional cultural change and adaptability on both sides—an issue that new institutional forms requiring deep collaboration (such as the museum school—see section 5.3) have been forced to address.

Programs Aimed at Granting Agencies: In some cases, museums have responded with lessened emphasis on the traditional school market in favor of a greater focus on highly specific segments of the formal education sector. In most cases the incentive is grant money. In the United States, one such grant program is Upward Bound, a government initiative that provides funding to agencies that assist children to become the first in their families to attend a university. Grants offered via this program have been pursued with much success by museums such as the Miami Museum of Science and Planetarium. Such grant programs can in fact become significant revenue centers for museums, which over the past two decades have for various reasons been forced to increase the percentage of revenues from self-generated sources. But while very much needed, they typically serve far fewer students than traditional museum education programs, and can have the effect of redirecting scarce internal resources away from these broader service programs.

Teacher Training: Like many of the other trends, museum-based teacher training is a service area that has been developing for some years. While teacher training ensures that teachers make the best use of the museum's resources in a way that respects the type of affective learning found in museums, it is also a form of outreach, intended to generate awareness of the museum and how it can benefit schools. Teacher training programs often serve as a bridge between the two pedagogies, to provide the tools teachers need to plan and lead their own museum visits, as opposed to relying on museum staff,[7] and to provide teachers with a sense of control, since teachers sometimes have very little influence on the ideas taught or the experiments conducted on a typical school museum visit.[8] In this regard, teacher training is part of the museum's attempt to position itself as a resource for teachers and a service provider, but it also recognizes the fact that some teachers lack a complete understanding of the ways in which a museum can contribute to their pedagogical goals, or of museum-based learning in general.

Whatever one's personal opinion of the marketization of the relationships in question, the evidence suggests that the quality of museum programs intended for the formal education sector has improved as a result.[9] Yet new opportunities have emerged that go beyond the readjustment of existing programs (or the development of new ones) in response to changing market conditions—in fact, there are structural changes afoot in the relationship between schools and museums. The next section focuses on the museum school, a creative new direction in museum-based learning, representing a new kind of synthesis between the formal learning of the traditional school sector and the informal learning so well-suited to the museum.

5.3   AN INNOVATIVE PARTNERSHIP: THE MUSEUM SCHOOL

What is a museum school? There are a range of museum-based learning initiatives that can be so labeled, from small "schools in museums" which are often operated solely by the museum, to "museums in schools" operated solely by a school district, to near-merged institutions that bridge the informal (museum) and formal (school) learning institutions via intensive partnerships. This is to say that no dominant model has yet emerged; the museum school as a concept is evidently still under construction.

Despite the vagueness of the term, the American researcher Kira S. King has defined *museum school* as an institution "that is collaboratively designed and implemented through a partnership between a school district and at least one museum in order to implement museum learning with at least one of the following three application activities: object creation, exhibit creation, and museum creation."[10] In fact, they may be defined even more broadly than that. These innovative concepts can involve a number of community organizations beyond the museum and the school district, including universities, colleges, and other cultural institutions.[11] Clearly there is room within the museum school concept for partnerships of considerable breadth.

Several of the trends noted in this chapter have provided impetus for the development of the museum school. The various aspects of a narrower, more formal regime in North American and other public schools—the new curriculum, the impact of disincentives to underperformance (schools that do not perform up to standard can face punitive sanctions), and the drive for greater accountability at the school and district level—have in fact opened a gap in students' education that museums are particularly well-suited to fill. More than one researcher has noted that the imposition of more rigid standards on public school systems has restricted learning opportunities in the school curriculum. This process is blamed for "stifling the potential to pose counter models and to envision alternative possibilities," while the imposed standards "[distract] us from paying attention to the importance of building a culture of schooling that is genuinely intellectual in character, that values questions and ideas at least as much as getting right answers."[12] Most important, the more formalized learning structures now in place in the traditional education sector are at odds with the need for schools to prepare students for success in the creative economy, which is increasingly being recognized as crucial for economic success in the twenty-first century.[13] Museum schools therefore offer an attractive opportunity to escape the rigidity endemic to the curriculum in most North American and some other school districts at present.

The rise of the museum school can also be linked to financial pressures in the formal education sector, since cash-strapped school districts have a greater incentive to seek partnerships with other public education institutions to help fill pedagogical gaps and to help them meet the performance standards imposed upon them by governments. According to Carolyn Jabs, writing in *Edutopia* in 2004, "daunted by the costs of creating schools from the ground up, school districts have begun to explore the idea of sharing facilities with local organizations from museums and zoos to health-care centers and retail outlets." Operating costs are shared between the museum and the school, and corporate sponsors can be sought to provide additional operating support.

Yet the predominant driving force in the development of museum schools is pedagogical in nature. While marketization is no doubt a factor, the emergence of the institution known as the museum school is more directly attributable to increasing pedagogical formalization in the public school system. In fact, museum schools represent an alternative type of school reform—a type that is almost exactly the opposite of the "3-Rs"-focused test-based school reform efforts implemented in many parts of North America and elsewhere over the past several years. The result is a dramatic new experiment in combining the best aspects of informal and formal learning in the museum school.

COMMUNITY-CONNECTED SCIENCE EDUCATION: SOUTHWEST VIRGINIA'S NEW MUSEUM HIGH SCHOOL

Michael L. Bentley

Jay Lemke has argued that, "science and science education, as traditionally understood, may already have become either obsolete or overspecialized."[1] New challenges to schools in educating students for democratic citizenship include globalization, unending wars against a dispersed enemy, accelerating climate change, environmental degradation and loss of biodiversity, regional collapses of the carrying capacity, and the revolution in technology. This twenty-first century new reality is reflected in the inclusion of the K–12 (kindergarten–grade 12) curriculum content area, "Science in Personal and Social Perspectives," as one of eight content areas in the United States's National Science Education Standards (National Research Council, 1996).[2]

Virginia is a state that has received good marks for its standards and testing program by *Education Week*'s annual "Quality Counts" ranking.[3] First mandated in 1995, the Virginia Standards of Learning (Board of Education, 2003) curriculum framework for K–12 science provides many jumping off points for environmental education, especially in the state's standards for ninth grade earth science.[4] Unfortunately, in Virginia, the best students often skip the earth science course so they can take more advanced courses in other sciences for their third science course. Ninth grade earth science is also typically populated with many "inclusion" students, an extra pedagogical challenge for many of those who teach the course.

For this and other reasons, such as the widespread perception of teachers that superficial coverage of many topics helps students better prepare for high-stakes tests than in-depth study of fewer topics, the public secondary schools in Virginia are limited in being able to address the new economic and environmental challenges to democratic society. Linda McNeil affirms that an unintended outcome of the imposition of state standards on public schools is a narrowing of learning opportunities in the school curriculum, "stifling the potential to pose counter models and to envision alternative possibilities."[5]

A LOCAL CURRICULUM INITIATIVE

A consequence of a narrowing of the public school curriculum in Virginia and across the United States—a result of the 'No Child Left Behind' Act— has been a loss of diversity of curriculum models for K–12 education. In east Tennessee and in southwestern Virginia, where I work and live, there has also been a decline in teacher morale and a growing dissatisfaction with the rigid state-mandated curriculum and its high-stakes testing program. Brooks and Brooks point out that, "Educational improvement is not accomplished through administrative or legislative mandate. It is accomplished through attention to the complicated, idiosyncratic, often paradoxical, and difficult-to-measure nature of learning."[6] Elliot Eisner has also warned that the standards movement distracts us from the deeper issues of education: "It distracts us from paying attention to the importance of building a culture of schooling that is genuinely intellectual in character, that values questions and ideas at least as much as getting right answers."[7]

The loss of curriculum diversity and creativity in the public schools provided the context in 1999 when a group of families decided to organize themselves and undertake a project to create an opportunity for a different kind of schooling for adolescents in the Roanoke Valley area, one that would better address the challenges of educating students for democratic citizenship. What emerged in 2001 from the efforts of two-dozen or so people was Community High School (http://www.communityhigh.net), a unique local expression of the museum school concept.

Many of those who worked on the Community High project were parents of children enrolled in Roanoke's Community School (http://www.communityschool.net), a not-for-profit nontraditional prekindergarten-to-grade-8 private school dating to 1971 that annually serves a diverse population of 145 students (40 percent of whom receive financial aid). In 2001, Community School's board of trustees took the high school project under its wing and thus became the new school's parent organization. While continuing strong ties, Community High (CHS) and Community School are now governed by separate boards with overlapping membership. Each institution has its own tax-exempt status and is located at a separate site in the community.

CHS was designed to serve a student body of sixty secondary school students. During the two-year planning period, working relationships were formed with informal educators at the many cultural institutions situated in the Roanoke area, including:

Mill Mountain Theatre
The Roanoke Symphony Orchestra
The Science Museum of Western Virginia
The Art Museum of Western Virginia
The History Museum of Western Virginia

The Virginia Museum of Transportation and O. Winston Link Museum
Mill Mountain Zoo
Virginia's Explore Park
Opera Roanoke
Roanoke Ballet
The Harrison Museum of African American Culture
The Salem Museum

In planning for the new school, the curriculum design team was advised by the University of Virginia Curry School's Thomas Jefferson Center for Educational Design in Charlottesville (http://curry.edschool.virginia.edu/centers/jefferson/home.html). This multidisciplinary research center was created in 1996 and is dedicated to the study of effective learning. Its mission is to monitor, evaluate, and promote innovative educational design through publications, consulting, and conferences. In addition, the CHS project involved faculty and administrators from the area's higher education institutions, particularly Hollins University. The Community School campus is located adjacent to Hollins University and the two institutions have had a long-standing cooperative relationship.

Community High School opened in September 2002 with about a dozen students, two full-time teachers, a part-time director, and several part-time instructors. Each succeeding year the numbers of students has increased, with a 2005–2006 enrollment of forty-four full-time and several part-time students. The first four-year class graduated in June 2006. Accreditation is currently pending with the Southern Association of Colleges and Schools (SACS).

CHS was initially located in the Jefferson Center, a renovated former public high school in downtown Roanoke in the heart of the Roanoke Valley's museum and cultural community. As home to a number of cultural and service institutions, the Jefferson Center provided multiple performance venues for CHS students, no doubt contributing to the evolution of the school's arts-rich curriculum. By 2005, CHS had outgrown its space in the Jefferson Center and was moved to a larger and more flexible downtown facility, across from the *Roanoke Times* (the local daily newspaper) and the Roanoke City Municipal Center. The new location is within walking distance of the Jefferson Center, the new YMCA, the Virginia Transportation Museum, the O. Winston Link Museum, the Roanoke Higher Education Center, and Center-in-the-Square, which houses Mill Mountain Theatre, the Science Museum, the Art Museum, and the Historical Society.

THE MUSEUM SCHOOL CONCEPT

Museum schools are an educational innovation, with some forty schools of this type now operating in the United States, but a much lesser number that are high schools.[8] In museum schools the curriculum, instruction, and assessment of students are aligned with a museum or other cultural institution. Some museum schools are housed on site at a museum, zoo, or related institution, while in other such schools students and teachers visit a museum on a regular basis. Since a variety of cultural institutions are involved, curriculum varies widely among museum schools. While museum schools represent a variety of designs, most are connected to a single museum and all involve utilizing their related cultural institutions in the education of students. According to Sonnet Takahisa and Ron Chaluisan, codirectors of the New York City Museum School, organizing and implementing a museum school is territory on the frontier of education today:

> The Museum School necessarily involves a paradigm shift: requiring new organizational structures, new role definitions for teachers and museum personnel. Faculty (must have) a willingness to move in new professional directions, an interest in interdisciplinary learning, a commitment to urban education, a sense of themselves as learners, an openness to team teaching and collaborative modes of curriculum development, and a sensitivity to the school's diverse community of students and their families.[9]

THE DESIGN OF COMMUNITY HIGH SCHOOL

The curriculum design of CHS was built upon Community School's tradition of experimental education, characterized by such features as:

learner-centeredness
community-connectedness
low student-to-teacher ratio
integration of environmental education in an interdisciplinary curriculum
infusion of the visual arts, drama, movement, and music into the curriculum.

CHS imitates other features of Community School as well. Community School's program encourages student self-confidence and self-management. Teachers use periodic student-parent conferences and narrative achievement reports instead of grades and report cards to help students take responsibility for their own progress. Parents play an important and active

Figure 5.1. Infusion of Visual Arts into the Curriculum Allows This Student to Develop Painting Skills

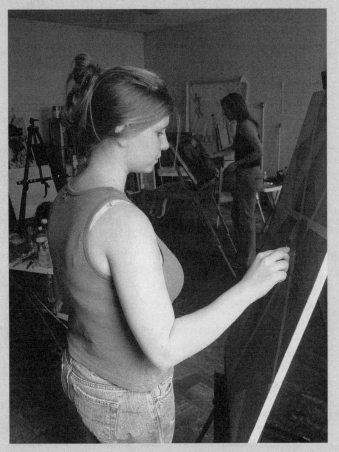

COURTESY OF COMMUNITY HIGH SCHOOL. PHOTO BY SARAH COX.

role in school life, creating a nurturing and supportive learning environment, helping in classrooms and in field studies, serving as trustees, and participating in a wide range of special activities.

Community High School is situated in the midst of the rich educational resources of the entire community. Students have opportunities to study and serve in the valley's business, legal, public safety, and medical and health communities as well as with the many cultural institutions. The Roanoke Valley is a transportation center and a center for medical and health education.

As is the case with other pioneering museum schools, the CHS curriculum has evolved through the collaboration of students, parents, faculty, and educators working in the community. CHS occupies a new and unique educational niche in the Roanoke Valley, and can be a model for museum schools for similarly sized communities. The education program addresses academics through an experiential learning approach and with many options, including project-based learning, mentorships, online and college courses, and community service internships.

Several small grants were acquired to fund start-up costs for CHS, and additional small grants each year have sustained the school's development. Linda Thornton has been the school's director since its inception. The school's faculty have excellent academic credentials, with several having had experiences working in nontraditional, experiential educational settings and others having connections with the resources of the Roanoke Valley community.

Jay Lemke may well be right in saying that traditional schools are obsolete, and he speculates that the torch of education eventually will be passed on to museums and libraries. Museum schools such as CHS will help bridge that gap and, in the meantime, take on the challenge of educating students for democratic citizenship. You are invited to follow the progress of this new museum high school on the Web at http://www.communityhigh.net.

A SAMPLER OF U.S. MUSEUM SCHOOLS

The American Association of Museums National Roster (1998) was the original basis of this list, which has been updated to 2006 for this chapter. Information provided is from articles and school Web sites.

B. F. Brown Arts Vision School
185 Elm Street, Fitchburg, MA 01420 ph. +1 978-345-3278
http://www.fitchburg.k12.ma.us/BFB_Arts_Vision.htm

Partnering Institution: Fitchburg Art Museum
This is a model of what a museum school can look like in a nonurban area. The presence of the school has influenced the Fitchburg Art Museum's acquisition and educational policies. All subjects in the Massachusetts Curriculum Frameworks are taught in the museum's galleries through the study of collection objects and the pursuit of studio art activities. The school initially served students in grades 5–8 and was created by two elementary school teachers. In 2000, it expanded to include the high school grades.
Date Started: 1995

Brent Museum Magnet Elementary School
330 3rd Street SE, Washington, D.C. 20003 ph. +1 202-357-1697
http://www.k12.dc.us/schools/brent/
Partnering Institution: Smithsonian Institution

Brent Elementary is a magnet school created by the District of Columbia Public School System and the Smithsonian Institution, which serves students in grades prekindergarten to sixth and is located close to Capitol Hill. One feature of this school is systematic professional development: faculty have one afternoon free a week to plan and one day off a month for seminars/workshops at the museums. At the end of the year, the school becomes a museum exhibition. Each student makes a display and each classroom becomes a themed exhibit. Student docents lead visitors on guided tours of their model museum.

Date Started: 1996

Charles R. Drew Science Magnet School
1 North Meadow Dr., Buffalo, NY 14214 ph. +1 716-816-4440
http://www.buffaloschools.org/
Partnering Institutions: Buffalo Museum of Science and Buffalo Zoo

This museum school partners with both a science museum and a zoo. Students in second through sixth grades at the Drew Magnet School study at the science museum; the seventh and eighth grade students study at the Buffalo Zoo.

Date started: 1990

Children's Museum of San Diego Elementary School
555 Union Street, San Diego, CA 92101 ph. +1 619-236-8712
http://museumschool.sandi.net/
Partnering Institution: San Diego Children's Museum (Museo de los Ninos)

This small museum school is a charter school. Using innovative methods of staffing, curriculum, and instruction, the school is linked with the learning opportunities of the Children's Museum/Museo de los Ninos and other community resources.

Date started: 1998

Exploris Middle School
207 E. Hargett Street, Raleigh, NC 27601 ph. +1 919-821-3168
http://www.exploris.org/learn/midschool/
Partnering Institution: Exploris Museum

Located next to the museum, this grades 6–8 independent charter school takes an integrated approach to learning in which the academic disciplines and basic skills are addressed through broad themes and projects, and authentic, real-life experiences. The principles and practices of Exploris Middle School are based on Exploris's understanding of how young adolescents learn best.

Date started: 1996.

Flagstaff Arts and Leadership Academy
3100 N. Fort Valley Road, #41, Flagstaff, AZ 86001 ph. +1 520-779-7223
http://www.fala.apscc.k12.az.us/
Partnering Institution: Museum of Northern Arizona

Located on the museum's campus, this public charter high school was heralded by the U.S. Department of Education for its academic rigor, unique learning environment, and academic/arts partnership with its museum partner.

Date started: 1996

Henry Ford Academy of Manufacturing Arts and Sciences
PO Box 1148, 20900 Oakwood Boulevard, Dearborn, Michigan 48121-1148
ph. +1 313-982-6200
http://www.hfacademy.org/
Partnering Institution: Henry Ford Museum and Greenfield Village

One aim of the academy is to demonstrate that students can receive a high-quality education outside of a traditional school. The school is located in the museum and village, so that students have access to millions of artifacts representing American history. Thus, students might learn English in the house where Robert Frost lived while at the University of Michigan as poet laureate, conduct science experiments in Thomas Edison's Menlo Park laboratory, or do research in the museum library, containing more than 25 million historic papers and primary sources. The academy is surrounded by Ford Motor Company facilities where students have access to advanced facilities such as Ford's Design Center.

Date started: 1997.

Museum Magnet School
Rondo Education Center, 560 Concordia Ave., St. Paul, MN 55103
ph. +1 651-325-2600
http://museum.spps.org
Partnering Institution: Science Museum of Minnesota

The original idea behind the creation of the Museum Magnet School was to design a program that allowed students to become exhibit developers, installers, and presenters. This kindergarten-to-grade-6 school develops strong academic skills of reading, writing, and mathematics to create a school museum with exhibits made by children. Science experiments, engineering projects, art, and technology combine with research in the library and at the museum, along with a strong emphasis on language arts, to give students a chance to show what they've learned and learn more as they exhibit.

Date started: 2000.

Museum School 25 and Museum Middle School
79 Warburton Avenue, Yonkers, NY 10701 ph. +1 914-376-8450;
    Middle School 565 Warburton Avenue, Yonkers, NY 10701
    ph. +1 914-376-8425
http://museum.ypschools.org/home.asp
Partnering Institution: Hudson River Museum

The kindergarten-to-grade 5 Museum School 25 is next door to the grades 6–8 Museum Middle School, which is down the block from the Hudson River Museum. The schools are part of a unique museum-school triad, each having a stunning view of the Hudson River and Palisades. Museum School 25 is a multilevel facility that winds its way from classroom to classroom and gallery to gallery displaying its students' works-in-progress. The elementary school opened in 1986 and the middle school in the mid-1990s.

New York City Museum School
333 West 17th Street, New York, NY 10011 ph. +1 212-675-6206
http://www.nycmuseumschool.org/
Partnering Institutions: Brooklyn Museum of Art, Metropolitan Museum of
    Art, Jewish Museum, American Museum of Natural History, Children's
    Museum of Manhattan

The New York City Museum School (NYCMS) is a high school that develops student scholarship through use of primary resources in the sciences, history, literature, and the arts. Museum collections offer evidence, illustrate ideas, stimulate curiosity, provoke questions, and offer alternative ways of presentation. Instruction is enriched with developmentally appropriate museum-based projects related to state and local curriculum. NYCMS has a heterogeneous group of students who represent a diverse community and a range of academic experiences. The faculty includes licensed teachers and museum professionals who collaborate to design projects to support the intellectual, social, and emotional growth of the students. At the conclusion of their studies, students present their findings to an audience of peers, faculty, and families. All academic courses at NYCMS are college-preparatory.

Date started: 1995.

North Hollywood High School
5231 Colfax Ave, North Hollywood, CA 91601-3097 ph. +1 818-769-8510
http://www.lausd.k12.ca.us/North_Hollywood_HS/Info/index.html
Partnering Institution: Los Angeles Zoo

Its proximity to the zoo allows NHHS to utilize all of the facilities at the Los Angeles Zoo. Students attend docent lectures, go on behind-the-scenes tours, use the library, and attend special lectures by zoo research staff on specific subjects as arranged by their instructors. Science classes have zoo assignments that explore the animal and plant collection of the zoo. Students enrolled in this Magnet program come from around the Greater Los Angeles area.

Date started: 1981.

Science Center School
700 State Drive, Los Angeles, CA 90037-1295 ph. +1 213-744-7444
http://www.californiasciencecenter.org/Education/AboutUs/ScienceCenter
    School/ScienceCenterSchool.php
Partnering Institution: California Science Center

The building of the Science Center School was part of the California Science Center's twenty-five-year master plan, and resulted from a decade of work with the Los Angeles Unified School District. The school site is part of the Science Center complex, and includes a new building to house most of the school's classrooms and the newly renovated Wallis Annenberg Building for Science Learning and Innovation. That building houses eight classrooms, administrative offices, a multipurpose room, and the school library. In addition, the building includes over 80,000 square feet (7,432 sq. m.) for the Science Center's education division, the Amgen Center for Science Learning. Thus the school is directly adjacent to facilities that house many of the Science Center's programs including community programs, summer science camp, camp-ins and a burgeoning teacher professional development program.

Date started: 2004.

Stuart Hobson Middle School
410 E Street NE, Washington, D.C. 20002 ph. +1 202-698-4700
http://capitolhillclusterschool.org/_wsn/page7.html
Partnering Institution: Smithsonian Institution

Located near Union Station and the National Mall, Stuart Hobson Middle School offers a curriculum based upon the collections of America's national museums and the expertise of museum staff. As a magnet school, Stuart Hobson works with the Smithsonian to go beyond traditional education and emphasize the power of museums as keepers of the human heritage. Teachers and students have the opportunity to teach and learn in ways that museum specialists do, pursuing authentic questions about nature and culture and employing investigative methods to prepare exhibitions. Grades 5–8 students are educated through object-based learning, where students collect, study, and interpret objects or artifacts in order to learn

about various aspects of life and culture. These objects may be actual artifacts from a museum or an object created or collected by the students
themselves.

Date started: 1997

Zoo School: The School of Environmental Studies
12155 Johnny Cake Ridge Road, Apple Valley, MN 55124 ph. +1 612-431-8755
http://www.isd196.k12.mn.us/schools/ses/
Partnering Institution: Minnesota Zoological Gardens

The School of Environmental Studies is an optional high school in the
Rosemount/Apple Valley/Eagan School District outside St. Paul, Minnesota,
and is located on a twelve-acre site on the grounds of the zoo. The school
is organized into two houses of approximately one hundred junior and senior students. Within each house, students are organized into pods of
approximately ten students. Pods are physical as well as social spaces. The
pods are set around a large space (the *centrum*) that is the primary instructional area. Tables and chairs, rather than desks, serve to make this space
flexible and easily reorganized based on the needs of learners and instructors. Teachers work with students for extended periods of time, and strong
personal relationships are developed. Teachers help students connect with
appropriate community specialists in areas of student interest. Members
of the local community—artists, horticulturalists, architects, and others—
act as mentors to students. Field studies and theme courses provide opportunities for students and teachers to pursue particular goals. An ongoing
relationship with the Lever Corporation and the National Park Service
provides student internships in Yellowstone National Park each summer.

Date started: 1995

Other resources on the Web:

List of School Virtual Museums: http://www.fno.org/museum/list.html

NOTES

1. J. L. Lemke, "Encounters with complementary perspectives in science education
research," http://academic.brooklyn.cuny.edu/education/jlemke/papers/jrst4.htm, 2000.

2. National Research Council, *National Science Education Standards* (Washington,
DC: National Academy Press, 1996).

3. "Quality Counts at 10: A Decade of Standards-based Education," *Education Week*
25, no. 17 (January 4, 2006).

4. Board of Education, *Science Standards of Learning for Virginia Public Schools*
(Richmond: Commonwealth of Virginia, 1995).

5. L. McNeil, "Creating New Inequalities: Contradictions of Reform," *Phi Delta
Kappan* 81, no. 10 (2000): 734.

6. M. G. Brooks and J. G. Brooks, "The Courage to be Constructivist," *Educational Leadership* 57, no. 3 (1999): 20.

7. E. W. Eisner, "Standards for American Schools: Help or Hindrance?," *Phi Delta Kappan* 76, no. 10 (1995): 764.

8. M. Phillips, "Museum-Schools: Hybrid Spaces for Accessing Learning" (San Francisco: Center for Informal Learning and Schools, 2006).

9. S. Takahisa and R. Chaluisan, "New York City Museum School," *Proceedings, Museum School Symposium: Beginning the Conversation* (St. Paul: Science Museum of Minnesota, 1995), p. 24.

5.3.1   Integrating Distinct Institutional Cultures

For any museum school, there are a number of challenges at the outset that relate to the very different cultures of the informal and formal learning sectors.[14] Creating such partnerships often requires change on behalf of all players. While there can be much diversity regarding the depth of integration between the partners, depending on the museum school model employed, in most cases the efforts to create a museum school require some development of a common language, as well as a mutual understanding of each other's resources and staff expertise.[15] Achieving such goals is no easy task, and must be based on shared understanding of the common goal backed up by intensive planning—and lots of teamwork.

5.3.2   The Nature of Learning in the Museum School

The common feature in museum school programming is experiential learning with a degree of self-direction, the type of learning best facilitated by a museum. Transferring this kind of learning to a more formal educational setting is the key, and often the difficulty, since programming at the museum school cannot be as informal as for casual museum visitors. A delicate balance must be achieved. Some believe that museum-based schools can be more powerful if attributes of formal learning are introduced, such as interacting mentors and long-term engagement with learners.[16] But defining museum school education too strictly within the confines of the publicly mandated curriculum can choke off the spontaneity of informal learning, suggesting that the charter school format (which has more freedom in this regard) may be the most promising model for museum schools of the future.[17] A charter school is a publicly funded institution that operates independently of the local school board, through a charter exempting it from selected provincial, state, or municipal rules and regulations, often with a curriculum and educational philosophy different from other public schools. In a charter school the freedom of museum-based educators (often in collaboration with the children themselves) to choose learning materials produces wide variations and more diversity in what topics are covered. Performance evaluation varies from traditional schools as well, with children free to manage their own time during the day, but ultimately held responsible for completing tasks.

Collaboration is often a key feature of program development, with teachers and students determining the curriculum together, or in partnership with other staff and consultants.[18] Thus the lack of control over content experienced by teachers during a conventional school visit to a museum is no longer an issue. Moreover, collaboration is important in the learning process itself, as it is consistent with the learning styles of young children. The collaborative link is important here: in museum education programs, collaborative learning occurs not only between docents or teachers and students, but also among the students themselves. Interdisciplinary learning also comes more naturally within a museum setting than in a formal classroom, particularly given the more rigid subject lines encouraged by new curriculum standards.

In this search for the best balance between formal and informal learning, the museum school is perhaps the most fascinating—and most radical—partnership between museums and traditional schools. In the museum school, a different mindset emerges in the classroom, with children utilizing museum *processes* of knowledge generation—they become active rather than passive learners. Although museum schools are too new and the research too embryonic to draw definitive conclusions, these children are more likely to emerge as critical thinkers and problem solvers who will pursue lifelong learning, which is the ideal in a creative knowledge-based economy.[19]

5.4 UNIVERSITY MUSEUMS

Another very different relationship between the formal and informal sectors is that of the university with the museum, particularly with museums that are part of universities. Here, as Susan Taylor and Dr. Caroline Harris's case study on Princeton University Art Museum in this chapter makes clear, there has been a strong movement toward multidisciplinarity, in order to involve a much broader spectrum of the faculty than just those professors whose specialties happen to lie within the museum's subject discipline. University art museums need to find ways to involve professors from science or business faculties, while science museums need to build links between their discipline and the humanities. Like all museums, so too are university museums being asked to justify their existence, and in many cases cannot take continuing institutional support for granted. Broadening their audiences and bases of support are important ways of doing so.

A growing feature of university museums, as exemplified by the Student Advisory Board at the Princeton University Art Museum mentioned in the case study, is the involvement of students in programming decisions and development. Lord Cultural Resources has done several university museum studies that showed surprisingly little student interest or involvement in the museum unless museum personnel make a concerted effort to reach out to students and give them an opportunity to participate in shaping the exhibition and events program. This is not at all to surrender curatorial or academic decision making in these matters, but rather to see the development of museum programs as providing an opportunity for students to learn by working with museum professionals and university professors in adapting programs to meet student interests and concerns—again to broaden the museum's audience, but also to add value to the students' courses of study.

The third movement among university museums, also exemplified in the Princeton case study, is outreach from university museums to the broader community surrounding the campus. Whereas university museums have traditionally suffered in attendance (for reasons that include poor accessibility, low visibility, and lack of marketing, and very often the reluctance of persons without a university education to come onto a campus to visit them), focused outreach programs can involve the community and make the university a much more valuable asset to the city or town in which it is located, and an important educational resource for all residents.

5.5 CONCLUSION

Relationships between museums and the formal education sector are changing rapidly due to forces emanating from both within and without the institutions in question. The specific qualities of museum-based learning—its informality, its affective character, its transformative nature—can be an advantage for school districts that have come under intense ideological and financial pressure from governments and the general public, particularly in North America, to focus on rote learning and the type of "school intelligence" best reflected by standardized tests. This can be equally advantageous to museums, allowing them to pursue their missions as public education institutions in new and creative ways—and helping them generate new revenue streams.

While museum-based school programs cannot have all the attributes of the type of informal learning experienced by the casual visitor (for example, the voluntary aspect), their inherently experimental and hands-on approach allows school districts to foster the kinds of creative intelligence neglected by forced cuts to formal arts or music programs (for example), yet still connect to the topics and subject matters favored by legislators and the general public (such as science). As financial pressures and resulting cuts to traditional field trips and the like have made it difficult for teachers and their students to take advantage of all that these museum-based programs have to offer, there has emerged an opportunity for museums to offer school districts a pedagogy that is not always available in the classroom—in other words, to fill a gap.[20]

Meanwhile, at the postsecondary level of formal education, the university museum is experiencing change, involving its faculty in multidisciplinary ways, getting students to participate meaningfully in the development of programs, and reaching out to the surrounding community to make the institution of greater service to the people living around it.

Thus there is significant potential in the informal learning process to contribute to the transformation of twenty-first century education, from the old model developed to serve yesterday's industrial society to a new model designed to support today's knowledge economy. The museum-school (and museum-university) nexus has the potential to generate some of the most promising new developments in museum education—and perhaps also in the ongoing school reform debate—as formal and informal education institutions work together to refine the synthesis in the years to come. Together these trends suggest an emerging new relationship between museums and the formal education sector that presents challenges to all, but that can result in an enhanced museum learning experience at all levels, from kindergarten to post-graduate studies.

SERVING STUDENTS, FACULTY, AND THE COMMUNITY AT PRINCETON UNIVERSITY ART MUSEUM

Susan M. Taylor and Caroline Harris

In the year 2000, director Susan Taylor and the Princeton University Art Museum staff began a strategic planning process designed to update the museum's mission, and re-evaluate its goals and objectives. The museum's primary mission has remained the same since its foundation in 1882: to give Princeton University students access to original works of art to complement and enrich the instructional and research activities of the university. In defining the museum's priorities, the staff also recognized the importance of integrating into the museum's mission Princeton University's goals of teaching, research, and service, reinforcing the museum's clear obligation to serve the local community, the region, and beyond. To better fulfill the museum's commitment to its various constituencies, a Department of Education and Academic Programs was established in 2002 with the appointment of the first curator of Education and Academic Programs, who reports to the director and is an active participant in all curatorial affairs.

One of the curator's most important new initiatives was the institution of quarterly staff meetings to discuss upcoming installations, exhibitions, and related programming, and interpretive strategies in order to develop a long-range plan for learning and interpretation. This level of advance preparation helped to target key audiences, expand public programming, and facilitate collaborations with other university departments. It also provided the necessary time to incorporate members of the museum's audiences into the planning process. For example, teacher focus groups have been critical to the development of online teacher resources. Community focus groups, including discussions with parents and young professionals, have helped the museum create programs and a marketing plan to serve a wider public.

The museum has a successful array of outreach projects. The Princeton University Art Museum Docent Association leads tours for approximately 10,000 visitors per year. Over 8,000 of the participants in public tours are school children, demonstrating the museum's commitment to elementary and secondary education. Saturday morning family programs, which consist of a talk by a museum docent followed by a hands-on project led by a professional art teacher, attract approximately 800 people per year. Hundreds of families attend an annual Family Day in June, which focuses on a particular area of the collection such as Asian art. Weekly gallery talks bring roughly 1,500 people to the museum for in-depth discussions by faculty, staff, graduate, and undergraduate students of works of art in the permanent collection and special exhibitions. In 2006, the Department of Education and Academic Programs began its first program for visitors who are blind or visually impaired, reaching out to an underserved group.

In addition to these ongoing programs, the museum staff is dedicated to developing new projects that take advantage of a university museum's unique ability to draw upon and engage the intellectual resources of the academy and to build bridges from the academic community to a broader public. Cosponsorships and collaborative programs have proved to be the key to the success of these initiatives. Working with university faculty, staff, students, area institutions, and the local community is essential for the creation of educational programs and events that appeal to a university audience and the general public.

The programs in conjunction with an exhibition presented at Princeton, *Mir Iskusstva: Russia's Age of Elegance*, February 25 to June 11, 2006, provide a model of such efforts. The exhibition included over eighty paintings, bronze sculptures, ceramics, prints, and drawings by artists of the *Mir Iskusstva* (World of Art) movement that flourished in Russia at the turn of the twentieth century. Under the motto "art for art's sake," artists from all disciplines—music, dance, theater, literature, and the visual arts—united in a period of extraordinary cultural creativity.

The museum's curators and operations staff collaborated with a team of scholars to develop programming and resources related to the exhibition. Faculty and staff from Princeton University's Slavic Languages and Literature Department, Music Department, Cotsen Children's Library, and the Program in Theater and Dance were assembled early in the planning stages, guaranteeing that members of the museum's target audience were invested in the exhibition and programming. The team also served as ambassadors to their constituencies, sharing information about the exhibition that encouraged more collaborations and a broader audience, making *Mir Iskusstva* a true catalyst for campuswide programs and events.

Janet Kennedy, author of *The "Mir Iskusstva Group" and Russian Art 1898–1912* (1977) and professor of the history of art at Indiana University, served as a visiting professor in Slavic languages and literatures and gave a public lecture, ensuring that the exhibition was integrated into the university curriculum. In addition, community auditors were encouraged to take her course. Princeton University professor Ellen Chances developed an on-campus colloquium, featuring faculty from the Slavic Languages and Literature Department and the Department of Spanish and Portuguese

Languages and Cultures. She also organized several public lectures, including three by Marian Burleigh-Motley, lecturer, The Metropolitan Museum of Art, as part of the university's Eberhard L. Faber Lecture Series.

The academic programs for *Mir Iskusstva* were advertised to the university community and the general public. All were well attended by faculty, staff, students, and the local and regional community. This crossover appeal illustrates the power of programming that has multiple applications, serving the needs of several of the museum's constituencies, including undergraduates and graduate students who are studying the art and culture of the period, and the museum's general audience who depend on the museum for lifelong learning opportunities. For example, as part of one of the museum's popular *After Hours at the Art Museum* series, Princeton University students read in Russian and English from the Pushkin poem *The Bronze Horseman* to an audience of over one hundred students, faculty, and community members.

For family audiences, Cotsen Children's Library presented *Art to Art*, a series of four workshops for children led by professional artists and inspired by different aspects of the exhibition. The art produced in the workshops was exhibited at the university. Cotsen also mounted a related exhibition of children's book illustrations by artists associated with the *Mir Iskusstva* group.

Princeton University's Richardson Chamber Players gave a sold-out concert *Music from Diaghilev's World* in the museum galleries. The University's Program in Theater and Dance produced *L'Après-midi d'un faune*, featuring Vaslav Nijinsky's original choreography and replicas of artist Leon Bakst's sets and costumes. Performances were featured as part of the opening events for the exhibition, ensuring a large audience for the students' performances that included university and museum members.

Finally, the exhibition inspired collaborations between the museum, the community-based Princeton Symphony Orchestra, and the American Repertory Ballet. The Orchestra presented a concert featuring composers of the period—Debussy, Budashkin, Lanner, and Stravinsky—which was augmented by the choreography of the American Repertory Ballet's Artistic Director Graham Lustig for the ballet *Petrouchka*. A sold-out performance was followed by a reception and viewing of the exhibition by over three hundred concert-goers.

While a long-range plan for public programs is critical, the museum has continued its strategic planning in other areas of outreach as well. The curator of Education and Academic Programs oversaw a task force charged with how to make the museum an integral part of the undergraduate experience. The committee included representatives from the university administration, the faculty, museum staff, and undergraduates. The group focused on ways to make the museum more accessible to students, effective marketing strategies for a university audience, the long- and short-term benefits of student involvement in and awareness of the art museum, and measures of success. A series of recommendations for programs and marketing strategies is being implemented over the years, 2006–2009.

The museum has also reiterated its commitment to the development of the next generation of museum professionals. To further that mission, the Department of Education organizes a highly competitive eight-week paid summer internship program, recruiting approximately eight to ten undergraduate and graduate students per year. Interns work in curatorial, administrative, and the registrar's offices. The program is structured to help students understand and participate in the functioning of the museum, and includes a summer-long project in one department as well as weekly orientations with other museum departments.

The task force identified as a priority the creation of a student advisory board for the museum. The curator of education recruited ten students for the board in 2005–2006, including two graduate students, one senior, four juniors, two sophomores, and one freshman. In the fall semester of 2005, the Student Advisory Board established a series of evening events at the museum designed to include a behind-the-scenes talk with a faculty member or curator. The board hosted four events in the 2005–2006 academic year, targeted to specific e-mail lists such as class officers. The events were successful, attracting twenty to thirty students per evening. Based on that success, the board has decided to move forward with more events on this same model. They also hope to establish the Student Friends of the Princeton University Art Museum as a permanent organization.

Four years after the Department of Education and Academic Programs was founded, the museum has developed relationships across campus and in the community that help bring new audiences to the museum for inspiring and educational programs. As the department moved into its fifth year, the curator of Education and Academic Programs determined to focus on extending the institution's impact to all undergraduate students, making its resources and programming an integral part of their experience at Princeton. The museum can create both means and opportunity to educate students to appreciate the importance of art in society. An informed understanding of the overall value of cultural institutions in contemporary life is essential as these students will assume leadership roles in the philanthropic, corporate, not-for-profit, and government sectors, both national and international. In these capacities, they will have the opportunity to shape and affect the future of the cultural experience.

In addition to its long-range exhibition and permanent collection planning that includes representatives from faculty of many departments, the museum has established an endowed position with the support of the Andrew W. Mellon Foundation that will work with faculty from various disciplines to develop programs and courses based on the permanent collection. At the core of this initiative is a belief in the museum's unique ability to promote object-based scholarship as an essential part of the academic experience. Moreover, the museum in turn can take advantage of these academic resources to develop programs and gallery spaces that engage the imagination, and the intellectual and aesthetic sensibilities of all its audiences.

NOTES

1. In this chapter these are understood primarily to mean schools and museums respectively, although the terms *informal* and *formal* learning institutions can encompass other types as well.

2. The term *marketization* has appeared in Nobuko Kawashima, "Privatizing Museum Services in U.K. Local Authorities—New Managerialism in Action?" in *Public Management: An International Journal of Research and Theory* 1, no. 2 (1999): 163, as well as elsewhere in the literature.

3. As reported by Hanna Gould in *Settings Other Than Schools: Initial Teacher Training Placements in Museums, Galleries and Archives* (Yorkshire Museum, Libraries and Archives Council, June 2003), p. 1.

4. This discussion primarily applies to North American public schools, but is also found elsewhere.

5. Institute of Museum and Library Services, *True Needs, True Partners: Museums Serving Schools: 2002 Survey Highlights* (Washington, DC: IMLS, 2002), p. 9.

6. IMLS, *True Needs, True Partners*, p. 4.

7. For a description of one such program at the Museum of Fine Arts in Boston, see Margaret K. Burchanal, "Thinking Through Art" in *Journal of Museum Education* 23, no. 2 (1998): 13–15.

8. As discussed in J. Guisasola, M. Morentin, K. Zusa, "School Visits to Science Museums and Learning Sciences: A Complex Relationship," *Physics Education* 40, no. 6 (November 2005).

9. According to the 2002 IMLS survey cited earlier, nearly two-thirds of museums that report an impact from educational reform on their programs say that the result has been increased service to teachers, more school partners, and higher numbers of museum visits.

10. Kira S. King, "Museum Schools: Institutional Partnership and Museum Learning," paper presented at the American Education Research Association (AERA) annual meeting, 1990, p. 3.

11. See Michael L. Bentley, "Community-Connected Science Education: Creating a Museum High School for Southwestern Virginia," http://www.ed.psu.edu/CI/Journals/2002aets/s1_bentley.rtf.

12. Linda McNeil and Elliot Eisner, respectively, quoted in Bentley, "Community-Connected Science Education."

13. Appreciation of the significance of the creative economy has grown exponentially since the publication of Richard Florida's *The Rise of the Creative Class and How It's Changing Work, Leisure, Community, and Everyday Life* (New York: Basic Books, 2002).

14. http://www.edutopia.org/magazine/ed1article.php?id=art_1193&issue=nov_04.

15. Kelly O. Finnerty, Debra Ingram, Douglas Huffman, Karen Thimmesch, and Wayne Gilman, "Finding a Common Language for Museum Process: Science Museum of Minnesota Museum Magnet School," *Journal of Museum Education* 23, no. 2 (1998): 3.

16. Christine Klein, Jean Corse, Vivian Grigsby, Sharonica Hardin, and Cheryl Ward, "A Museum School: Building Grounded Theory as Two Cultures Meet," paper

presented at the American Educational Research Association (AERA) annual meeting, 2001, p. 10, http://eric.ed.gov/ERICDocs/data/ericdocs2/content_storage_01/0000000b/80/0d/6b/b4.pdf.

17. Paul Krapfel, "How Museums Can Shape Public Education: Chrysalis Charter School," *Journal of Museum Education* 23, no. 2 (1998): 12.

18. Ibid., p. 13.

19. Klein et al. "A Museum School," p. 2.

20. Much of the preceding discussion was drawn from Kira S. King and Theodore Frick, "Transforming Education: Case Studies in Systems Thinking," paper presented at the American Educational Research Association (AERA) annual meeting, 1999.

CHAPTER 6

Involving the Community
The Museum as Forum for Dialogue and Learning

SPENCER R. CREW

Throughout the years one key issue with which museums have wrestled is their role as educational institutions and their relationship to their audiences. This conversation is critical as it gets to a core question concerning how museums provide value as community institutions. While education is one of their most important tasks, the form it should take has not always been as clear. The choices have ranged from employing a Socratic approach to using a more authoritarian technique. With the former their task was to understand and respond to the interests of visitors, while with the latter they sought to expose visitors to artifacts and ideas in which they may not have an initial interest but that the staff believed visitors needed to understand better. To accomplish this goal museums saw themselves as knowledgeable tutors who led their students down the road to enlightenment even when the students resisted. Museum staff knew visitors eventually would realize how much the experience benefited them.

6.1 VISITORS AND THE MUSEUM

A museum's final decision about which relationship to its audience it would embrace depended on where the institution believed its best chances of success lay. Some of the early nineteenth-century museums focused on visitors as customers and as critical revenue sources. They believed that education could be entertaining and engaging as well as profitable. These institutions sought to create experiences that attracted people who came because they believed what was offered at these institutions was worth the price of admission. Places like the Peale Museum in Philadelphia and the American Museum in New York followed this strategy. Charles Peale and P. T. Barnum were entrepreneurs committed to finding ways to attract visitors to their institutions because of the power of the objects and the environments they created around them. They considered the preferences of visitors first as they crafted the presentations in their museums and marketed them to the public.

They believed that education did not have to be grueling or boring, but could be both enjoyable and effective.[1]

Other institutions did not follow this path. As their primary support shifted from the general public to the wealthy movers and shakers of society, their emphasis changed as well. More museums saw themselves as the preservers and reinforcers of prevailing cultural values. Consequently, their goal was to highlight the quality of the artifacts they held in their collections as well as to generate awe and reverence for the cultures that created them. Museum staff in the United States wanted to reinforce the idea of the progressive improvement of American society and technology. For these institutions their responsibility to their visitors was to expose them to the values and cultural norms intertwined in these objects. This meant their most important role was to collect and preserve these significant cultural icons. Their key audience was not the general public, but the patrons who supported the acquisition and preservation of the artifacts. Museum staff focused in this manner worked hard on improving professional standards for the field. In the process they sought to prove that they could properly care for and study these objects, and that they were worthy of the trust placed in them by donors. The educational goal in this case was to increase staff knowledge of the objects and to illustrate the importance of the artifacts as cultural icons.[2] How the general public felt about these while on view was less important than making the objects available to illustrate important cultural concepts visitors should know about the world in which they lived. If the public was wise enough to take advantage of what the museums offered that was good. If they did not make use of the opportunity it was their misfortune and poor judgment.

While not every museum followed this pattern precisely, this mode of increasing professionalization characterized the trajectory of the museum field for much of the twentieth century. The objects, the exhibitions, and the programs produced were directed toward reinforcing traditional history, culture, and knowledge while ignoring nontraditional perspectives. The lives and the material culture of the successful, the movers and shakers, and the wealthy dominated the narratives presented in these institutions. There were exceptions like the Newark Museum, directed by John Cotton Dana, who believed museums needed to be more responsive to the general public. But this perspective was in the minority.

6.2   THE LATE-TWENTIETH-CENTURY MUSEUM

The manner in which museums viewed their relationship with the general public did not begin to shift again until the latter part of the twentieth century. Then a number of factors came into play to cause the change. Sources of funding support for these institutions began to broaden as local and national governmental funding increased in importance. These agencies were interested in how the cultural institutions that they supported served their local communities, and asked them to demonstrate their impact. National foundations followed a similar pattern as they sought to maximize the impact of the dollars they provided cultural organizations. In addition, more visitors demanded that museums broaden the topics and the artifacts they highlighted in their presentations. Civil rights activists across the nation raised important questions about whose culture, whose history, whose narrative was included in these institutions. These potential customers were not content with only traditional interpretations. They wanted the discussion broadened, made more diverse and more inclusive. At the same time, new scholarship in the academy offered information about the contributions many different people had made to the United States. The history of African Americans, Latinos, Asian-Pacific Americans, women, American Indians, and numerous other groups experienced a renaissance as their stories and contributions became more readily available.[3] Representatives of those groups wanted this information included in the narratives featured in museums. They felt that excluding these stories created a biased and unacceptable image of a rich and diverse American culture.

As the pressure mounted, museums began to adjust and think more about the rich variety of stories they could access and include in their presentations. They began to recognize that maintaining their relevancy as institutions in a rapidly evolving world meant that they must embrace new ideas and new perspectives. One of the first illustrations of this new thinking was the publication in 1984 of *Museums for a New Century* by the American Association of Museums. The core message it highlighted was the importance of pluralism in American society and the responsibility of museums to recognize and help translate its meaning to its visitors. They acknowledged that this is not a simple task as it sometimes means mediating competing points of view. However, they saw it as an essential role that museums could not ignore.

Another publication by AAM in 1992 reinforced the ideas set forth in *Museums for a New Century* and carried them further. *Excellence and Equity: Education and the Public Dimensions of Museums* encouraged museums to shift the paradigm of how they saw their relationship with their audiences. It emphasized the educational role of museums in the broadest sense and promoted more and deeper collaboration between museums and their visitors. The authors strongly believed that museums could no longer position themselves as omniscient sources of authority who best understood what their visitors should learn and need not ask their opinions. Instead, they argued that partnerships made more sense—partnerships that respect the knowledge brought to the conversation by all of the participants, and which incorporate that collective perspective into the exhibitions and programs created by the museums.

The good news is that rather than stubbornly resisting the idea many institutions began to take the concerns and opinions of their visitors more seriously. They recognized that the changing demographics of the communities where they were located demanded more flexibility if they were to remain viable. The leisure-time options available for potential visitors were expanding rapidly. Sporting events, concerts, theater, and numerous other activities gave visitors many more choices. The challenge for museums was insuring that they remained high in value as people made choices. Asking visitors what interested them and including them in the decision-making process in creating new activities helped. If visitors saw their history, their culture, their stories in the museums, they were much more likely to visit and to find value in the work of these institutions.

As it turned out, this argument for a different relationship with audiences had merit, as the popularity of museums, many of whom began to embrace this new mindset, climbed upward in the years that followed. A conference at the White House in 1995 on travel and tourism illustrated the growing importance of cultural institutions in the eyes of the public. In a report on how people spent their time while on vacation some interesting facts surfaced. There were certain key activities that consistently topped the list for vacation travelers. Number one on the list of activities was shopping. In many ways this is not at all surprising. But second on the list was visiting cultural institutions such as museums, science centers, zoos, or cultural festivals. The report pointed out that people liked to go to these institutions because they offered experiences that vacationers felt enriched the quality of their visit and deepened their understanding of the history and culture of the area. In response to this statistic tourism bureaus indicated that they would more actively feature museums as one of the highlights of their states.

The popularity of museums continued to rise in the years that followed, as another study published by the AAM in 2001 illustrated. The report found that visits to museums of all types had reached about 865 million per year. This meant that about one-third of Americans said they had visited a museum, aquarium, science or technology center, or a zoo within the past six months. Nearly a quarter of Americans had gone to one of these places in the past year, and one in five had been there more than a year ago. This data was notable as it indicated that at the time of the report attending museums was one of the most popular things people did. It had not reached the level of attendance at sporting events, like auto racing for example, but it was rising in importance. This was great news for museums and reason for them to feel excited about the future and their place as significant institutions in the eyes of the public.

6.3   THE POST-9/11 MUSEUM

In the light of these studies someone looking at the state of the field in early 2001 could have predicted a very bright future. But circumstances change quickly, and so did the environment for museums. Most significantly the events of September 11, 2001 shook the nation as well as our institutions. This catastrophe paired with a weakening economy had a dramatic impact upon attendance at cultural institutions and their viability. Sites like Colonial Williamsburg (Virginia), Sturbridge Village (Massachusetts), and the Smithsonian Institution (Washington, D.C.) witnessed significant slumps in their visitorship, sales, and, consequently, income. Other museums across the United States witnessed similar reductions in visitorship and income. The recovery from these setbacks has been slow. It has created a reason for us to look again at our relationship to our visitors and to consider very seriously the challenges of operating a museum in the twenty-first century. In fact, as we contemplate the present state of the field, how we position ourselves as relevant social entities in a world that has changed significantly in just the last few years is a critical core issue.

Wrestling with this question brings up once again the issue of the role of museums as educational institutions and the nature of the relationship they need to forge with visitors. The ideas put forth in *Museums for a New Century* and *Excellence and Equity* are still important cornerstones in this conversation about engaging audiences. What increases the complexity of the discussion is the necessity of expanding the definition of diversity and how we think about this concept in the broadest possible way. In the twenty-first century, discussions on diversity must cover more than race, gender, and ethnicity, which were the most often discussed focal points of the last quarter of the twentieth century. A new array of characteristics such as age, learning styles, and computer literacy are all variables that need inclusion under expanded discussions of diversity.

At core, the challenge is how our institutions engage new ideas, new ways of operating, and new modes of communication. In earlier discussions discomfort often sprang from moving away from traditional ways and opening oneself up to new possibilities. It is critical that our institutions are not bound by tradition. This is not to argue that traditional ways of operating and presentation do not have value. But they are not the only way to see and connect to the world and our audiences. The challenge is how to seek out and use the best of the old and the new. It is also to make the effort to explore which approaches are most effective in consolidating the relationship between our institutions and our audiences. We need to find ways to provide experiences for our visitors that offer meaning to their lives, and position our organizations as places that have an important societal role to play.

Often the hardest step is to allow oneself to move into uncomfortable territory. A good example is a project recently undertaken by the Chicago Historical Society titled "Teen Chicago." It began as an effort to capture what it meant to be a teenager in Chicago from 1900 to the present. The initial approach was pretty straightforward. The society used students from across the city to conduct about a hundred oral histories with older residents about their experiences as teenagers in Chicago. The students were to explore what teenagers thought about, wore, listened to, and how they lived in the past. The Chicago Historical Society saw this as a great way to study the history of the city through a unique perspective. The society also thought it was a great way to make history come alive for the students doing the interviews.

What the staff at the Historical Society did a bit differently was to make the teenagers they recruited partners in the project from the very start. This "Teen Council" helped fashion the questions, selected whom they would interview, and offered ideas on how to share the information they acquired with the public. The results were much different than the staff originally imagined. The students became very enthusiastic about the project and infused it with their own ideas and views. In particular, they wanted a say in how the exhibition resulting from their interviews would look. The issue for the staff was the degree to which they were willing to share their control over the exhibition and the programs accompanying it. To their credit they chose to give the students an opportunity to have a major influence on the design and execution of the project. The students' input impacted the colors used, the musical styles, and the presentation techniques. The resulting exhibition had an aesthetic much more recognizable and inviting to a younger generation. It was not what the typical visitor might expect at a place like the Chicago Historical Society. The show was very much in a style familiar to the MTV generation. The colors were bright, the music often livelier, and the modes of presentation innovative. For example, they presented some of their interviews on screens set in lockers like the ones used by students in high school.

The programming around the exhibition also followed a different direction because the activities were heavily teen oriented. They had poetry slams, rap performers, as well as break-dancers and skateboarders outside the building on different occasions. The goal was to make the exhibition, and more importantly the building, feel user-friendly and inviting to teenage visitors. For example, at events like the poetry slam extra uniformed guards were not put in place, despite concerns about possible violence. The staff felt it more important to let students attending the events see that the historical society was treating them like any other guests coming to an event in the building.[4]

The results were gratifying for the institution. Teens flocked to the museum to see the work of their colleagues as well as to experience this exhibition that talked about issues of interest to them. They began to see the museum as a teen-friendly place. It no longer was the staid, threatening building they once pictured. Their increased attendance helped lead to a dramatic increase in visitorship to the Chicago Historical Society.

Thus, despite the worry of some of the more traditional supporters of the historical society and some staff, the experiment paid dividends. The exhibition and related programming illustrated the importance of listening seriously to and responding to the interests of specific audiences. It also illustrated how to target and engage specific audiences as well as the success that can follow when they feel included and welcomed. This is neither an easy process nor a comfortable one. To achieve success an institution must be prepared to explore new directions and commit to truly sharing the process of creating new and unique experiences within the building. If we are to remain relevant and engaging entities this is one of the commitments we will have to make as the twenty-first century stretches before us.

6.4   TECHNOLOGY IN THE MUSEUM

Museums also need to work harder at better integrating technology and innovation into the visitor experience. This issue is still an area of debate for the field. An example is a recent discussion among AAM colleagues about an award for which several museums had been nominated. The awards sponsored by the Themed Attraction Association recognized innovative presentations in these institutions. A very lively discussion ensued concerning how people felt about the issue of receiving recognition from the "theme park" world. The debate revolved around the question of the differences between museums and places like Disney World. Some people were not at all bothered by the connection and embraced the concept that there was much we could gain from emulating some of the things done at these parks. Others firmly believed that the association was not good. They felt museums would suffer in the comparison and lose their unique identity. In their view museums could not compete on the "gee whiz" level with for-profit theme parks. The resources the parks could put into their experiences far surpass the monies and people museums have available. Also, by not staying focused on our special characteristics we place ourselves in jeopardy. Among the special aspects of museums are the artifacts, the scholarship, and the context they provide visitors. Most theme parks could not match this expertise, and museums should play to their strengths rather than trying to emulate the things theme parks did best, said these participants.

This is a debate that has stretched over many years. But in the twenty-first century choices around this issue are taking on a new urgency. In an age of sophisticated technology and information-rich environments museums cannot afford to sit on the sidelines. Computers, technology, touch screens, film, and interactives are the norm in today's world. They impact nearly every aspect of our lives. This is even truer when we consider younger visitors to our institutions. They have been raised on this technology and are extremely comfortable with it. Because technology is second nature to them they expect to have access to information in a variety of forms and platforms. They are used to working with large bytes of information and using technology to receive it and to manipulate it. They are not alone in this mindset, as more and more retired visitors are using and becoming comfortable with technology as well. They use it to buy airplane tickets, to preplan vacations, and to send e-mails to children and—more importantly—grandchildren. More and more, for them, technology is just another tool they expect to have available.

This reality does not leave many options for museums. Technology has to be among the choices available to our visitors. And, we need to use that technology in creative ways. It is not enough to have it serve as an alternative way to present labels or information in greater depth. This application is no more exciting than reading a long label attached to the wall. In fact, reading it on a computer screen can be even more annoying and is not the best use of the medium. The wonderful aspect of technology is that it has tremendous flexibility and opportunities for creativity. At its best, technology has the ability to draw visitors into ideas and topics they might not have investigated otherwise. It can reveal the awe and wonder many of us find in the material we work with and use, but which may not have the same innate appeal to others. It is important to examine closely how to leverage technology to its best advantage.

Effective education and engagement does not come in one prescribed format. Effective educators are flexible. Traditional approaches can intersect with less traditional techniques in very valuable and appealing ways. This can in the end persuade visitors to spend more time in our institutions, and to return. Science centers and children's museums have been very smart about this issue. By using technology and hands-on learning environments they have created new ways to connect to visitors. The Exploratorium in San Francisco and the Indianapolis Children's Museum are two good examples. More traditional institutions need to look at these places and find ways to apply their successes in their own settings—even when it feels a little like we are getting close to resembling "theme parks."

An example is the environmental theater that is part of the experience at the National Underground Railroad Freedom Center in Cincinnati. Instead of creating a traditional film experience or an IMAX theater the Freedom Center constructed an environment that allows visitors to join a young enslaved woman running from Kentucky through Ohio to Canada on the Underground Railroad. The setting is a wooded area along the banks of the Ohio River in Kentucky across the river from the state of Ohio sometime prior to 1860. Visitors enter as trees, stars, chirping crickets, owls, fog from the river, and fireflies surround them while they take their seats. Once settled, the drama begins as they join the fleeing woman who is hotly pursued by slave catchers and baying dogs. In the process of her adventure shots are fired that seem to whiz by visitors, she plunges into the river, and eventually makes contact with black and white participants in the Underground Railroad. During the escape there are a number of tense moments that help visitors understand how truly dangerous it was to participate in this endeavor, and that a successful outcome was not guaranteed.

The television presenter Oprah Winfrey is the narrator of this very powerful and moving experience. It brings to life the realities of the Underground Railroad in a very forceful way. Visitor reaction to the presentation has been uniformly positive. In surveys it is one of the highest rated activities in the Freedom Center. Teachers, students, and other visitors comment on how real the experience feels and how it allows them to connect to the Underground Railroad experience in a very unexpected but powerful way. In short, they learn something new and touching as a result of the experience. In this instance technology is a useful and powerful tool that enhances the visitor experience and has not caused it to suffer because of its similarity to theme park experiences.

Technology is not an evil in itself, and neither is the use of immersive environments, high-end technology, or creative media applications. They are simply tools available to help create better connections with visitors. Museums should not retreat from or avoid experimentation in these areas. Rather they need to seek imaginative ways to integrate these tools to add to the power of the information they provide visitors. It is important to remain open to looking at techniques used by entities other than museums. There are lessons worth learning there that can be successfully applied or modified in our places. This can be done while still maintaining the special attributes of our institutions. Tried and true techniques of presentation still have their usefulness, but they also have their limitations. Today's visitors are much more sophisticated in their expectations, and if museums fail to rise to the challenge they risk losing their value and importance. Potential visitors have numerous options concerning how and where they will spend their limited leisure funds. The factors that influence those choices in one direction versus another are often intangible and subtle. Museums must take advantage of every opportunity to make their offerings difficult for potential visitors to bypass.

THE DIALOGUE ZONE AT THE NATIONAL UNDERGROUND RAILROAD FREEDOM CENTER

Spencer R. Crew

The mission of the National Underground Railroad Freedom Center is an inspiring and prescriptive concept that highlights the work of individuals involved in the Underground Railroad as well as later generations of people who also worked actively on behalf of freedom. The goal is to encourage each of us to take our own steps toward making a difference. The key challenge in executing this mission is to create experiences that inspire visitors to think seriously about issues of civic engagement and social responsibility.

The exhibitions, films, and computer interactives at the Freedom Center provide experiences that very effectively carry this message. They encourage the kinds of social interactions among visitors that are a valuable part of a visit to a cultural institution. But the goal of the Freedom Center is to go further. In the language of the Underground Railroad the aspiration is to create a "safe house" for reflection and conversation about the important issues of race, racial cooperation, diversity, and personal engagement that are core to the mission.

The area created to focus primarily on this goal in the Freedom Center is the Dialogue Zone. It is a room crafted with the specific purpose of allowing visitors an opportunity to reflect on what they have experienced during their visit, what immediate impact it has had on them, and what longer term impact they think it will have. It is an opportunity to process their journey through the Freedom Center in a safe and supportive environment. The space is not elaborate. It contains movable chairs, writing material, AV capability, carpeted floors, and warm colors on the walls. It is located in the final exhibition area of the Freedom Center titled "Reflect, Respond, Resolve." This area creates simulated situations for visitors that highlight present-day issues that raise questions around the definition of freedom and access to it by different individuals and groups. The answers to the issues raised are not straightforward or easily solved. Like many challenges in life, the answers are complicated. The goal is to encourage initial conversations among visitors that reinforce many of the ideas they encountered in other areas of the building. The Dialogue Zone provides a space to continue those conversations, rather than leaving visitors to sort through their reactions by themselves.

Essential to providing the best possible environment for these conversations are the staff members present in the space. They are trained facili-

Figure 6.1. Discussion in the Dialogue Zone

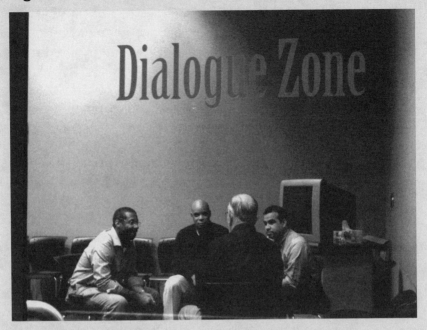

COURTESY OF NATIONAL UNDERGROUND RAILROAD FREEDOM CENTER.

tators who shape the experience to assure that the people engaged in the conversation feel they can speak openly and candidly with the understanding that their thoughts will be affirmed and validated, not attacked. The objective is to create dialogue, not debate. It is not to win everyone over to one point of view. Indeed, there are no right or wrong answers. What is most important is having the opportunity to hear different perspectives and to understand why others might see things differently. This can be a very powerful and useful experience. It also can change how one thinks about an issue or how one might see the actions of others in new ways. It is an opportunity to learn.

The guiding spirit of the space is a psychologist who is a joint hire between the Freedom Center and Xavier University in Cincinnati. She has many years of experience in community-based psychology, which has impacted the framing of the experience provided for visitors. A team of advisors from across the state of Ohio contributed to the development of the format for the conversations that take place in the Dialogue Zone. All of the facilitators undergo a training process that provides them with the rationale and guidelines for the dialogues they will lead. Ground rules are created for the conversations, and facilitators are prepared for the expected and unexpected reactions that can occur with charged discussions pertaining to race or cultural diversity. Skilled professional practitioners from the Cincinnati area, as well as graduate student trainees working toward their doctorate in clinical psychology at Xavier University were invited to work in the Dialogue Zone. The unique setting of the Freedom Center offers the graduate student trainees the opportunity to increase their awareness of the ever-expanding role of diversity in our lives. The trainees are exposed to the rich tapestry of human beings who venture into the museum space. Trainees are encouraged and challenged to examine their personal values and lifetime experiences and the potential impact those experiences might have on their effectiveness with people similar to and different from themselves.

Dialogue Zone facilitators are managing conversations that friends do not engage in easily, let alone people who have just met. Facilitators have to be prepared for typical and atypical emotional responses to the subjects discussed. When the discussions go well they are thought provoking and engaging. Participants are grateful for the opportunity to process the ideas and thoughts stimulated by their visit. It adds a dimension to the experience that is not usually available in cultural institutions.

Indeed, one of the challenges of the Dialogue Zone has been encouraging visitors to take advantage of the opportunity. Many school groups and scheduled tour groups request the opportunity to spend time in the Dialogue Zone as the last part of their visit to the Freedom Center. The feedback from these visitors has been quite positive and encouraging about the value of that experience. They have said discussions enhance their visit as well as reinforce the mission of the Freedom Center.

In the case of individuals or family groups, getting them to take advantage of the space has been a greater challenge. A leap of faith often is necessary to enter a room, no matter how inviting, and share one's personal perspectives. Visitors can be wary of taking that chance, yet getting them to take the first step is critical. Sometimes observing conversations already taking place in the space can draw them in, but more often it takes proactive steps on the part of the facilitators to engage these visitors. Instead of remaining inside the Dialogue Zone and waiting for visitors to look through the glass walls and walk in, the facilitators stand outside and engage visitors in conversations about their experience. In this way they seek to introduce visitors to the usefulness of the Dialogue Zone and to get them to take the time to utilize it. This process has enabled the facilitators to get more visitors to take advantage of this valuable resource. Reports about the usefulness of this experience from this category of visitors have paralleled those of other groups.

For the Freedom Center, the Dialogue Zone is a learning space for visitors and for staff who want to learn better ways to have discussions about race and diversity. We hope to increase our own skills and create models for effective dialogues on difficult topics like these. We also hope to share our learning with facilitators, educators, diversity trainers, and others who can apply these skills in their own work. The Dialogue Zone embodies the overall spirit of the Freedom Center, which encourages exploring new ground with the belief that everyone will benefit from the learning gained as we move forward.

These considerations also extend to the intellectual and emotional style with which museums approach the information they present. They need to be provocative, questioning, and emotionally impactful. This does not have to dominate every presentation they make, but it does need to be a part of the array of ideas present in these institutions. As places of education, a museum's goals in part should focus on sharpening the critical thinking skills of its visitors. Museums need to offer visitors ways of viewing the world that help them navigate it, as well as find avenues through which they can, if they choose, make an impact.

The experiences of the past decade or so can make taking steps in this direction feel a bit nerve-wracking. The cultural wars of the 1990s in the United States certainly made many museums cautious. The controversies which emerged over exhibitions at the National Air and Space Museum (*The Enola Gay*), the Library of Congress (*Back of the Big House)*, the Royal Ontario Museum (*Out of Africa*), and the slave auction reenactment at Colonial Williamsburg, to name a few, were sobering. Individuals bothered by the content and interpretations of the presentations in these institutions certainly made life difficult for the staff at these museums. But it is also true that there were many others who supported these presentations and found them informative and quite appropriate. It is important that the voices of dissent do not totally drown out what may be a larger percentage, the silent majority, of our visitors.

A recent survey of museum visitors argues that visitor expectations may be more varied than we believe. A poll conducted of museum visitors in Canada and Australia showed that 70 percent thought it was appropriate for museums to look at contentious topics. For them the key was the positioning of these presentations. They wanted museums to give them the information on all sides of the controversy. They wanted the opportunity to analyze the information themselves and to perform their own sorting of the data. Then, if the museum presentation offered its perspective, the visitors could decide for themselves what they thought about that point of view.

But there is a further step that we can consider as we look at what additional value museums can provide. It is the opportunity to actively encourage visitors to contemplate their role and place in the world: to think about the challenges and responsibilities that lay before them as concerned and hopefully involved world citizens. Embracing this task carries museums into a more heavily prescriptive role than they have normally adopted. It gets them involved in openly offering value judgments and seeking to shape directly the way visitors think about civic engagement and social responsibility. It entails strongly encouraging visitors to believe that their decisions can have a positive impact in shaping the places where they live. They *can* make a difference if they so choose.

In adopting this philosophy and mission museums who follow this path are consciously positioning themselves as places of transformation: institutions that believe they should impact how their visitors connect to and engage with their fellow citizens and the society of which they are a part. This is not a role many museums embraced previously. Most often they saw as their primary role to inform and perhaps to offer new perspectives, but not to aggressively advocate civic engagement or social activism. However, there are a group of institutions adopting a different perspective, which argues for a need for change as we move into a new century.

The places that have come to embrace this positioning see themselves as "museums of conscience" and are taking a much more aggressive and prescriptive posture. The leading institution among them is the United States Holocaust Memorial Museum in Washington, D.C. Its mission includes the task "to encourage its visitors to reflect upon the moral and spiritual questions raised by the events of the Holocaust as well as their own responsibilities as citizens of a democracy." There is no doubt in these words that through its presentations the Holocaust Museum takes a very clear point of view with the intent of emphasizing the responsibility we each have to prevent injustices like the Holocaust from occurring again. This is not just their goal for a single exhibition, but it is the mission of the institution. It is not neutral on this subject, but rather quite forthright and forceful about the lessons it wants its visitors to embrace.

There are other institutions such as the Birmingham Civil Rights Institute, the Museum of the African Diaspora in San Francisco, the Museum of Tolerance in Los Angeles, the Lower Eastside Tenement Museum in New York, and the National Underground Railroad Freedom Center in Cincinnati that have followed similar paths with their missions. For example, the National Underground Railroad Freedom Center highlights the stories of the people who participated in the Underground Railroad with a focus on the diverse, interracial nature of this movement. It focuses on the willingness of these individuals to work collectively to defeat slavery and to support freedom. The emphasis is on the impact that determined and committed people can have when they make a conscious choice to make a difference through the choices they make. This lesson applies not only to the period of the Underground Railroad but to the present day as well. Through its exhibitions, touch screens, multimedia presentations, interactive computer programs, and a Dialogue Zone (see the case study in this chapter), the Freedom Center constantly reminds, prods, and questions its visitors about issues of civic engagement. In particular, the Dialogue Zone provides a safe space where visitors, with the help of trained facilitators, can reflect on the ideas they encountered during their visit and how these concepts impacted them. The goal in this space and throughout the Freedom Center is to educate and inspire visitors to find ways to make a difference. Another outstanding example is described in the case study on Constitution Hill in South Africa, also in this chapter.

The Freedom Center, Constitution Hill, and other museums of conscience hope that by illustrating past inequities and the struggle to overcome them they can show what can happen when engaged and committed citizens work to create a more just society. They show their visitors that the choices they make with regard to others can have an impact. Further, they point out that a socially responsible citizen finds ways to get engaged and to make a difference. These institutions are seeking to inspire their visitors to understand that their decisions can have consequences that make the world a better place. They are seeking to touch the conscience of their visitors and remind them of their responsibilities to others.

To take this position does entail some risk. There are organizations and interest groups who disapprove of the stands taken by these institutions. And some of these groups are quite influential. But these museums of conscience have determined that the message they offer is important enough to risk the negative reactions they might receive. Their belief is that there is strong support from the majority of their visitors for this very clear message. What they firmly believe they are providing is guidance and ideas for people as they seek to navigate a complex and sometimes confusing world. They believe they are serving as reference points to help their visitors find ways to add more value and meaning to their lives. In a world that has changed significantly over the past few years more people are looking for ways to navigate this new landscape and to add meaning through the choices they make. Museums of conscience believe they can offer guideposts to help in this journey. It is certainly an idea that other institutions may want to consider as they look to the future.

It is not necessary to create a new institution in order to generate meaningful civic dialogues, as at the National Underground Railroad Freedom Center. Numerous places have crafted thoughtful programs and exhibitions that generate similar experiences for their visitors. The goal is to provide a broader context for the topic presented. Visitors are then encouraged to think about and express their reactions. The Henry Art Gallery at the University of Washington, the Wadsworth Athenaeum, the Andy Warhol Museum, and the National Japanese American Museum have all had successful activities using this approach, and are places we might look at more closely.

The Warhol Museum created a community dialogue on race as part of the *Without Sanctuary: Lynching Photography in America* exhibition that the museum hosted. Rather than downplay the potential controversy that might accompany the exhibition, they chose to embrace it and use it in a constructive way. In partnership with several organizations in the city of Pittsburgh they held dialogues that discussed the images and feelings they evoked in the light of racial conflicts occurring in the city. About a thousand people participated in the dialogues during the course of the exhibition. The conversation generated new positive relationships between the museum staff and community members which have made a difference in the way the Warhol is seen by its neighbors, who now see it as an institution with value for them.[5]

SERVING THE PUBLIC INTEREST: THE ROLE OF EDUCATIONAL AND PUBLIC PROGRAMMING IN ADDRESSING COMMUNITY NEEDS IN SOUTH AFRICA

Danielle Melville

Museums and public spaces have an intrinsic mission to serve public interest and education through effective, interactive, and accessible programming. All museums have the distinctive ability to serve public awareness and education in an interactive and engaging manner. As public spaces, they offer people of all ages access to a nation's culture and heritage. Constitution Hill seeks to achieve this through comprehensive education and public programs together with key partnerships. As a mixed-use heritage development in the inner city of Johannesburg in South Africa and the home of the Constitutional Court, Constitution Hill is a unique living heritage site built on public participation. The site consists of the Constitutional Court, the historic fort prison complex, the former women's jail, and, in the near future, a retail, residential, and hospitality development. The buildings of the site starkly echo the abuses of the past (as symbolized by the former prison buildings) and the hope and enlightenment of the future (as symbolized by the new Constitutional Court).

The content underpinning program and exhibition development at Constitution Hill can be divided into six key areas:

1. The site—the history of the old fort, the jails, and the Boer War
2. The location and the immediate community—Johannesburg in transition from northern suburbs to Braamfontein and Hillbrow, the regeneration of the inner city
3. The ex-prisoners—the freedom struggle, society, incarceration (the oral history)
4. Physical objects—artifacts and other archival material
5. The Constitutional Court—that Constitution Hill is the chosen home of the Constitutional Court gives us a platform and ensures that Constitution Hill will continue to be relevant
6   The Constitution—its story and the values, rights, and freedoms on which the new South Africa is based and which the Court upholds, namely, dignity, nonracism, nonsexism, freedom, democracy, social justice, the rule of law, and reconciliation

The following guiding principles underlie all of the programming and its content at Constitution Hill, and directly link to the development of South Africa's constitutional democracy:

- Public participation
- A global symbol of human rights, democracy, and reconciliation
- A rights-based society
- A platform to get South Africans talking (a *lekgotla*)[1]
- A meeting place for the celebration of our rights and freedom
- A unique platform for South Africa's heritage and culture
- Every South African should experience the journey of the site at least once

If one were to create community categories, the Constitution Hill community can broadly be divided as follows: South Africans at large; the exprisoners and exwarders of the site; the immediate neighborhoods of Braamfontein and Hillbrow; key civil and social organizations or groups; and international visitors.

In the past (and with particular reference to Apartheid), South Africans have been divided along various lines. The introduction of democracy led to the development of what is colloquially termed "the rainbow nation" which is based foremost on the African principles of *Batho Pele* and *Ubuntu*. Batho Pele means putting people first, and Ubuntu means human dignity, deriving from the African saying, "I am human because you are human." These two principles are commonly used to describe what it is to be South African in the context of the new South Africa. This new patriotism stems from the key values of the Constitution that underpin our constitutional democracy and which make us uniquely South African. The key values of the Constitution include democracy, social justice and equity, equality, nonracism and nonsexism, ubuntu (human dignity), an open society, accountability, the rule of law, respect, and reconciliation.

Therefore, in determining its communities, Constitution Hill, by its very nature and mandate, serves every South African in a multicultural environment. This may be further supported by the recent move by museum and heritage practitioners in South Africa to combine heritage, arts, and culture into one sector, thereby increasing each institution's reach. This arguably stems from the growing belief that if "heritage" is culture from the past that one has the benefit of enjoying in the present and the task of preserving for the future, then in serving the public interest, museums should aim to ensure public ownership of and participation in culture, heritage, and the arts. Programming at Constitution Hill has therefore been created and developed to accommodate this unique mandate that at the same time allows for effective public participation.

Constitution Hill's mandate can thus be described as follows:

- to tell the stories of the site
- to promote the values of the Constitution
- to promote a rights-based society by encouraging public ownership of and participation in the process of democracy
- to ensure true depictions of the history
- to create awareness along with the opportunity for (public) interpretation, debate, discussion, and representation
- to provide an interface between the courts, the site of the prison, the tenants on site (the community of nongovernmental organizations), and ordinary people
- to ensure that visitors have an interactive learning experience and effective interpretation of the content through a range of programs
- to attract diverse audiences, in order to obtain a range of experiences, opinions, ideas, and values so that programming is truly representative and inclusive
- to ensure public ownership of culture and the arts (broadly understood)
- and to create an outlet for performance and culture.

There are two aspects of public participation to consider:

1. *Formal participation* which refers to program categories, program content, and program values.
2. *Informal participation* through which people are encouraged to make use of the site as a platform and take ownership of the site, its programs and spaces.

SERVING THE PUBLIC INTEREST

In order to achieve Constitution Hill's mandate and be truly accessible to a range of audiences, our focus has been on the creation of programs that are dynamic, evolving, and interactive, and not limited to static two-dimensional experiences or a strict inflexible programming structure that appeals only to specific audiences. In terms of accessibility and reach, apart from content, Constitution Hill requests a minimal entrance fee, there is a free day every Tuesday, all public programs are free and accessible to all, and every person who goes through the site's educational programs receives material to ensure that the experience and impact of the site is extended.

THE 'WE, THE PEOPLE' PROGRAM

Constitution Hill's *We, the People* program is an ongoing nationwide outreach public participation program that aims to "take the Hill to the nation and bring the nation back to the Hill." South Africa belongs to all who live in it, united in our diversity. *We, the People* strives to uphold this by listening to stories, preserving the memories, and validating the experiences of all who share in this country's living heritage. *We, the People* offers all visitors to the site the opportunity to participate in the building of Constitution Hill, and to lay down their own memories and experiences for future generations by leaving messages for the court, leaving a memory behind in the Memory Booth, or simply telling their story. The *We, the People* program is illustrated by the *We, the People* Wall, the Dignity Book, and the Memory Booth:

- The *We, the People* Wall records the opinions and impressions of visitors to Constitution Hill. It is comprised of handwritten messages from visitors to Constitution Hill that are etched onto copper "bricks" and added to the wall, providing a people's record of the first twenty-five years of Constitution Hill. The messages reflect simple and honest responses to what it means to be South African, and are a reflection of the views and expressions of South Africa's myriad peoples in one singular space.
- The Dignity Book has been established and will be displayed in the former Number Four prison alongside one of the chief warder's old prison registers. All exprisoners to the site are invited to inscribe their names, and the dates of their imprisonment, in the Dignity Book.
- The Memory Booth is a place where you may record your experiences on the Hill or of the Hill, and what it means to you as an individual, as a family, as a victim, or as a South African.

THE PERMANENT EXHIBITIONS

As the dominant visual experience on the site, the permanent exhibitions provide an important opportunity to interpret both the core values of the Constitution and the heritage value of the prison spaces. Exhibitions, as a mode of interpretation, help create a clear and defined visitor experience. The exhibitions at Constitution Hill were conceived to be minimalist so as not to overshadow the sacred nature of the heritage spaces and the raw experience. In many museums and heritage spaces, the core experience is the passive observation of key exhibits. However, at Constitution Hill many of the exhibits prompt the viewer with questions. This is another means of engagement, challenging viewers to question and consider different points of view, and leave behind their written response for others to read, ponder, and hopefully discuss.

EDUCATION PROGRAMS

Through the educational programs, Constitution Hill aims to provide children and learners with an interactive, dynamic learning experience that makes the Constitution tangible, real, and alive, and enables Constitution Hill to be a crucial site of learning. The Schools Program aims at reaching families through the school learners in order to lead an awareness campaign on human rights and the Constitution. The educational programs aim to educate people of all ages, and include the Children's Room, the Schools Program, and Adult Education:

The *Children's Room* and "*Constitution Kids*" was conceptualized with the community of the inner city in mind. The need for a safe appropriate community space and a space for children to play and learn was highlighted during the initial conceptualizing phase of planning. The Children's Room is aimed at educating children between the ages of three and twelve, and brings to life the Children's Bill of Rights in a unique African, tactile, fun, and interactive way so that children can work alongside their families and caregivers in beginning to experience and understand their attitudes, feelings, values, responsibilities, and rights.

The *Schools Program* ensures that a visit to Constitution Hill is relevant and meaningful for both learners and educators. The mission of this program is to foster active engagement with the values of the Constitution and human rights. This we hope will assist both learners and educators to

Figure 6.2. National Children's Day Festival

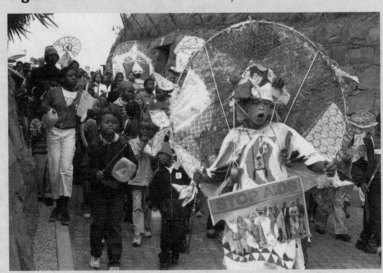

COURTESY OF OSCAR GUTIERREZ.

understand and reclaim the heritage and memories of the site, its lessons for reconciliation in the present, and its call for continued participation and citizenship in the future. The Schools Program makes clear links with the national Department of Education curriculum and meets cross-curriculum outcomes. The programs are diverse, from on-site and off-site tours to ex-prisoner *lekgotlas* and mock Constitutional Court trials. Through the Schools Program, Constitution Hill has been able to provide innovative and mission based support material to schools.

Adult Education is the third program that is aimed at ensuring that every visitor is provided with the opportunity to participate in a lively and informative tour. The program provides a platform for visitors to experience, question, and engage with other visitors locally and internationally. Tours are the foundation of the visitor experience at Constitution Hill. They are a tool that aims to educate visitors not only about our history but also about the stories of contemporary Hillbrow, Johannesburg, and South Africa.

PUBLIC PROGRAMS

Public programs are another means for the public to connect with the vast content of the site. The public programs are divided into categories that were strategically created to structure the mission and content of the site—that is, to enable active engagement and public participation. The variety of categories allows for flexibility and enables us to embrace current issues, celebrate days of national significance, address matters of public interest, and create a forum for public debate.

The following categories were developed:

Lekgotlas—Lekgotla means the coming together of individuals to talk, share, and debate. Based on the traditional concept of elders gathering to ponder and question, the spirit of Lekgotla is echoed in the architecture of the site. The series of Lekgotlas are organized to provide visitors with the opportunity to use and explore the history and offerings of the site, to inspire debate as well as discussion around important contemporary issues. They are a means of providing individuals with the resources and space to define their place in a changing South Africa. Four kinds are offered:

- *Encounter Lekgotlas* facilitate meetings between decision makers such as judges, politicians, policymakers, and members of the public. The aim here is to encourage dialogue and public accountability.
- *Dialogue Lekgotlas* are more informal interactions. They happen between groups of learners, nongovernmental organizations, or community audiences with an invited guest speaker who may or may not be a decision

maker or a policymaker. For example, Jewish Voices *Lekgotla* on "the Jailor and the Jailed" brought multicultural learners to interact with local and international speakers from an exprisoner to a member of the Conscientious Objectors of Israel.

- *Debate Lekgotlas* follow the formal structure of a debate. To date we have pursued these in partnership with the Wits Debating Union and have hosted both national and provincial school debating tournaments.
- *Rapid Response Lekgotlas* are intended to pick up on the hot issues and conversations of the day. This series responds to issues raised by the courts (in particular matters heard by the Constitutional Court), current affairs, and other contemporary challenges. The format for these is one of a talk show, and there is a voting component to the *Lekgotla* that becomes a means of measuring public opinion.

BUA! Speak Out!—The BUA strand is a lively forum based on the Beat Poet Movement for young poets and rap artists to workshop and perform around themes related to democracy, social justice, freedom, nonracism, and nonsexism.

Skills Development—The skills development program focuses on democracy, community development, and leadership skills. This program aims to encourage active citizenship and the building of democracy and social justice through dialogue and community action and leadership skills. Although this program is still evolving, our most successful skills development program is the Hillbrow Street Lights, which takes street children from neighboring Hillbrow and uses art, music, and dance to tell stories of their experiences, and creates a platform for their needs and rights. The Street Lights perform at many of the public programs as an integral part of the program's content.

Public Seminars—Public seminars are a platform for one or a series of speakers to present research, interpretations, or a set of ideas on a relevant topic. The audience is encouraged to ask questions and engage with the speakers.

Events—Through a series of events, Constitution Hill seeks to showcase and celebrate different cultures, diverse linguistics, and promote tolerance and human rights. Constitution Hill also aims to promote new types of experimental performance and those performances that would not be showcased in conventional theatre venues.

Temporary Exhibitions—These exhibitions are hosted to provide yet another voice, that of the visual or performance artist, who wishes to comment on social, political, and cultural issues that are pertinent. These exhibitions have attracted a key arts audience that may not otherwise have engaged with Constitution Hill.

ENSURING SUCCESSFUL OUTREACH AND PARTICIPATION

Partnerships are an integral part of all program generation at Constitution Hill and are initiated with the purpose of creating more substantial, sustainable, and comprehensive programming, maximizing resources and targeting as many people as possible with a focus on the immediate communities of the site. The ultimate goal is to establish *sustainable partnerships* among government structures, the private sector, and civil society through the following:

- Using community groups as service providers on site, such as catering, sound, entertainment, and the like. This enhances their profiles, provides them with opportunities for development, and creates reciprocal relationships. In addition, it is a way of addressing the lack of resources and restrictive budgets and at the same time promoting local initiatives.
- Encouraging partners and visitors to take ownership of the site through creating and managing programs continuously.
- Positioning the site as a platform for inclusive social, economic, and political dialogues with the neighboring community and various stakeholders.
- Increasing awareness of the site as an educational information resource.
- Increasing public participation and promoting the site as a campus for human rights both locally and internationally.
- Developing enriching and qualitative programs on site as a result of a network of strategic partnerships.

CONCLUSION

With such a vast community to serve, Constitution Hill faces the constant challenge that public interest is an ever-changing, ever-developing dynamic. Ultimately though, we have discovered that a solid structure of educational and public programs provides effective interactive tools for public engagement, awareness, and education—a sustainable structure that the community can take ownership of.

NOTES

1. *Lekgotla* means "the coming together of individuals to talk, share, and debate." It is based on the traditional African concept of elders gathering to ponder and question; the spirit of *Lekgotla* forms the basis of Constitution Hill and is echoed throughout the site.

6.6   CONCLUSION

There are no guarantees that the ideas suggested in this chapter—such as emulating museums of conscience, experimenting with technology, or forming more intimate working partnerships with our visitors—will prove the keys for success. There is no blueprint for creating a powerful and valuable experience for our audiences. History has told us that much. Audience expectations and needs change from era to era, as have the positioning of museums. Our work is very much an art form where one must have the willingness and ability to improvise. Experimentation is not something to fear, but to embrace.

What is true is that we are now part of an era where change is the norm. The ideas that hold sway one minute are subject to revision and new interpretation the next. The world is very different now than it was five years ago. Our audiences have come to expect this constant movement and change. They are not always comfortable with it, but they recognize the reality of it.

In the light of this environment it is essential that our institutions have flexibility and a willingness to experiment. They need to think about and stay ahead of the needs of their audiences, and consider the best way to respond to and provide for those needs. It is how they will continue to create value as institutions. This is the biggest challenge we face as twenty-first century institutions. We must stay attuned to our audiences and their needs. Our visitors are changing and evolving and we must change along with them. In many ways we need to update and follow the efforts of our predecessors like Charles Peale and John Cotton Dana who kept their ears attuned to the preferences and needs of their visitors. They understood that this commitment demanded constant learning, flexibility, and a willingness to accept the missteps that come with the process. Here is a tradition well worth preserving. It is a lesson from the past that will be critical to our success as we go forward. The path it will cause our institutions to follow will not always be comfortable for many of us. But it is important that we learn to live with that discomfort. It is the same lack of surety our visitors are experiencing while navigating this new century. In this way we will share that journey with them, and hopefully provide learning and growth along the way that will prove invaluable to everyone.

NOTES

1. G. Kulik, "Designing the Past: History Museum Exhibitions from Peale to the Present," in W. Leon and R. Rosenzweig, eds., *History Museums in the United States* (Urbana and Chicago: University of Illinois Press, 1989), p. 4.

2. H. Skramstad, "An Agenda for Museums in the Twenty-first Century," in G. Anderson, ed., *Reinventing the Museum: Historical and Contemporary Perspectives on the Paradigm Shift* (Walnut Creek, CA: AltaMira Press, 2004), pp. 120–21.

3. E. B. Gaither, "Hey! That's Mine: Thoughts on Pluralism and American Museums," in I. Karp, C. M. Kreamer, and S. D. Lavine, eds., *Museums and Communities: The Politics of Public Culture* (Washington, D.C.: Smithsonian Institution, 1992), pp. 56–64.

4. C. Elderkin, "Coming of Age," *Museum News* 84, no. 4 (July-August 2005): 11–14; also conversation with Lonnie Bunch, president, Chicago Historical Society, March 11, 2005.

5. See B. S. Bacon, P. Korza, and P. E. Williams, *A Museum and Community Toolkit* (Washington, D.C.: American Association of Museums, 2002), pp. 9–13; and E. Hirzy, *Mastering Civic Engagement: A Challenge to Museums* (Washington, D.C.: American Association of Museums, 2002), pp. 77–78.

PART III:
HOW
Resources for Museum Learning

Introduction

Barry Lord

Part I examines the rationale for museum learning, and its potential for a knowledge-based society that depends on lifelong learning for personal, social, and economic fulfillment. Part II considers who should be served at this banquet of learning—we discuss families, school groups, and reaching out to adults, adolescents, and children from all communities, including those whose stories were not previously told in most museums. Here, part III turns to the ways at our disposal to achieve these learning objectives with our visitors and the users of our programs.

My own chapter 7 puts the initial focus on the indispensable museum educator, professional, or volunteer, the people whose dedicated careers have made possible the dramatic reorientation of museums to serving their visitors with sensitive, focused learning experiences. One case study in that chapter by Barbara Gordon acquaints us with the outstanding volunteer docent program operated by the Chicago Architecture Foundation to provide learning experiences of the built environment in that great city, while another by Charlie Walter refers to the organization, management, and budgeting decisions involved in the highly effective and acclaimed learning programs of the Fort Worth Museum of Science and History.

In chapter 8, Heather Maximea takes us on a tour of the spaces that can be provided for museum learning, and shows how they can be enhanced to optimize the learners' experience in them. Heather's analysis also shows how a sensitive museum planner like herself can help architects and designers to meet the needs of museum learners of all ages.

Hugh Spencer's chapter 9 indicates how interpretative planning can affect the ways in which we communicate in exhibitions and other museum learning programs. Keri Ryan's case study in that chapter of a traveling exhibition called *Go Creative* that was a hit in two very disparate locations—China, and Trinidad and Tobago—shows how a profound understanding of the purpose of an exhibition can generate an interpretative plan that is expressed in something as simple as three mascots who personify and communicate the show's messages to a primarily adolescent target audience. Hugh then proceeds to a more detailed consideration of an important contemporary method of museum learning—electronic programs on the Internet. In the early twenty-first century, Web-based learning has emerged as an important part of any museum's learning program.

Dr. Barbara Soren also has her sights partly on the World Wide Web in chapter 10, in her case study on evaluating the Web exhibitions and Internet museum learning programs produced by the Canadian Heritage Information Network (CHIN) for the Virtual Museum of Canada. Barbara has a wider reach, however, as she draws our attention throughout her chapter to the importance of qualitative evaluation of the outcomes of exhibitions or museum learning programs. Her case study of an evaluation program for four smaller museums in southern Ontario focuses on the need to demystify visitor experience evaluation programs so that they can become more useful to museum professionals, especially the many overworked individuals struggling with insufficient budget and staff in smaller institutions and communities.

Chapters 11 and 12 relate to a recurring theme throughout the entire book—the fact that museum learning depends crucially on the motivation of the museum visitor or program user. Good marketing can inform and inspire motivation among visitors, as Amy Kaufman shows in chapter 11. Like Barbara, Amy is especially concerned to assist the marketing programs of smaller institutions with limited budgets.

Finally, in chapter 12, Mira Goldfarb addresses the challenge of sustaining our audiences—especially our adult audiences—for museum learning. Mira acknowledges that more sophisticated museums have now adopted a strategy of multiple points of access for their diverse visitors, but asks the open-ended question of how museums can encourage "re-entry" through these multiple points. In an illustrative case study, Sara Knelman describes how the Art Gallery of Hamilton in Ontario, Canada, has met this challenge by providing meaningful museum learning experiences that are related to a wide range of motivations among its community of visitors and users.

Thus from the recruitment, training, organization, and management of staff and volunteers through the spaces, techniques, evaluation, and marketing procedures for museum learning, we conclude with a consideration of its sustainability. But prior to examining each of these functions in turn, we need to address two of the most basic and important resources for museum learning, which should precede and embrace them all: a museum learning policy and museum learning plans.

A *museum learning policy* or *education policy* should be adopted by the governing body of the institution and should include the following features:

- The institution's commitment to serve its visitors with a program of museum learning, expressed in terms of a commitment to providing the staff, space, facilities, equipment, and funds necessary to achieve its learning objectives.
- A mission statement for museum learning that is integrally linked to the mission of the entire museum.
- A commitment to professional standards in museum learning practices, whether delivered through paid staff or volunteers.
- A commitment to ensuring that all staff and volunteers, especially those working with minors, are competent and trustworthy and have been vetted according to legal requirements and the moral responsibility of the museum.
- A commitment to remain abreast of current research, theories, and practices both in the academic disciplines appropriate to the subject matter of the museum, and in the field of informal education.
- A commitment to interpret the museum's permanent collections, museum research programs, and temporary exhibitions, with a clear statement of priorities among them.
- The section of the museum's collection policy referring to hands-on, living and/or loan collections that may be held for learning purposes.
- A commitment to interpretative planning and evaluation prior to, during, and following each exhibition or learning program, with a provision for applying the findings of each experience to future programs.
- A commitment to work with the museum's partners where appropriate and possible in order to deliver effective learning programs.
- A commitment to maintaining the highest academic standards of objectivity in the museum's learning programs, while aiming to make those programs relevant to the motivations and interests of as diverse a community of visitors and users as possible.
- A commitment to provide an effective learning environment for all visitors and users irrespective of age, ability, or capability.
- A statement of the museum's policy on languages of communication, both spoken and written, in the museum and on screen.
- A commitment to review the museum's learning policy and plans at least once every three years to ensure compliance with this policy and to make changes in accordance with the evolving objectives of the museum.

Based on such a policy, a *museum learning plan* or *education plan* should include:

- A mission statement with a summary of the objectives expressed in the institution's commitments in the museum learning policy

- A staffing plan, showing the present and future organization chart of the education or museum learning department, including links to other departments and the role of volunteers as well as paid staff.
- A training plan for staff and volunteers, including both in-house and other resources for training and development of personnel at all levels.
- A space plan that identifies all spaces in which museum learning will take place, plus the support areas both public and nonpublic, indicating all dimensions, occupancy limits, safety and security provisions, and rules of access.
- An equipment inventory listing such items as video monitors or recorders, audio equipment, slide projectors, screens, computers, office equipment, and supplies, with rules of access and provisions for loan or rental if applicable.
- A resources inventory referring to library, archival, photographic, video, audio, software, and other learning resources; hands-on, living, or other educational collections, loan collections, and traveling exhibitions.
- A program plan that lists all current learning programs whether in-house, external, or online, and projects those scheduled for future development, with a calendar showing dates of initiation, operation, and termination of each program.
- An institutional context summary, showing the museum's relationships with formal educational institutions, other museums, organizations, clubs, and associations.
- A marketing strategy, including target market identifications for each program, and provision for reports on and evaluation of marketing programs.
- An evaluation strategy, listing long-term and ad hoc evaluation programs, qualitative as well as quantitative, and the use of evaluation reports.
- A budget and financial plan, identifying salary and other costs, program-generated revenue, and grant sources, with a calendar linking the budgeting process to the museum's overall financial planning.

Such a policy and plans should facilitate the operation of the museum learning or education department as described in the pages of this section.

CHAPTER 7

The Centrality of Museum Educators

Organizing and Budgeting for Museum Learning

BARRY LORD

One Saturday afternoon in the early 1960s I stopped in to the Vancouver Art Gallery to pick up something I had forgotten from my assistant curator's office, only to find a distraught receptionist delighted to see me because she was facing down a group of disgruntled young men from a local correctional institution, and their two angry minders, who had brought them to the gallery for a tour that seemed to have slipped off the booking clerk's list. She immediately told them, "Ah, here is Mr. Lord, now, he will give you the guided tour."

My impromptu tour began where the hostile group was standing, at the entrance to the Emily Carr Gallery, which we had just reinstalled. Sensing their feelings of alienation that had been reinforced by their initial discovery that the gallery had apparently forgotten them, I took them through the Carr paintings biographically, explaining how she had been isolated as an artist in early twentieth-century British Columbia, how her alienation had led her to abandon painting altogether, and then how her kinship with West Coast First Nations people (of whom there were several in the correctional institute group), and her identification with the awesome landscape of Canada's Pacific coast, had allowed her to achieve the power and majesty of her later works.

As the tour progressed, the mood of the group changed, as more and more of the young men, and even their minders, saw how their own lives had parallels to that of the artist. We ended in a gallery of contemporary art produced by local painters and sculptors, and several heads nodded when I said that young men just like them often felt a similar alienation, and expressed it in works like those they could see around us.

It was a 1960s incident. Postmodern art historians have subsequently qualified Carr's heroic life story (although the essential facts are undisputed), and the approach to contemporary art that stresses expression of alienation was already somewhat dated by the advent of pop and minimal art, as I knew at the time. But the broader lesson of the experience for me was the potential that we, as museum educators, have to help visitors find their way in, to discover the relevance of what the museum has to offer, and to make it part of their lives. Museum educators can make a difference.

Hence the title of this chapter: "The Centrality of Museum Educators." *Any consideration of organizing and budgeting for museum learning must begin with the staff and volunteers who are at the center of the museum learning experience for many visitors.* Of course, curators and exhibition designers aim to communicate directly with the visitors, and graphics and audio tours can be powerfully effective. We want the unaccompanied visitor to enter deeply into the learning experience, and he or she need not be dependent on a guide. But wherever visitors have the opportunity for engaging human contact, their comments in visitors' books or assessment sheets invariably attest that person-to-person communication is the most convincing learning experience that the museum can offer. Quite aside from other advantages, the in-person museum educator is *also* a learner, so that the experience is one of sharing and exchange, not a one-way procedure in which the visitor is assumed to be passive. *Museum educators are at the core of the museum learning experience, and their centrality should be reflected in the museum's organization, whether they are paid or voluntary.*

7.1   VOLUNTARY OR PAID DOCENTS

The first case study in this chapter—The City is Our Museum by Barbara Gordon—illustrates this centrality graphically in the example of the Chicago Architecture Foundation's guided tours, where the collection consists of the remarkable built environment of the city. Barbara's case study is particularly significant because it stresses the importance of volunteer docents, who remain the core deliverers of the informal educational experience at a wide range of institutions.

Indeed, one of the fundamental challenges of planning, organizing, and budgeting for museum learning is to determine the optimal relationship between paid and voluntary educators in situations where they are working together. As Barbara's case study indicates, the Chicago Architecture Foundation has found one solution. One key is the purposefully demanding program of training, preparation, and evaluation that volunteer docents must undergo before they are permitted to join the elite corps of the CAF. In my experience, this is crucial: volunteers must know that they are being given the opportunity to participate in an advanced learning experience, however informal, so that those who qualify take pride and care in providing a high-quality experience that is solidly based on up-to-date and accurate scholarship. I suggest a general rule:

> Broadly speaking, the more demanding the training, preparation, and evaluation programs are, the higher the morale and the more effective the performance of the volunteers who survive the introductory process and become part of the daily learning life of the institution.

From this general observation follows the importance of the *volunteer coordinator*—itself sometimes a voluntary position—and the *booking clerk*, who schedules the volunteers. In virtually all cases where great difficulties are reported in working with volunteers I have found that there is either an insufficiently demanding training and evaluation course, an inadequate or nonexistent volunteer coordinator, or an inefficient booking clerk. Volunteers must be asked at their initial interview what hours they will be able to commit, and these must be respected—and changed when necessary—throughout their life at the institution.

The best way to show respect for volunteer docents is to present them with a *volunteer contract* that records their time commitment, even in the training period. The contract must also set the terms of their evaluation, and make it clear that failure in the training period and dismissal due to a poor evaluation are possible. Only on this basis can a highly motivated corps of volunteer docents be developed. The volunteer contract is also an opportunity to point out that all volunteers must first be museum members, to situate the museum's education program in the context of the museum's mission, to specify the relationship between voluntary and paid staff, and to identify standards of conduct expected of the volunteer corps.

Annual—or even more frequent—recognition of the contribution that volunteers make to the institution is extremely important. These annual events are where volunteers are formally "paid" by the museum, so it is crucial that the director, curators, and board members all attend and participate, and that volunteers' families are invited to enjoy the refreshments and to see that their family member's contribution—which takes him or her away from the family circle—is appreciated by the highest ranking persons in the museum. If local or regional politicians can be persuaded to participate and present some of the honors, all the better. Some years ago I happened to be at the Orlando Museum of Science the morning after the annual Volunteer Recognition Night—that was the morning that the director, curators, and board chairman were given the date of next year's Recognition Night, so that they would keep it in their calendar, and be there.

Even with challenging training programs, effective volunteer coordinators and booking clerks, clear volunteer contracts, and regular volunteer appreciation nights attended by senior museum personnel, it is commonplace that due to social changes, volunteers have become harder and harder to recruit and keep. Families in which both parents have to work, and the retirement income that necessitates a part-time or full-time job for the pensioner, leave little time for volunteering for a large number of people. Even more fundamentally, the knowledge economy, with its demands for much longer working hours than much industrial or office employment, has thinned the ranks of prospective volunteers.

To some extent, this difficulty has been overemphasized. As the CAF case study shows, it is still possible to inspire and develop a vibrant volunteer force even in a large busy city like Chicago. Similarly, in some parts of the world it is said that the volunteer culture is foreign, and won't work in this country or region because it doesn't fit with the culture: yet in Kuwait The Scientific Center has proven that it is possible to operate a revenue-generating summer holiday program of internships throughout an excellent science center and aquarium for hundreds of adolescents aged 15 or 16, and then to offer volunteer postings as docents to the best of them throughout the rest of the year. So it is always worth probing to determine where the resistance to volunteers is—whether it is really in the community, or actually inside the institution itself. Establishing and maintaining effective volunteer programs takes dedication and consummate people skills, and if these are lacking the institution may find it easier to hire paid docents, if the budget allows.

Another path to museum learning that some institutions have taken with school groups is to rely on teachers to become the museum educators during a school visit, in some cases with the aid of kits provided either physically or virtually to the teachers. Although this may save the time needed to develop an effective volunteer program, and/or the cost of professional docents, it must be very carefully done if it is not to lower the quality of the learning experience for the affected groups. Merely providing a written guide to busy teachers, and expecting them to acquire the confidence and expertise to guide students through a complex exhibition experience seldom works. If this strategy is combined with intensive teacher training programs, especially if teachers in training can get credit from their training schools for hours spent with classes in the museum just as if they were in the classroom, then it may be possible for the museum to develop an effective teacher-guided learning program.

Still another approach, which may save on the docent staff budget, is to position educators in the galleries, where they are available to answer questions and to inspire visitors in both formal and informal groups as they enter each gallery. Stationed docents, as distinct from docents who take tours through the galleries, may be particularly appropriate in historic houses or in constricted circulation environments, such as a historic ship's confined spaces below decks. It is tempting, but it can be dangerous, to replace security guards with such educators, or to recruit and train guards who can serve as educators. It is too easy for a two-person team of thieves to distract such a multitasked person by engaging him or her in conversation with one thief, while the other undertakes the theft or vandalism. Security consultants warn against this practice, and experience has shown that a person stationed in a gallery can be either an educator or a guard, but cannot be expected to do both at the same time.

Paid docents, either stationed in the galleries or taking tours, should be recruited, trained, evaluated, and compensated as professionals. Since they will provide the spark for much of the museum learning that will happen in the museum, they must be treated with respect, and expected to perform to a high level of competence. Having been recruited due to their educational qualifications—in art history, science, human history, or a technical specialization—they must be given training in the informal learning process that can happen in the museum. They may be historical technology demonstrators, teaching scientists, aquarium divers, or living history role-playing actors, as well as tour group docents. They should not be accorded permanent status until their aptitude for their demanding roles has been determined. When it has been determined, they should be fairly compensated, and provided with dedicated restrooms equipped with showers where needed, a lounge for lunches and breaks, and a sufficient work space for study and preparation.

THE CITY IS OUR MUSEUM! THE DOCENT AND TOUR PROGRAM AT THE CHICAGO ARCHITECTURE FOUNDATION

Barbara Gordon

Finally, all the planning is complete! The speakers are confirmed, the homework assignments for each week are prepared, the sponsors are matched up, and we've double-checked that all the buildings are still standing! As we put together the Docent Education Program for the upcoming training class each January, we get a rush of excitement knowing that soon we will initiate a new class of fifty enthusiastic men and women from many different backgrounds. Each of these docents-in-training comes together in the name of one mission: to educate the public about architecture and the built environment in Chicago. We're always amazed that people wait in line to join this program each year! In the next ten weeks, they will be working on homework for two hours each night, spending approximately four hours each week outside looking at buildings, and practicing, revising, and practicing again!

Each docent-in-training starts his or her career at the Chicago Architecture Foundation with two downtown, or loop, walking tours. *The Historic Skyscrapers Tour* highlights commercial buildings from after the Great Chicago Fire of 1871 until the beginning of World War II. *The Modern Skyscrapers Tour* focuses on modern and postmodern architecture from 1950 to present-day commissions. The Volunteer Services Department and the Docent Council's Education Committee prepare a course in which speakers from all over the city of Chicago are invited to discuss issues related to these two loop walking tours. In the weeks ahead, the docents-in-training will meet architects, urban planners, university professors, and construction workers. Experienced Chicago Architecture Foundation docents will introduce them to theme building, creating cohesive tours, and presentation skills.

The Chicago Architecture Foundation (CAF) is a not-for-profit organization dedicated to advancing public interest and education in architecture and design. It is the only organization dedicated exclusively to enhancing the public's awareness and appreciation of Chicago's outstanding architectural legacy. CAF pursues this mission through a comprehensive program of tours, exhibitions, lectures, special events, and youth education programs. Started by a handful of volunteers in 1966 to save the Glessner House (1886, architect H. H. Richardson) from destruction, CAF

Figure 7.1. Visitors Boarding an Architectural Bus Tour

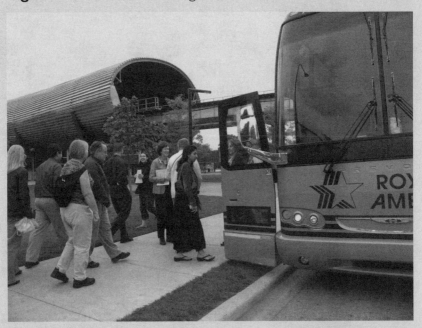

COURTESY OF THE CHICAGO ARCHITECTURE FOUNDATION. PHOTO BY VINCENT CHUNG.

has become a strong and respected organization in Chicago and the architectural community. Concentrating our efforts on educational programming and city area tours, we no longer own or operate Glessner House, or take on preservation advocacy.

In the early 1970s, CAF began docent-led architectural tours to raise money for the restoration of the house. The tour program has expanded from two tours offered in 1971 to more than eighty-five in 2005 (in which we served nearly 185,000 individuals!). Our tours are conducted on foot, by bus, boat, bike, and train, and cover the Chicago metropolitan area. Topics range from specific Chicago architects or neighborhoods to a general survey of the downtown buildings.

Each CAF tour has been the inspiration and creation of a docent, and has been executed through the Docent Council's Tour Committee, which monitors the quality of these tours. The committee meets monthly and is comprised of approximately ten members, including both recent graduates and experienced docents. Staff members also sit on the committee to provide advertising, budgetary, and attendance information, as well as to provide the link between staff and docent activities.

Figure 7.2. Participants on a Chicago Architecture Foundation Bicycle Tour Take a Break Along the Chicago River.

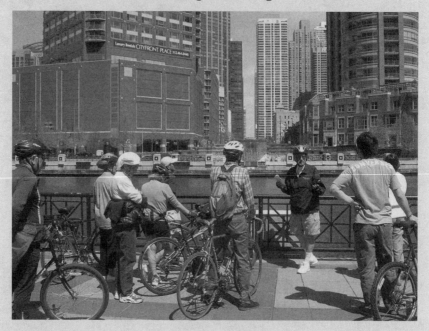

COURTESY OF THE CHICAGO ARCHITECTURE FOUNDATION. PHOTO BY BRENT HOFFMAN.

THE DOCENT BODY

Our intense Docent Education Program was developed in 1971 to prepare volunteers to lead a wide variety of architectural tours throughout metropolitan Chicago. More than 1,500 docents have completed this program. We currently have close to 450 docents who are actively giving tours.

CAF docents demonstrate a civic pride for Chicago, an enthusiasm for intellectual challenges, and a strong sense of sharing. Docents come from all over the metropolitan area of Chicago, including city neighborhoods and suburbs, and include younger men, who are scarce at most art and history museums. Many occupations are represented among the docents, including university professors, television producers, architects, homemakers, paralegals, and nurses. The majority of applicants learn about our volunteer program through other docents or on a CAF tour. Docent candidates are highly intrigued by the subject of architecture and want to be among a group of people who share their interest. Many candidates have planned for years to become CAF docents.

DOCENT TRAINING

Prior to that first public tour all docents must take a ten-week training program in which they meet once a week from 9:00 a.m. to 4:30 p.m. The success of our training and tour program starts with flexibility. The training course is offered on Thursdays and Saturdays, and tours are conducted seven days a week. Lectures, tour demonstrations, tour practice, exercises, and games that solidify facts, observations, and interpretation techniques are all part of the training course. Each week, homework is assigned that helps trainees to develop and write their own tours. Docents-in-training are also matched up with a sponsor, an experienced docent who mentors them through the entire process from the first day of class.

Docents are encouraged to write their tours using themes. Early in docent training, they are asked to incorporate a unifying thread that creates a cohesive tour. Themes for the downtown walking tours might be the philosophy of the First Chicago School of Architecture, zoning laws, or technological advances that made the skyscraper possible. Docents interpret the architecture objectively in order for the public to form their own opinions, while describing a building's visual organization, historic importance, and design influences.

DOCENT PROGRAM EVALUATION

The first required evaluation is a follow-up tour with the sponsor that is to be completed at the end of the docent's first year of doing public tours. Subsequently, once every three years docents are eligible to be observed on a tour by a trained peer reviewer. Written feedback is filed with the Volunteer Services Department, and any problems are reported to the Docent Council's Standards Committee, who will coach the docent through the problem. In the event of a complaint from a tourist, the Standards Committee will contact the docent in writing about the nature of the complaint and ask for a written response to the problem. Should the docent receive multiple complaints, the committee will send a representative to observe the tour.

CONCLUSION

What makes CAF unique in comparison to other cultural organizations is that the city is our museum. Our collection of buildings old and new is constantly evolving through politics, financial agreements, and market trends in

Figure 7.3. With eighty-eight different tours, the Chicago Architecture Foundation docents offer their expertise in and around the Chicago area.

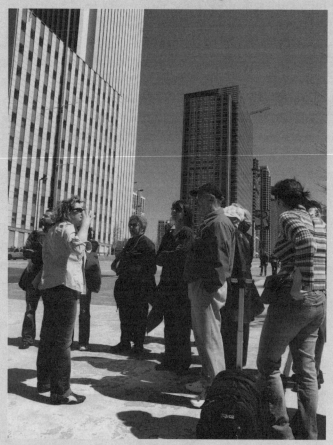

COURTESY OF THE CHICAGO ARCHITECTURE FOUNDATION. PHOTO BY ANNE EVANS.

Chicago. Therefore, we have a rich variety of public programming opportunities. It is inspiring to see the dedication toward our mission that remains very strong with each new graduating docent class. Without the docents there would be no Chicago Architecture Foundation!

7.2 MUSEUM LEARNING WITHIN THE MUSEUM ORGANIZATION

Whether paid or voluntary, museum educators are involved in an energy-consuming occupation that requires imagination, concentration, patience, and skill that must be exercised repeatedly with unpredictable—or sometimes too predictable—groups of visitors. Maintaining their morale is therefore important, and depends crucially on the leadership provided to them, and the status that leadership has within the institution.

When I took over as head of Education Services at the National Gallery of Canada in 1970, I found that curators at that time would routinely decline to meet with the paid docent staff to take them through an exhibition that they had just installed. I had to insist, and in one or two instances go and get them from their offices to bring them to a tour that had been scheduled for the docents. This was not surprising, neither to me nor to the docents, because at that time it was accepted that museum educators had relatively low status within the organization. They were literally viewed as "handmaidens" of the curatorial staff. Educators were not consulted about the content of exhibitions, but were expected to follow whatever direction the curator had established, even if that curator declined to leave his or her office to meet with the educators.

Under the leadership of the National Gallery's director, Dr. Jean Sutherland Boggs, and with the cooperation of some of the dedicated young curators she had recruited, all that began to change. Not only was I encouraged to demand curatorial participation in training the docents but, as head of Education Services, I began to be invited to at least the initial planning meeting for exhibitions. Similar changes have been made in many institutions since that time—although as Dr. Claudia Haas points out in chapter 4, there are still many museums where educators are accorded relatively low status.

The status of museum learning within the institution is reflected by its place within the museum's organizational structure. The structure recommended in our *Manual of Museum Planning* (1997) is a tripartite division of administration, collections, and public programs, with all three headed by an assistant director (or comparable title), reporting to the executive office of the director. On this model the head of public programs has equal status with the chief curator and the senior administrator (however that position is described), and all three report to an executive director. Among other advantages, this organization accords equivalent status to the three essential components of museum organization, and therefore should establish a climate in which sufficient respect is paid to the learning experience that is the focus of the public programs division.

Under the leadership of a director of public programs, this division may comprise departments dedicated to exhibitions, special events, theater programs (such as an IMAX), a planetarium, online services, membership, and other programs as well as an education or learning department. In smaller museums, the entire department may be headed by one person, or in any case the director of public programs may also be the head of education services. In slightly larger institutions, the head of education or learning services should be supported by a booking clerk (who may double as secretary but has the essential task of maintaining the calendar of scheduled group visits and the docents who will serve them), and a volunteer coordinator, as well as the corps of trained docents. In many institutions the projectionist or other audiovisual or multimedia staff may also report to the head of education. The organizational chart (figure 7.4) provides a generic example.

Whether large or small, it is important that the leader of the museum's learning services grasps his or her role as one of "training the trainers," preparing professional or volunteer educators who in turn provide the actual firsthand learning experiences to the visitors, whether as individuals or in groups. Although the leader should, from time to time, take a school tour in order to refresh his or her firsthand experience, it is important that the leader of the education or learning department should not be exhausted by directly serving the public: instead, he or she should be focusing time on planning and writing programs, and training and evaluating those who actually do provide the frontline services.

7.3   JOB DESCRIPTIONS

This section provides job descriptions for positions relevant to the museum's learning programs consistent with the approach to staffing outlined in the pre-

Figure 7.4. Programs Division Organization Chart

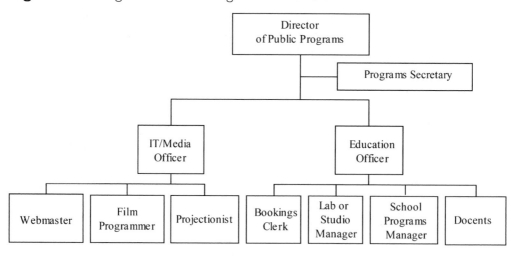

COURTESY OF LORD CULTURAL RESOURCES.

ceding sections of this chapter. Of course every museum will have staffing specific to its needs. In some institutions one brave soul may undertake most or all of these functions—although in most such cases that individual will immediately launch a volunteer program, or recruit interns to help. On the other hand, larger institutions may have many specialized educators, such as cultural animators, actors, demonstrators, and IT staff.

To begin, we assume a museum large enough to have both a director of public programs (who would also be responsible for exhibitions and related activities) and an education officer who reports to him or her:

Director of Public Programs
Reports to the chief executive officer (director), and is responsible for:

- the development and management of exhibitions and audiovisual programming, activities, materials, and events which attract and serve a wide range of audiences including schools
- liaison with the school system to increase awareness of the museum as an educational resource
- liaison with exhibit designers and fabricators, technical program suppliers, and artists
- meeting revenue and attendance targets as set out in the marketing plan
- supervision and performance of staff within the public programs division.

Qualifications: advanced degree in an area related to the museum's specialization and/or in museum studies; experience in a management position in a cultural attraction; proven management ability; knowledge of visitor behavior and needs; knowledge of the museum's collections; knowledge of evaluation methods; entrepreneurial orientation.

Education Officer
Reports to the director of public programs and is responsible for:

- managing and developing partnerships with schools to offer curriculum-based programs related to the museum's collection, in the museum and/or in schools
- setting standards for all educational programming
- ongoing liaison with schools, community groups, and other target audiences to arrange a program of field trips consisting of guided tours and/or demonstrations
- contributing to the design of exhibitions and other public programming to enhance its educational value
- achievement of school attendance and revenue targets
- preparation of publications or media-based products to schools

- preparation of promotional copy for all aspects of the educational program
- developing and implementing adult education programs related to the museum's collection
- developing training programs for volunteer docents.

Qualifications: Advanced degree in education or in an area related to the museum's specialization, or in museum studies; experience in the education and/or program area of a museum or cultural attraction; ability to design and implement educational programs including the preparation of exhibits and publications; demonstrated ability in communications and museum education techniques; knowledge of the objectives and curricula of the school system; knowledge of the museum's collections; knowledge of evaluation methods.

Certain core staff are common to most museum learning or education departments: a bookings clerk and a school programs manager are almost universal, unless the education officer is directly responsible for school programs. Some institutions have managers for school programs and a separate position for other learning programs for adults. Educators or docents, including demonstrators and actors, will report to either the education officer or the school programs officer.

Bookings Clerk
Reports to the education officer and is responsible for:

- booking school groups and public group tours
- booking paid staff or volunteer docents to meet group tours
- liaison with schools, community groups, and tour operators.

Qualifications: High school graduation; knowledge of and demonstrated ability in word processing, data entry, and scheduling software; excellent accuracy and communication skills.

School Programs Manager
Reports to the education officer and is responsible for:

- design and delivery of programs for school groups
- preparation of school kits and resource materials
- liaison with teachers and schools
- coordination of part-time museum teachers
- training and evaluation of volunteer docents
- field trip programs.

Qualifications: Degree in education or museum studies; experience in a museum education department or related institution; knowledge of objectives and curricula of the school system; knowledge in the area of the museum's collections; knowledge of evaluation methods.

Educator/Docent

Reports to the education officer or to the school programs manager and is responsible for:

- planning and provision of tours of the museum's galleries for schools and other groups, for both permanent collection and temporary exhibitions
- planning and provision of other museum educational programs
- collaboration with teachers on educational use of the museum.

Qualifications: Undergraduate degree (at least) in the museum's subject matter, or in education; experience as a teacher, docent, or in other educational work; excellent communications and requisite language skills; knowledge of the collection.

For many museums, the theater or auditorium is a focus of their learning programs. If so, a museum theatre manager, a film programmer, and a projectionist, who can double as a technical specialist for audiovisual and interactive exhibits, will be needed.

Museum Theater Manager

For museums with theaters, the manager reports to the director of public programs and is responsible for:

- coordinating all performances, activities, and special events in support of the museum's overall programming and revenue goals
- preparation of promotional copy and program notes in cooperation with other program staff
- liaison with other education staff to schedule school visit-related performances
- scheduling, box office operation, ticket sales, front of house operations
- operation of the museum theater to maintain acoustic standards and ambience.

Qualifications: Certificate in arts administration, theater, or performing arts or equivalent in experience; experience and proven ability in theater operations and management; good supervisory skills; knowledge of computerized ticketing systems; entrepreneurial orientation.

Film Programmer

For museums with extensive film programs, reports to the theatre manager or the deputy director (public programs), and is responsible for:

- developing and managing a series of film programs in support of the museum's overall programming and revenue goals
- preparation of promotional copy and program notes
- coordination of scheduling, sales of tickets, and program delivery in collaboration with the theater manager and education
- liaison with schools and other target audiences.

Qualifications: Degree in film, communications, or the equivalent in experience; experience in film programming at a museum or cultural institution; proven ability to develop audiences and meet revenue targets.

Projectionist (Lighting and Sound Technician)

Reports to the theater manager or the education officer and is responsible for:

- projection of slides, film, video, and other audiovisual programs
- technical support services for all exhibitions, performances, and productions
- maintenance and upkeep of museum theater equipment
- maintenance and repair of all audiovisual components of the museum's exhibits.

Qualifications: Certificate or other training in electronics; demonstrated ability to maintain and operate sophisticated lighting and sound systems.

Given the growing importance of online learning programs described in Hugh Spencer's chapter 9, an officer responsible for information technology (IT) and/or a Web master have become essential positions on the museum's education staff:

IT/Web master

Reports to the director of public programs or the education officer and is responsible for:

- planning, design, and production of public programs in all media, including Web cast, IT, film, video, electronic, computer, and multimedia programs
- operation and maintenance of these programs, including updating of the Web site

- research and development of applications of imaging and graphic technology to the museum's public programs, in the galleries and online
- evaluation of the museum's IT, Web, and media programs in consultation with the evaluation officer

Qualifications: Experience in IT, Web, and multimedia planning, design, and production; knowledge of the collection or of the museum's subject matter.

If the museum has a laboratory or art studio, its manager is an important position.

Lab or Studio Manager

For museums with science laboratories or visual arts studios, reports to the education officer and is responsible for:

- development, implementation, and evaluation of a program of after-school and weekend classes for all ages in a variety of arts and technical disciplines
- recruitment and coordination of science demonstrators, professional technicians, and artists to instruct in this program
- achievement of attendance and revenue goals established for the program
- liaison with schools, community groups, and other target audiences
- preparation of all support materials
- preparation of promotional copy.

Qualifications: Degree or certificate in relevant science disciplines or in visual art; teaching laboratory or visual art studio experience; experience in a museum or related institution; proven ability to design and implement educational experiences for students and families.

In some museums a very large proportion of attendance visits on the occasion of special events. For others, special events are an important revenue source as well as an opportunity for more extensive or intensive museum learning. In either case, a special events manager is needed. A sometimes related position is that of an outreach officer, often called a community relations officer: this is not a public relations position, but part of the museum learning staff, oriented to providing museum learning services off-site, sometimes through traveling exhibitions, or by placing docents or demonstrators in schools or shopping malls, or else bringing in groups from underserved populations in the community.

Special Events Manager

Reports to the director of public programs and is responsible for:

- the design and delivery of lecture series, demonstrations, film series, festivals, and other special events to complement exhibitions and other programs
- recruitment and coordination of speakers, instructors, and facilitators
- achievement of attendance and revenue targets for the unit.

Qualifications: Degree or certificate in adult education or museum studies or the equivalent in experience; experience in a museum or related institution in the area of public programming; demonstrated ability to create programming in this format and an entrepreneurial orientation.

Outreach Manager/Community Liaison Officer
  Reports to the education officer and is responsible for:

- developing and implementing outreach programming aimed at bringing underrepresented groups into the museum as visitors, and/or at extending museum services into the community
- liaison with community groups and other community services.

Qualifications: Experience and ability in the outreach or community development area of a museum or related institution; knowledge of the school system and of community organizations and services; excellent communication skills.

A key position in the education staff of a great many museums is the volunteer coordinator, who has the vital task of supervising recruitment, training, and deployment of volunteers, often working closely with the bookings clerk. This may be a paid position, or may itself be part of the volunteer corps.

Volunteer Coordinator
  Reports to the education officer and is responsible for:

- recruitment, training, and supervision of volunteers in collaboration with all program coordinators and activities which require volunteer staffing
- placement, scheduling, and booking of volunteer assistance
- maintenance of records and mailing lists
- creation of a benefit program for volunteers, such as a newsletter.

Qualifications: A degree in museum studies or an area related to the museum's specialization; demonstrated supervisory skills, preferably with volunteers in a museum setting; experience in and knowledge of the field of volunteerism; excellent communication skills; may be a volunteer, or a former volunteer.

Not all institutions can afford a full-time evaluation manager, however desirable that may be. In many instances, this may be a contract position, engaged for the review of the effectiveness of specific exhibitions or programs. Here we assume it is a full-time position.

Evaluation Manager
Reports to the director of public programs and is responsible for:

- measuring and documenting the public's perception of the relevance of the museum's products and services
- the design and implementation of the museum's evaluation plan
- design and implementation of visitor and nonvisitor surveys
- gallery and exhibition evaluation
- program and special event evaluation
- participation in the design of exhibitions, public programming, and other public products and services.

Qualifications: University degree in psychology or psychometry, or equivalent in experience; knowledge and proven ability in the design, implementation, and interpretation of visitor studies and surveys; experience in evaluation in a museum or other cultural attraction.

Finally, a related position that is sometimes separate but can be advantageously incorporated in the museum learning division of a museum is that of a communications or publications manager.

Communications or Publications Manager
Reports to the director of public programs and is responsible for:

- coordination and supervision of all printed materials produced by the museum such as annual reports, books, catalogues, guide books, film and lecture materials, newsletters, research journals, and all historical, photographic, and graphic reference works
- format and editing of all graphics and labels in the galleries and on screen
- editing all material and maintaining editorial standards of language, grammatical, and stylistic form
- ensuring all graphic design projects the museum's desired image
- achievement of revenue targets from publications
- distribution of materials in relation to print-runs.

Qualifications: Degree in journalism, public relations, communications, or marketing; proven ability and extensive experience in all aspects of publishing, editing, print production, and distribution; experience working in a museum or related organization.

7.4   BUDGETING FOR MUSEUM LEARNING

The second case study in this chapter—Cost and Revenue of Museum Learning at the Fort Worth Museum of Science and Learning by Charlie Walter—provides some useful lessons from a museum that really considers itself a learning institution first and foremost. It will be seen that as such it not only budgets for costs but also for revenues, and aims to balance these where possible. Too often the museum's learning services are seen as a cost center only, with their revenue potential not being recognized.

To this end it is useful if revenue from the learning experiences provided in an IMAX theater or a planetarium, for instance, are credited to the learning department. But even more so it is important to grasp that teacher training, for instance, can be a revenue opportunity, if the museum is recognized by formal education bodies or levels of government as a vital part of the teacher training program, either for incoming new candidate teachers or as a site for upgrading and updating the knowledge and skills of science or history teachers. The operation of a museum preschool and a weekend museum school can be put on a revenue-producing basis, with the aid of appropriate subsidies and grants to make these services affordable to at least some families in the community, as the Fort Worth example shows.

A fundamental question is whether school groups or other tour groups should be charged. Where admission to the entire museum is free, this may be moot. But where visitors are charged an admission fee, the question of whether and how much to charge school groups or other groups is a challenging one. A reduced charge per student—that is, less than that student would pay if he or she entered as an individual or as part of a family visit—is almost universal. When there is a charge, it is left to the formal education sector—sometimes to the individual school or class—to decide whether the entrance fee per student will be paid wholly or partially by each parent or caregiver, or whether the school board will pay all or most of the cost. The charge, along with the cost of the school bus to get the class to the museum, adds to the barriers that a teacher or principal must overcome to get a school tour organized—impediments which have only increased in recent years, as Dr. Brad King makes clear in chapter 5.

There is yet another reason why a museum may wish to reconsider whether it should be charging, or how much it should be charging, per student. The museum may find it far more remunerative to provide education services to schools, at least within its city or county boundaries, for free or for a more reduced rate, in exchange for public funding that the government of that constituency extends for this purpose. Thus—as is illustrated again by the Fort Worth case study—budgeting for museum learning must be seen as a process that involves government subsidy, grants for specific projects, and revenue from particular programs such as an IMAX theater, a planetarium, a teacher training program, school tours, or a museum preschool, just as much as a calculation of the cost of paid docents, hands-on materials, or interactive technology.

Online learning programs are providing a whole new frontier of museum learning, opening up possibilities for reaching far greater numbers of individuals over a vast range—indeed, worldwide—as well as serving specific groups such as teachers throughout a country, state, or province. In her chapter on evaluation, Dr. Barbara Soren discusses the ways in which these programs are affecting the planning and execution of virtual exhibitions, are now often seen as educational accompaniments to physical exhibitions in the galleries, or are increasingly offered as educational experiences in their own right. Online museum educators who conceive, plan, design, produce, and manage these programs are becoming a dynamic new component of many museum learning departments today. Here again the budgetary implications—revenue from project grants or other sources, as well as costs—are emerging as important factors in the ongoing management of a museum learning department.

Museum educators today should expect to be central to deliberations not only for planning new exhibitions, but about the fundamental issues of fulfilling the museum's mandate. The "Cinderella" status of the education department that worked hard and earned grant money, but was accorded low prestige within the institution, is or should be no more. On the contrary, the fact that museums and the governments that fund them now understand learning as essential to their mission, and the opportunities afforded by the emergence of online and other new technologies (as reviewed by Hugh Spencer in his chapter) point to an exciting future for museum educators and their public everywhere.

COST AND REVENUE OF MUSEUM LEARNING AT THE FORT WORTH MUSEUM OF SCIENCE AND HISTORY

Charlie Walter

One of my earliest memories as a new vice president was sitting around the table with my department heads and asking them, "What is the ultimate goal of this organization?" As we went around the table, all department heads commented thoughtfully on a number of things, all related directly to the museum's mission. I opened my briefcase and pulled out a finance textbook from my MBA program and read, "The ultimate goal of any organization is to survive." I shut the book and commented that 80 percent of the decisions I had observed the museum make over the past five years had been as much about survival as they had been about mission. In my mind's eye I saw light bulbs clicking on over the heads of each of my staff as the expressions on their faces reflected their thinking on this dynamic of institutional mission and survival.

At the Fort Worth Museum of Science and History, we have spent years cultivating a culture of learning. A key aspect of this learning culture is trying to be systemic in our thinking. This means that when we are talking about designing a new program, our conversations range from the foundations of education theory that influence the program's design to the financial implications, marketing opportunities, and development potential of the project. In the best learning organizations, all elements are connected and aligned, moving in the same direction. By introducing organizational survival into the process, planning on a departmental basis is more holistic in the sense that each department more fully appreciates the challenges facing the overall museum.

Foremost among these challenges are sustainability and accessibility. Any program's viability depends on its ability to generate revenue. This revenue will be some combination of program fees, private philanthropy, and/or public support. There is a balance here in that museum programs must serve the entire community. Keeping program fees as low as possible, and thus programs as accessible as possible, is important. The key is finding the right combination of revenue streams (program fees, private support, public support) that will keep programs sustainable and accessible to broad audiences over the long-term.

Before proceeding to draw some lessons from our practical experience, it is useful to glance at our organization chart, illustrated here.

Figure 7.5. Organization Chart for the Fort Worth Museum of Science and History Board of Trustees

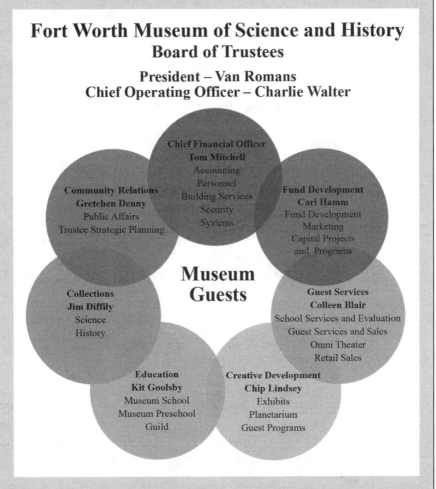

Fort Worth Museum of Science and History
Board of Trustees
President – Van Romans
Chief Operating Officer – Charlie Walter

Chief Financial Officer
Tom Mitchell
Accounting
Personnel
Building Services
Security
Systems

Community Relations
Gretchen Denny
Public Affairs
Trustee Strategic Planning

Fund Development
Carl Hamm
Fund Development
Marketing
Capital Projects
and Programs

Museum Guests

Collections
Jim Diffily
Science
History

Guest Services
Colleen Blair
School Services and Evaluation
Guest Services and Sales
Omni Theater
Retail Sales

Education
Kit Goolsby
Museum School
Museum Preschool
Guild

Creative Development
Chip Lindsey
Exhibits
Planetarium
Guest Programs

COURTESY OF THE FORT WORTH MUSEUM OF SCIENCE AND HISTORY.

- Its most important feature is that the museum's guests—our visitors— are at the heart of our organization. All of our departments, not just guest services, are focused on serving our guests, without whom we are literally out of business.
- The second feature is that each of the departmental circles overlaps, suggesting an interrelated chain of areas of competence, rather than a hierarchy of reporting relationships.
- Within that chain, education is situated between collections and creative services, which is where it belongs.

- And in turn, creative services is next to guest services, while collections links to community relations. All of these departments need to be coordinated in their policies, plans, and programs with education.
- And beyond those circles are the departments of fund development and the chief financial officer, which brings us back to the relationship between museum learning and the budget.

Now to tell you a few of the most important lessons we have learned in our practice.

SOME NUTS-AND-BOLTS THINGS WE HAVE LEARNED

Throughput is important. In the mid-1980s, the museum's board questioned the operation of our planetarium. Numbers seemed stagnant. The board challenged staff to look at ways to improve utilization of the facility. The one action that had the biggest impact was changing from a 45-minute show to a 25-minute show. This doubled the planetarium's capacity and increased revenues dramatically.

Another area of the museum that has high throughput is our museum preschool program. Children enrolled in this program meet two hours each week for thirty weeks. The museum has five classrooms dedicated to preschool, and there is a morning and an afternoon session in each room with twenty students in each session. The math here adds up to one thousand preschool-aged students coming to the museum for two hours each week for thirty weeks! Current preschool tuition is $600 per student. Because of its high throughput, museum preschool generates $600,000 in revenue for its fall/spring session.

Have a portfolio of offerings at a variety of prices. Our teacher professional development programs are approached in this manner. We have found that some teachers want to come on a Saturday for a two-hour session, and will pay (either themselves or their district) $35 to $50. Others may want a day-long fossil excursion and pay $100 for the experience, or an even longer, multiday field course for $500. Districts may want to contract a multiple-day professional development experience for their teachers for $6,000 to $15,000. Having this range of experiences gives your program many entry points, and relationships built over time lead to teachers participating in multiple programs.

Try something new each year. Intentionally looking for innovative ideas is critical to a program's viability. It's easy to get caught in a pattern where you offer similar programs in the same way year after year after year. A number of years ago we received a call from a colleague in the field asking if we would be interested in a project to explore new uses of digital technologies for learning. Our expertise in this area was very low, and we agreed to participate as a learning partner. Three years later we were able to wrap what we learned into an $890,000 grant targeting under-represented youth and technology fluency.

Another new program was started at a meeting with a school district official. We came to the meeting fully expecting this individual to ask us to conduct some teacher professional development programs for his district. Instead he surprised us by asking for help in developing a program to engage families in their children's learning. Two sessions were prototyped in that first year, and family science nights were launched the following year. In our most recent fiscal year, fifty family science nights were held with schools paying a fee of $600 to help defray costs. The museum has also generated $50,000–$100,000 through grants and contributions annually to support this effort

Talk to your customers. Our museum school, school services, and special programs areas of the museum continually survey and dialogue with program participants and adjust programs based on this feedback. For years

Figure 7.6. Texas Center for Inquiry, Building Capacity for Classroom Inquiry. Teachers Involved in Stream Table Inquiry Experience

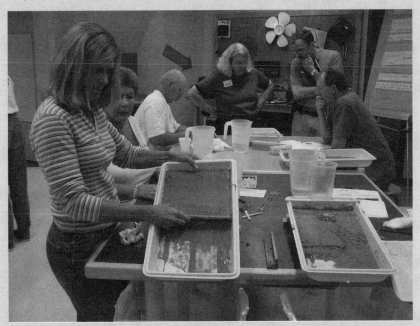

COURTESY OF THE FORT WORTH MUSEUM OF SCIENCE AND HISTORY.

Figure 7.7. Texas Center for Inquiry, Building Capacity for Classroom Inquiry. Teachers Involved in Stream Table Inquiry Experience

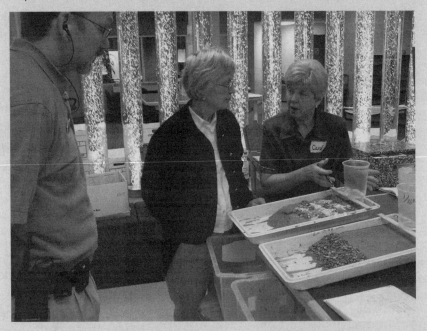

COURTESY OF THE FORT WORTH MUSEUM OF SCIENCE AND HISTORY.

our museum school operated its programs based on a model where parents came each week for six to eight weeks. Feedback from parents indicated that their lifestyles no longer allowed them to commit to this length of time, so now most programs are daylong Saturday programs in the fall and spring, or weeklong programs in the summer, allowing parents more flexibility in their scheduling.

Fast, Cheap, High Quality—Pick Any Two. This mantra of engineering and exhibition design is equally true of museum learning programs. The most important thing you can do in designing informal learning programs is to ensure the highest level of quality possible. It has been our experience that children, parents, and teachers flock to our programs for two important reasons:

1. Because we give them access to our rich collections and exhibits.
2. We very purposefully design our learning experiences around age appropriateness and a strong commitment to creating comfortable, exciting learning environments where each learner has quality one-on-one time with program faculty. *Every hour of new program delivery takes two hours of preparation and one hour of evaluation.* We incorporate these hours into

our program budgeting models and target revenue accordingly. These steps help us to ensure a high quality experience for our guests.

As stated above, finding the balance between sustainability and accessibility is critical when developing these programs. Our most accessible programs are 100 percent funded through grants. Others generate enough in program fees to cover all of their direct costs and contribute a large share toward their indirect or overhead costs. Development efforts have led to scholarship money that helps to make programs more accessible. In planning your programs, thinking through issues of quality, throughput, variety, customer feedback, and innovation will help you build sustainable programs that are accessible to the entire community.

Finally, here is a sample of some of our museum learning programs, their approximate number of participants, the revenue they generated in the year reported on (in U.S. dollars), and a brief comment on each.

Table 7.1 A Sample of Fort Worth Museum of Science and History Learning Programs

Program Examples	# Participants	Revenue Generated (U.S.$)	Description/ Comments
Museum Preschool	1,020 (Fall/Spring) 454 (Summer)	$525/child - $582,000/Year $11.50/hour	Cost includes a Family Membership to the Museum ($75 value). Program meets once a week for 34 weeks. Ages 3, 4, 5.
Museum School	400 (Fall/Spring) 608 (Summer)	$8.00–$8.50/hour - $92,200/Year	6–8 Saturday Sessions usually 9am–2pm. Weeklong Sessions
Camp-In	2,300	$35.00/person - $69,690/Year	Predominantly Girl Scouts
Summer Science Institute	20 K–12 Teachers	$6,000	Contract with local school districts. 5 days. 2 staff.

(Continued)

Table 7.1 A Sample of Fort Worth Museum of Science and History Learning Programs (Continued)

Program Examples	# Participants	Revenue Generated (U.S.$)	Description/ Comments
Inquiry Institute	26 K–12 Teachers	$15,000	Two preparation days budgeted for each program delivery day. 5 days. 5 staff.
Hands-On Science Partnership	3–5 Partnerships	$5,000	A 'bundle' of services: teacher professional development, class visits, one family night.
Family Science Nights	10,256 (26 schools)	$13,000 ($600/school)	$43,600 raised through development efforts
Traveling Exhibitions		$285,000/Year	Market-priced

CHAPTER 8

Space and Facilities for Museum Learning

HEATHER MAXIMEA

This chapter looks at the special spaces or facilities that museums need to present learning programs effectively. Increasingly, museums in every country are developing an understanding of lifelong learning, and extending the notion of education in museums to a wider audience, of all age groups and levels of literacy and formal educational understanding. Inviting this wider audience into the museum, and giving them the food for thought that they crave, is seen to be the only real way to build a new museum-going public that supports museum ideals. In turn, this means that the demand for special spaces in museums, with dedicated orientation to learning programs and needs, is also on the increase.

Galleries, lobbies, theaters, outdoor trails, and sculpture gardens all provide a setting for communication and for formal and informal learning as well as aesthetic and contemplative experiences. In addition to the spaces that house and interpret museum collections, museums increasingly invest in specialized spaces for education, ranging from seminar rooms, classrooms, and research laboratories to "discovery rooms," libraries and resource centers, theaters, and suites of auxiliary space including lunchrooms, cloakrooms, and preparation and storage facilities. Innovations such as railway museum cars and museumobiles also have their place in the development of interpretive and educational facilities. A primary distinction in museum spaces devoted to learning can be made between in-gallery facilities, education facilities that are external to the galleries, and auxiliary and support facilities. This chapter focuses primarily on facilities found outside the exhibition galleries of the museum.

Another differentiation to consider is whether projected programs for the education space include either self-directed experiences, or organized activities directed by museum docents, teachers, or animators, or a combination of both. This chapter considers each of these options.

8.1 EVOLUTION OF MUSEUM LEARNING FACILITIES

Education facilities in museums have evolved along with museum learning programs themselves, which in turn have evolved in response to changes in our perceptions of museums, and our demands on them as increasingly essential elements of human culture. The social role of museums as repositories and interpreters of our world and its wonders has come to include a role as informal educators. With that change has come the need for resources—staff, supplies and equipment, marketing, and facilities—to facilitate that role.

At first, the museum galleries themselves served as the primary educational spaces as they continue to do today. Almost from the beginning, informal guiding of groups and individuals through the galleries was offered. By the early years of the twentieth century, museums were hiring guides and museum teachers to interpret exhibits. Allowing space in gallery circulation for guided groups to gather or to flow through was one of the first impacts of museum learning programs on museum facilities design.

As learning activities in the museum expanded beyond the guided tour, galleries also accommodated activities such as drawing and painting classes and the lectures and demonstrations required by interest clubs and organizations. Having a group of students crowding a gallery for a lecture or demonstration was quickly seen to be an irritant to other visitors, an interruption to normal visitor flow, and not always ideal from the teaching point of view, since the opportunity for extended sessions or for wet or messy activities in the gallery was limited. A teacher or docent could bring a few additional specimens or examples into the gallery and hand them around, or remove items from cases for closer examination, but view lines and supervision could be difficult. Many museums left open space between the cases to serve as informal gathering spaces, or used open space for seated lectures or films, but as exhibition formats changed, much of this type of space disappeared.

The traditional docent-led lecture/tour continued, and is still going strong, but museums also developed the idea of bringing the student into the laboratory or into a classroom or lecture hall, where more students could have a lecture, demonstration, or even a hands-on activity that complemented, but did not replace, the gallery experience. Some such activities could be accommodated in back-of-house space such as workrooms and laboratories, but access and available space were generally severely limited. The need for specialized meeting, lecture, and demonstration spaces analogous to those in formal educational institutions became apparent.

These earliest dedicated spaces for museum learning were very similar to a university classroom or laboratory of the time, with abundant natural light or strong overhead lamps, shelves of specimens and equipment, counters and lab stools, or demonstration tables being the order of the day. Sometimes the space was organized as an amphitheater, similar to that found in science and medical schools of the day.

Initially the orientation was toward adult ideas of the educational process, using adult-sized facilities and adult-oriented techniques. This was slow to change, as museum staffs and hierarchies were dominated by men trained in universities, with little or no contact with the evolving primary school system and little concept of the learning needs of nonacademics or children. Slowly, however, museums began to assign staff to teaching, and, eventually, to hire trained teachers. These teachers, many of whom were women, began the movement to develop special learning spaces that reflected the needs of different museum audiences.

The Royal Ontario Museum in Toronto, Canada, serves as an example of how new is the concept of special staff and spaces for museum learning. The museum opened its doors in 1914. A true museum of its time, closely connected in its development to emerging educational systems in the Canadian Province of Ontario, it comprised expansive galleries for natural sciences, art, and archaeology, and had a basement workroom/laboratory, but no dedicated classroom. University students, naturalist groups, and school groups alike were accommodated in the galleries and the sole workroom. In 1918, an audacious woman—Miss Margaret MacLean—applied to the directors to be hired as the first guide, only to be met by tight-lipped resistance. She started her own unofficial guiding business—and was so successful in driving up a flagging attendance that in 1919 she was put on salary as an official museum employee.[1] In addition to tours and lectures to schools and other groups, Miss MacLean initiated Saturday afternoon adult lectures, and a Saturday study hour for children. However, it was not until 1928 that the museum hired a full-time teacher to conduct classes for school children in the museum. Throughout the 1950s, educational activities were conducted in the galleries, the laboratories, and the theater—only in the 1970s and 1980s were the first education classrooms and discovery rooms created at the ROM.

At the turn of the twentieth century, new ideas about how people learn were percolating through educational systems, promoted by advanced thinkers among teachers, education system planners, and others concerned with the issues of quality education as well as education for all. A seminal thinker about how people (and children in particular) learn was Dr. Maria Montessori. Her direct experience and observation led to the establishment in Italy, the Netherlands, England, the United States, and as far a field as India, of carefully designed classrooms and teaching materials. Still today, the Montessori School movement provides examples and sources for the design of progressive educational facilities. Dr. Montessori advocated expansive rooms filled with natural light, with views to the outdoors; furniture carefully scaled to each age group, with shelving accessible to the students themselves; and special stations designed for particular activities, whether growing live plants or demonstrating an art technique. Her ideas have had perhaps the most profound effect on museum learning facilities. At the same time, the best of museum learning facilities have gone far beyond the classroom model to create learning environments that are open, flexible, and stimulating to the creativity of children and adults.

In designing special educational facilities inside museums, educators have often been torn between the tried and true design of traditional classrooms and learning formats, and the grand opportunity to bring learning into a different physical context that values freedom over structure. One important development has been the evolution of various types of learning spaces for different kinds of museums.

8.2   SPACES FOR LEARNING IN DIFFERENT TYPES OF MUSEUMS

Museums of every type house educational programs and facilities. The following list of museum types brings into the mind's eye the gamut of architectural structures of every style, size, and material that comprise the world's museums:

- Aboriginal Museums
- Art Museums
- Children's Museums
- Eco-Museums
- Historical and Anthropological Museums
- Idea Museums
- Natural History Museums
- Outdoor Museums
- Science Centers
- Specialized Museums

Within these diverse museums, spaces for learning can reflect the diverse contents stemming from discipline or idea specialization. This is clear when we observe the art studio in the art museum, the laboratory in the science museum, the discovery center in the idea museum, or the nature trails of an outdoor museum. These spaces are reflective of subject disciplines and the specialized spaces they have evolved for their practice, and represent a transfer of discipline ideas into the museum. The challenge is always to modify the traditional discipline-oriented space (such as a natural science laboratory) to serve the needs of different groups of users, which may vary from primary school children and families with members of varying ages to adults with a particular interest.

A full-fledged natural science lab might be appropriate for high school or university students in a school setting, but in the museum setting and the short time frame of the museum visit, may not offer the right opportunities for learning about the natural world. Making an investment in laboratory technology capable of handling a full school class may also be prohibitively expensive. The museum educator, in conjunction with discipline specialists, must make choices as to what activities and experiences will be achievable and informative for target audiences, and use these choices to inform the development of types of museum space.

8.3 FACILITIES FOR DIFFERENT AGE GROUPS

One of the key challenges for museum learning programs is to provide an abundance of learning opportunities and possibilities for all its visitors, no matter their ages, state of health, or level of formal education. Getting a fix on who your audience is—the specific age groups and educational levels whom you target as your visitors—can help narrow the broad band of possibilities and allow the museum to make best use of its resources.

We understand today that people of different ages have different learning capabilities and learn in different ways; each age group needs to be presented with an optimal learning environment. Some of the insights of developmental psychology and other disciplines can be of help in discerning how these may play out in the museum environment.

Age groups may be characterized as:

- Infant/Toddler (accompanied by parent) Age Birth to 3
- Children Age 4–7
- Children Age 8–12
- Adolescents Age 13–18
- Adults
- Seniors
- Families—Multigenerational Groups

Infant/Toddler—Age Birth to 3

Infants and toddlers up to the age of 3 move from the sensorimotor stage of rapid physical development, movement and coordination skills, and perceptions, in which they perceive themselves as the center of the universe, to the preoperational stage, in which they are beginning to interact more cooperatively with others and to gain more advanced skills such as fitting together large puzzle pieces or riding a tricycle. Children at this stage need a stable and familiar physical environment from which to explore the world. They enjoy repetition in activities such as hand clapping games, familiar puzzles and stories, or simple coloring, and they may need help from adults.

A learning environment for very small children need not be very large but should be a contained area where they feel safe, can see their parents nearby, or be accompanied by parents. A low fence or barrier within a larger space can contain several play stations, a reading area with beanbag chairs or mattresses, and so on. Barriers and furnishings need to be free of sharp corners, with easily cleaned surfaces and nontoxic finishes, bearing in mind that the children may put almost anything in their mouths. Baby-changing facilities nearby are essential.

Children Age 4–7

The child aged 4 to 7 is still in the preoperational stage of development, but progressing with learning about him- or herself and about the world. His or her ability to conceptualize is growing and the child enjoys make-believe play and can understand rules and sharing. These children are at the questioning stage but like concrete answers. They are physically very active and need to burn energy, and will move away from their parent or teacher to explore new experiences.

The learning environment needs to include lots of opportunity to do things—more complex puzzles, discovery boxes with magnifying glasses and other simple tools, working with clay or plasticine, or turning a big crank to make a music box work are all popular. A large space with work and play stations can also house active play areas such as a tunnel or slide. An art studio or activity room can allow for projects with paint, paper, or clay, or a science area can allow for learning about animals, rocks, and the like through pictures as well as mounts and hands-on specimens. The dinosaur dig or archaeology dig is especially popular with this age group. Needless to say, the activity areas can get messy, and easy cleanup is essential. Tough surfaces that can withstand climbing, appropriately low tables and chairs, accessible hand wash sinks, and pinup boards and shelves for displaying projects are needed.

Children Age 7–12

From ages 7 to 12, children in the concrete operations stage are developing increasingly good motor skills, and verbal and mental skills to match. They are active and energetic and can operate on their own for long periods. They enjoy doing things with friends and in organized groups (such as Cub Scouts and Brownies), and being on sports teams. They like facts and information and are starting to ask why, how, and when.

Learning spaces for children at this stage need to take account of their need to *find out* as well as to *do*. Using the museum galleries as the arena of exploration, and carrying their findings back to the studio or activity lab, enables these children to put new knowledge to use. Films and videos become important for conveying additional layers of information. In the art studio, more intensive technologies such as papier-mâché or block printing may be required. In the lab or field station, children will want to examine specimens up close, measure and weigh, take notes, and make collections. The spaces used for these activities can be almost adult in scale and design, with some adjustments in table and counter height for younger children. Storage for equipment and supplies and ability to work on projects over a longer period of time is more important, as this age group loves activities such as a Saturday morning club.

Adolescents Age 13–18

From age 11 or 12 through adolescence, the child enters the formal operational stage of development and the cognitive structures increasingly resemble those of an adult. At the same time, the physical and emotional changes of puberty through adolescence can be challenging for many young people. "Putting it all together" for themselves is the concern of these years; both acknowledging and challenging authority, reliance on peers and peer judgments, and developing individual identity often seem at cross purposes. Youngsters need to be able to gain more sophisticated understandings in disciplines that they choose for themselves—and to choose for themselves whether to be alone or part of a group at any one time. The museum can offer an environment that has elements of containment as well as freedom, and also offers key opportunities for socializing and learning with peers.

The galleries of the museum are the outward and most obvious resource for learning at this age but, in fact, children and adolescents avidly seek more in-depth experiences and engagement in the disciplines they are attracted to, whether that be technology, sports, the arts, or archaeology. Although the museum library or media center, or the film theater, may feed some of this hunger, more behind-the-scenes engagement will be very attractive. Teen groups, special classes and workshops, and the opportunity to volunteer or intern working alongside museum professionals, are key. The ability to bring teens into the world of the creative studio or laboratory, and to give them their own "club" space in which to explore the chosen discipline, will be the enabling factor for the museum to attract and hold a teen audience.

Museums experimenting with spaces to attract teens and young adults realize that the element of "cool" (or in alternate parlance "hot") may distinguish the acceptable from the unacceptable space. The studio, media lab, seminar room, or amphitheater may be adult in format—but good design and capability to support hot new technology can bring it into the realm of cool. The ability of the space to allow teens to feel at least temporary "ownership" for the purposes of their meeting or project is equally key to acceptance: if space permits, a teen lounge, coffee room, or other hangout for young volunteers and visitors is highly recommended.

Adults

As adults, we continue to develop our cognitive skills, and our abilities to think logically, to conceptualize the abstract, and to hypothesize and come to conclusions. We are concerned with past, present, and future, and engaged in the wider social and political realm. D. A. Kolb[2] postulated an adult learning cycle (developing through childhood and adolescence), which moves from "concrete experience" through "reflective conservation" to "abstract conceptualization" and "active experimentation," returning to "concrete experience" again. To the extent that the museum allows for this cycle, and for variations in learning styles, it may increase the satisfaction of its adult audience.

Lifelong learning for adults is self-driven and self-selected. Adults may choose to supplement their visit to the museum galleries as a source of learning by visiting the museum library or resource center; signing up for lectures, films, and classes; or becoming volunteers, which in itself demands a training commitment. The opportunity to meet and socialize with like-minded individuals through lectures and classes may be an additional motivation.

The adult spaces for learning in the museum, beyond the galleries, may thus include a theater, library, art or craft studio, activity room or laboratory, or a seminar room or lecture hall. The standards for these spaces for adults are well understood by planners and architects, and the aim should be to design them to reflect the vision and needs of the specific institution in its environment.

Seniors

Many of the developed countries now report a growing population of older people—seniors—or in the terms of indigenous peoples, the elders. As retirees from active working life, seniors have more time to get reinvolved in community institutions and to re-engage in learning activities. As supporters and mentors of museums, as well as visitors, seniors should have an honored place. In some indigenous communities, the elders become the board members, the keepers of culture, and the teachers of culture and natural science within the museum setting.

The major change for most seniors in their use of the museum's many spaces is in difficulties with access caused by decreased mobility, sight, and hearing. Thus designing for accessibility is a key issue in enabling senior users of the facility. In addition to improved accessibility to all normally accessible museum space, seniors will be grateful for attention to visitor amenities and services such as tea rooms, lobby seating areas, and shaded outdoor seating.

As for designing spaces for the elders of indigenous peoples, there is an outstanding example in the sweetgrass ceremony space at the Cultural Heritage Center of the Smithsonian Institution's National Museum of the American Indian in Suitland, Maryland, just outside of Washington, D.C. Another fine instance is the room for viewing sacred objects for Aboriginal elders at the South Australian Museum in Adelaide.

Families—Multigenerational Groups

One of the best ways for people of all ages to learn is through social interaction, especially learning via interaction with family members. Though formal museum learning environments such as classrooms may be targeted to specific age groups, ideally there will be times—holidays, evenings, and weekends—when such facilities may be used for family programs. In designing each type of learning environment in the museum it is advisable to envision the presence of parents and/or grandparents along with teens and children, and to plan for their ability to share the museum experience. Small children and their caregivers need to be able to maintain fairly close contact at all times—the adult should be as active a participant as possible in the play or storybook areas. As children grow and their sense of independence increases, the parent still should be able to keep an eye on active children, and to step into the picture when needed.

When designing play stations or computer terminal stations for multigenerational use, consideration must be given to the different size, height, and weight requirements of children, adults, and seniors.

8.4   FACILITIES FOR SCHOOLS

As soon as groups of school children became a major visitation component, the first designated spaces for learning in museums—classrooms—were instituted. Today this connection between formal and informal learning has become a collaboration, between departments of education, teachers, and museums in many countries, in efforts to improve the quality of the total educational experience. As Dr. Brad King emphasizes in chapter 5, the museum experience is widely recognized to be "something different"—something not attainable in most classrooms—and therefore, the aim is not to replicate the classroom experience, but to go beyond it.

When students at any level from preschool through college age come to the museum, their primary learning experience should be in the galleries or exhibition halls. To support the gallery experience, museums have developed a range of spaces which are discussed in more detail below, and which allow the student a chance to participate in activities that may not be feasible in the normal classroom. These experiences may reflect actual behind-the-scenes activities of the museum and its artistic or scholarly disciplines, and give the young visitors a chance to be budding scientists, excavators, artists, and carriers of culture, in microcosm. The spaces they require reflect the qualities and capabilities of scientific labs, art studios, and field stations, to name a few of the options. Perhaps the best term to give these special spaces would be *exploration spaces*.

Where a school is actually attached to a museum (as described in one of the case studies in chapter 5), the school has actual classrooms, used daily as in a normal school; however, the students also have the opportunity, for part of their school day, to move into the exploration spaces of the museum for different and enhanced kinds of learning. In other arrangements, students from specific schools may come to the museum for an intensive study period of one or more weeks, with special projects guided by museum staff as one of the benefits.

8.5   FACILITIES FOR SELF-DIRECTED, OR ORGANIZED, PROGRAMS

Museum educational programs generally can be described as either self-directed, or organized, and either on-site or extension programs.

Self-Guided Programs—Examples
In-House:
- In-gallery programs—self-guided tours
- Audioguides and podcasting
- Self-guided discovery room
- Self-activated audiovisuals
- Self-activated interactives

Figure 8.1. Types of Learning Programs

	In-house	Extension
Self-directed	Self-directed In-house	Self-directed Extension
Guided	Guided In-house	Guided Extension

COURTESY OF THE AUTHOR..

Extension:
- Take-home discovery kits
- Web access from home or school
- Organized programs

In-House:
- In-gallery programs—guided tours and activities
- Lecture/film/performance/demonstration programs
- Studio and lab programs
- Back-of-house tours
- School programs—sequenced museum experiences using different spaces
- Special events—festivals

Extension:
- Distance learning
- Outreach programs
- Discovery cases and kits

In general, all the in-house programs require both front-of-house (public) space and back-of-house (support) space to come to life; the extension programs require only back-of-house (support) space in the museum, because they are activated in the home, the classroom, senior center, or community library as an extension venue.

8.6 LOCATION OF EDUCATION SPACE IN RELATION TO GALLERY SPACE

Another issue that often comes to the forefront when beginning to plan for museum learning spaces is whether these should be all grouped together, separate from the galleries, in an education center or classroom wing, or whether they should be integrated closely into the interpretive or gallery space.

This may be a matter of institutional mission or vision, or of organizational preference. The vision or mission may be to relate all educational activities very closely to what is going on in adjacent galleries—as the galleries change, the content and activities in the museum learning space change with them. This type of arrangement is closely allied to concepts of in-gallery learning, because it takes an activity that may not be possible in the gallery, or may compete with the gallery program, and gives it high-priority space as close to the gallery as possible. An example of how this works is in an art museum, which has a small activity space or hands-on room on each floor, sometimes directly open to the gallery space. When a textile exhibition is on, the activity space may be set up with a simple loom for weaving or yarn stitching activities and demonstrations; when the exhibition changes to photography, the activity space changes to different exploration activities.

Flexibility of room layout and facilities is therefore often key to the success of a hands-on room. The more frequently the gallery contents change, the more flexible the space may need to be. The range of activities we have seen in such a room include:

- A temporary Tibetan sand mandala
- Block printing or printing from natural specimens
- Archaeology or dinosaur "dig"
- Flint knapping pit
- Wood turning and finishing techniques
- Terraria or insectaria for observation and guided touching
- Visible storage arrays of artifacts and specimens with viewing and activity guides

At the same time, it may not be possible to include messy or "wet" activities so close to the gallery spaces, or space may not be available to accommodate workstations for a full school class or interest group. The sheer volume of users of the education program may be seen as overwhelming the capacity of the galleries.

Some institutions desire a separation between the gallery spaces, which they view as reserved specifically for display and interpretive activities, and education spaces, which may be viewed as noisy, messy, and generally disruptive to the gallery experience.

Many museums thus move to concentrate learning spaces in their own dedicated section of the building, which tends to be at a distance from the gallery spaces. As a rule, only part of the museum visit for schools and other groups is experienced in the galleries, with the remainder being routed to classrooms, studios, laboratories, libraries and theaters for different types of learning experiences.

8.7   DEDICATED MUSEUM LEARNING FACILITIES

Museum learning facilities outside the interpretive galleries comprise three essentially different types of space. These are:

- Dedicated learning spaces
- Auxiliary or visitor service spaces
- Support spaces

Dedicated Learning Spaces

Dedicated learning spaces within museums may include a wide range of space types, some of which come from discipline traditions, and some of which may reflect traditional learning or classroom environments. Some of these dedicated spaces are:

Meeting and Seminar Space: Virtually every museum requires space for staff and committee meetings, and for meetings of related users such as teachers, hobbyists, and other interest groups, and even for community users if there are no other community facilities available. By providing meeting rooms, the museum may offer a valuable community service and attract the support of other community groups. The seminar room may also lend support to the activities of a self-guiding teen group, which needs a "cool" but somewhat adult, independent space in which to formulate projects they may then take out into the galleries or activity rooms, or into the community at large.

The meeting or seminar room generally is designed for adult sit-down meetings or small seminar-type classes (high school or university age classes) ranging from ten to fifteen persons, up to thirty to fifty persons. Setup can be flexibly arranged to suit the group, with rows of chairs, or chairs set around meeting or demonstration tables. Blackboards or whiteboards, flip chart stands, an AV cart and projection screen, and for the larger rooms, a podium, make these rooms functional. Online network connections are also needed. Any or all of these may be either built-in or portable.

Classrooms: By this term we mean a traditional classroom similar to that found in a school or university setting. In contrast to meeting or seminar rooms, the classroom is static in design, with desks and chairs, teacher's desk, and blackboard, all in fixed positions. Before devoting precious museum space to a traditional classroom, the educator must ask, what is the value of replicating a classroom and, by inference, a traditional classroom learning style, inside the museum? While the traditional classroom may be familiar and comfortable to both students and educators, it may also be stultifying and restrictive, unresponsive to the themes and messages the museum wishes to convey. A museum school may be an institution that really needs classrooms, although even in those settings a more flexible setup may be preferred.

Art Studios: Art studios, by their very name, replicate the spaces in which artists work, and enable museum goers to experience art production for themselves within the walls of the museum. Some art museums run very active studio classes in a variety of media, and require both wet (with sinks and drains for dyes, paints, and clay) studios and dry studios (for drawing, weaving, spinning, and similar "clean" activities. Studios can be specialized for printmaking, glass or ceramics or textile work, or kept as flexible as possible to accommodate as many art techniques as possible. A large open space can allow for media to be spread on the floor and for each student to have ample creative space; however, many museums are restricted in space and lean toward table-based activities such as cut paper, clay modeling, watercolor painting, or calligraphy. Some walls should have pinnable surfaces to facilitate ongoing change of displays of the work produced.

Activity Rooms: An activity room or project room is a similar type of space to the studio, with sturdy surfaces, open floor space that can be set up with work tables, sinks for messy projects, and pinnable walls for displaying works in progress, but it may be found in science or history as well as art museums. In a history museum it may be a large open space for role-playing or historic reenactment, such as the Western Reserve Historical Society's spaces in Cleveland, Ohio, for reenacting encampments of the Civil War, yet be flexible enough to switch over to a project of making news clipping scrapbooks of Cleveland's labor and civil rights history. In a natural history museum, the activity range can be very wide, depending on the disciplines involved, including geology, paleontology, archaeology, and all branches of biology.

The activity or project room can also respond to the needs of a variety of age groups at different times, or can be specialized for a particular age group and school curriculum. It can be viewed as the all-purpose museum alternative to the standard classroom, in that it offers a high degree of creative flexibility, while ideally accommodating an entire school class plus teachers and other adult mentors.

Multipurpose Rooms: Some museums develop a multipurpose room as an alternative to the activity room. The idea is that one room can serve the needs of different groups of users with different activities at different times of day. Noneducation events, such as committee meetings, luncheons, and afternoon or evening films, fundraising events, seasonal fairs and craft sales, lectures, concerts, even community art shows, may be envisaged as uses of the multipurpose room. The danger for education programming is that these uses may be conflicting in time and space, and mutually incompatible in function. For example, the education program may lose use of the space for several weeks due to a seasonal event, or may have to clear away all project materials on a daily basis to leave the room clear for noneducation users. *While multipurpose rooms can be valuable where space is truly at a premium, the real needs of each program that will be using the space need to be evaluated to determine whether this is the best option.*

Labs and Discovery Centers: Labs and discovery centers in museums differ from activity or project rooms; they are generally designed for specific purposes and with more or less fixed equipment and fittings. These spaces generally have a number of stations, either of similar type such as computer workstations or microscope viewing stations, or several different stations each highlighting a different idea, activity or technique. An example might be a preschool discovery center with six to eight different work areas or play tables, each of which provides a different creative learning activity, and each of which can be activated by one to three small children at one time. Another might be a series of wood crafting stations where slightly older children can combine different shaped pieces and practice techniques such as pounding, drilling, and sanding. Labs and discovery centers can include "bug rooms" and other live plant and animal living and learning environments, so they can also have specialized support space needs.

> Some discovery rooms are set up with easy-to-carry "discovery boxes," which may be checked out and taken to low tables and workbenches for individual exploration. Nearly all labs and discovery rooms require attendant staff to assist users, help with tasks, and put away kits and equipment not being used.

Libraries: Many museums have libraries, either used strictly as research facilities for staff, or, in larger well-established museums, open to the public to at least some degree. The cost of operating a library is high, especially a specialized library which must keep up with scholarly publications and finely illustrated art or natural science books. Public access is often scaled back as the museum tries to reduce the costs of acquisition, staff, and space for a growing collection. At the same time, however, the museum is increasingly valued as a source of knowledge and judged on its ability to make information resources available to its public.

Resource Centers: Museums are beginning to explore new ways of making huge volumes of information available to visitors through new technologies. Access to information may not depend on a museum visit if the user can reach into a museum database or publications Web site from home or office. The new definition of a museum library may be an "information resource center" which has quite different facility needs from the traditional library.

As an educational facility, the museum resource center or knowledge center of the future will likely be less about stacks of books and journals or even about reading rooms and helpful librarians. The facilities slowly becoming a reality for museums are more about online computers (some with specialized or large-scale media screens or earphones) throughout the museum, small and intimate reading and viewing areas, media labs and back-of-house Web support, and production suites. The Orange County Museum of Art's Orange Lounge is an ultracool media lounge with a small media art gallery, currently located in a high-traffic shopping mall—this exemplifies the experimental nature of the museum's handling of media connections to its audience.

Loan Collections: A central concern of educational programs in many museums is to make collections—art, artifacts, and specimens—more accessible to visitors. Beyond access through gallery display and interpretation, opportunities for hands-on contact with real objects from the collections are highly valued by visitors. A few museums actually make selected specimens or kits available for visitors (usually members) or teachers to borrow and take home or to school. In facilities terms, a small loans area like a boutique where loan material can be selected by the visitor and processed by staff is required. Objects or kits have their own custom traveling cases, which may form the at-home or in-classroom display case or stand, and in some instances simple examination equipment can also be borrowed.

Community Galleries: An adjunct to the art studio and activity space of many art museums today is a gallery space that is more integrated with learning activities—the community gallery. This space is provided to showcase work being done in the museum's art programs, but also work being done at many levels in the community at large, which might never meet the curatorial criteria of the main exhibition galleries. In nonart museums, a community gallery may also afford a place where members of the community become the curator of short-term exhibitions developed by interest groups, individuals, families, collectors, or organizations, around themes that they propose through a community process. One such exhibition involved community representations of a traditional city neighborhood with its colorful street life—a way of strengthening community bonds.

In facilities terms, the physical requirements for a community gallery may be less stringent than those for other galleries. For example, security and environmental controls may be more relaxed, the scale of the space and materials more casual, and the gallery itself may be located either with a cluster of learning spaces or near the lobby with meeting and other public access spaces for maximum visibility to the Community.

Performing Arts Space: Performing arts—dance, music, role-playing, puppetry—may be seen as an integral part of what a museum is about, another way of expressing and understanding culture and society that cannot be disassociated from textual or other visual means of expression. Spaces in which the performing arts can be integrated into educational programs range from the galleries themselves, to multipurpose and activity rooms, to formal theaters and auditoria, to outdoor amphitheaters and dance circles.

These are mainly specialized spaces; however, part of the reason for maintaining flexibility in educational spaces is to allow for the possibility of bringing in the performing arts. Open floor space rather than inflexible seating arrangements, small movable stages or folding puppet theaters, or screens that can hide costume change areas and from which actors or dancers can emerge, all open the doors to creative expression through facilities design. More specifically, museums with a strong connection to music and music making, such as the Experience Music Project in Seattle, Washington, offer full-scale music labs as part of the interpretive and educational experience.

Audiovisual and Media Rooms: Spaces where individuals or groups of visitors may view film and video may be considered part of the interpretive space, but may equally be part of the museum's education programming space. A school group's experience of an exhibit may be enhanced by a video that ties into their specific curriculum requirements. People at all levels of society and in all age groups also experiment with making media products themselves, and these can be an adjunct to their learning and experiencing in the museum, a way of communicating their experience to others. As with knowledge centers, centers set up for production and sharing of new media products are beginning to appear in innovating museums in many countries. Vienna's children museum, ZOOM, provides one example, and is discussed in chapter 4.

Auxiliary or Visitor Service Spaces

Every museum needs space in which to receive its visitors, to make them comfortable and welcomed, to orient them to basic services such as washrooms and cafes, and to help them transition into the museum environment. Planning the learning program, which involves managing groups of children of different ages, as well as families, adult tours, and general visitors, also requires a clear understanding of the sequence of a museum visit, and the facilities a visitor requires at each stage of their museum experience. Although these are not instructional spaces per se, they are key to an effective education program. These spaces may include outdoor areas that lead from the parking lot or entry court to the main entrances, and indoor entry foyers, which serve as the hub to all visitor services.

Some of the spaces museums have evolved for serving visitors and users interested in learning include:

Approach and Arrival: The museum experience actually starts long before visitors arrive at the museum, as they plan for their visit. Part of their planning will be how to get there, and what they can expect to see and do on arrival. Will they be able to find the right freeway turnoff? Will the museum be recognizable (perhaps from a picture on the museum Web site) and will there be a parking problem? Is parking paid or free? If arriving by public transport, how far will visitors have to walk to reach the museum doors? These are some of the questions that good previsit orientation can help with—a form of education allied with visitor services. Providing this information in advance empowers visitors to effectively plan for their day at the museum and increases their enjoyment.

Visitors to the museum may arrive on foot, by car, via public transportation, or by school or tour bus. In every case, the distance people have to walk from their arrival point to the main doors to the museum is a key factor determining whether they begin their museum visit already tired and hot, or comfortable, eager, and relaxed. Shelter from the weather along the route to the museum, and good directional signage, are also key. If visitors have to wait for the doors to open or for family members to arrive, shelter at the main doors is also appreciated.

Bus Drop-off and Parking: Both school groups and special interest groups often arrive by bus, and an estimate of the daily number of buses that may need to be accommodated on the museum site (or parked at some other location) is needed in early stages of planning the building, and planning for the learning programs and facilities. In many cities, there is no room for buses to stay parked at the museum, so they drop off their passengers and leave to park elsewhere. The museum requires a safe drop-off zone for buses, ideally where passengers alighting will not need to cross a traffic zone before entering the building, and where traffic is heavy, separate drop-off and pick-up zones may be required. Rain and sun shelters at the drop-off and pick-up zones are needed for waiting passengers.

Group Entrance and Lobby: As the museum's learning program grows in scope and number of daily users, the question will be raised as to whether a separate entrance for education users would be beneficial. If school groups mainly come to the museum in the morning, and leave by early afternoon, their use of lobby and other spaces may not conflict with use by general museum visitors. However, having a space where groups can be gathered, where the teacher can do a head count and lunches and coats can be put away, and where museum teachers or docents can orient the students to their visit, is very useful. A short talk or video presentation is often used to give students who may never have visited a museum some tips on rules and behavior, location of amenities such as vending machines, and the length and structure of their visit. Each school class may be in the group lobby for only fifteen to twenty minutes before leaving to go to a classroom, gallery, or theater for the first experience of their stay; thus if arrival times are pre-arranged, a number of school groups can use the space at the same time or sequentially.

The group lobby is also the last space the school children will move through, as they prepare to leave. They will use the restrooms, pick up any stored belongings, visit the museum shop, and gather with their teacher to begin the journey back to school.

In late afternoon or evening hours, the group lobby may become a foyer space for adult learners to gather. For example, teachers who come for workshops need to hang their coats, check their registrations, pick up books and supplies, and perhaps grab a hasty snack or a cup of coffee before moving to a seminar room nearby. During class breaks, coffee tables can be set out in the group lobby, and this can also be a space for temporary display of project materials. Similarly, on weekends and holiday periods, the group lobby may be set up to serve the needs of Saturday clubs, science camps, family days, or other group events.

Restrooms: Following a long journey to the museum, the first thing the visitor looks for on entering is often the restroom. Restrooms—which may be called washrooms, toilets, or lavatories—should be in the unpaid zone of the museum, and immediately visible and accessible to all visitors. In most countries today, provision of facilities for the handicapped is mandatory. Some museums now provide a larger toilet and changing room for handicapped adult visitors, with space for their attendants. A family washroom and baby feeding room may also be required. At least some of the museum's restrooms should be located immediately adjacent to the group entrance, and others close to the various classrooms and lunchrooms. Both male and female washrooms should include baby-changing tables.

A museum with a very large program for children will wish to consider special children's restrooms with appropriate sized facilities. The number of stalls, urinals, and sinks required in the restrooms is in general a function of the peak visitation period (based on average length of stay) on the design day—a busy weekend day during the high tourism season. However, facilities for group tours, especially school groups, should be calculated separately, since whole busloads of school groups arriving within a short time period will place a severe demand on the capacity of the facilities.

Sick Room and Emergency Response: A medical problem can occur in any museum and could range from simple stomach upset or headache to situations that require an emergency response team. Every museum also needs to evaluate the potential need to respond to a mass emergency, and some museums are designated as refuges for the public in times of emergency. A small museum may need only a single first aid room shared by staff and visitors, where someone can rest, and where first aid supplies are stored and can be administered. Larger museums may need a sickroom for visitors near the main lobby and/or group lobby, and an industrial-level First Aid and ERT (emergency response team) room near the service entrances and workshops, with access for emergency vehicles. Consulting with local police, fire, and emergency services is strongly suggested as part of the planning process.

Coat and Backpack Storage: Depending on local conditions, learners arriving at the museum may need to store coats and boots, umbrellas, and backpacks to be out of the way. This is a compact storage solution that requires a minimum of staff attention, looks tidy, and allows the class teacher to control access and supervise her own class most effectively. A comparable solution is a set of large nets, one to a class, that are suspended and can be lowered from or raised to the ceiling.

Expensive gear such as video cameras, wallets, or purses should never be stored in bins or racks; ideally, some coin return lockers should be available for storing such items securely, or they should be turned in to a security officer.

A "lost and found" storage closet for items left behind is usually controlled by the security or visitor services staff.

Lunchrooms: The question of whether a museum needs to provide special places for school children to eat their lunches arises during the facilities planning process. Although the museum may have a café, the café operator will not be eager to see hordes of children taking over his space and eating home-packed lunches. Even if the children are buying their lunches, thirty or more kids can be noisy and messy—and not appreciated by other café patrons. However, a specialized lunchroom is a luxury when museum space is very constrained. Other options that may be considered are using the group lobby, studios, or classrooms as lunch spaces between 11:30 a.m. and 1:30 p.m., or, in clement weather, having children eat outside in a roofed patio or pavilion, or at picnic tables.

If a lunchroom is provided, it would be an open concept space, with tables and chairs suitable to the intended age group, and with a cleanup counter with hand-washing sinks and some cabinet storage for supplies. Garbage and recycling containers should be provided with children expected to do a basic cleanup after eating their lunches. Washrooms and sickroom should be adjacent, plus a janitor's closet, and vending machines for healthy snacks may be located in a hallway alcove. The lunchroom may be gaily decorated, and in many museums doubles as a revenue source, since it can be rented to families for children's birthday parties.

Vending: As discussed above, it is often advisable to make some provision for learners, both adults and children, to be able to purchase snacks from vending machines rather than the museum café. In fact, if a museum cannot afford to operate a café, vending machines are almost a necessity. It is well known that a visitor who is hungry or thirsty will not report a good visitor experience, and that once the visitor leaves to purchase meals or snacks, he or she most likely will not return to the museum.

To be as accessible as possible to the greatest number of patrons, the vending machines should be in a hallway area or lobby alcove, rather than in a room (such as a classroom that might be locked most of the time). Some museums locate a vending facility out of doors, or in a space accessible from outdoors but with a lockable enclosure to protect against vandals.

Support Spaces

Support spaces for museum educational facilities are in general back-of-house, invisible to the ordinary visitor, and accessible only to staff. Support facilities may be built into the actual classroom or studio space, or provided as separate rooms, which ideally will be nearby for easy preparation and supervision. Some of these include:

Preparation Rooms: If the learning program includes hands-on arts and crafts or science projects, or development of discovery boxes and self-guided tour materials, the education staff needs a place to prepare the materials in advance of the activity. Sometimes this can be done in the studios before the classes arrive or after they leave, but if the rooms are generally fully booked, other space must be found. Temporary storage for prepared materials on shelves or on a cart is useful so that a day's or week's worth of class material can be prepared well in advance.

The prep room generally requires a wall of shelving or cabinets for supplies and equipment, large sturdy work tables, and a counter with a utility sink for mixing paints or dyes. A special paint or clay drain may be required. Equipment such as a light table or paper cutter needs to be set up permanently. If there is equipment that children should not have access to, such as an oven or kiln, these can be located in the prep room where only staff and teachers have access.

Supplies and Kit Storage: Learning programs typically accumulate special equipment such as easels for painting, clipboards, supply carts, puppet theaters, clothing racks, microscope stands, and myriad other items that should be inventoried so that storage and activity space can be allocated for them. Some items may be stored in the prep room, some in the studios or classrooms, and some may be needed near the gallery floor. Discovery boxes or kits may need to be stored somewhere accessible for an outreach loan program.

Arts, crafts, and science supplies are also used by the education programs, and often are purchased in bulk and carry over from year to year. Since supplies are a valuable asset, storing them safely and being able to find them when wanted are essential. As with equipment, most supplies are stored near where they will be used, in built-in or freestanding shelving or cabinets within the education rooms; however, many nooks and crannies around the museum are typically called into service to store education supplies. Some ingenious storage systems include a movable storage wall that contains cabinets and also acts as a screen between two areas, and movable and stackable plastic bins, each of which is set up to hold supplies for a different age group or activity, are very popular.

Learning Collection Storage: Integral to many museum learning programs is the opportunity to use hands-on objects or specimens to make the learning experience more real. Museums set aside these objects in a special collection to be used by the learning program, and these need to be stored separately, but in similar conditions, to the rest of the museum collection. At the same time, the items need to be accessible for program use, so they cannot be stored offsite or in a collections storage area with restricted access.

Part of the regular collections storage area can be set aside for learning collections, as long as education staff can have reasonable access. This is often the best solution in terms of providing climate-controlled, secure storage at the lowest cost. Large museums may have the option of setting a whole room aside (it need not be a large room), as long as it can be at suitable relative humidity and temperature levels for the learning collection.

Offices: Education staff require office space, meeting rooms, and copy and print facilities for administrative, planning, and coordinating tasks on a daily basis. These can be centralized with other museum offices, or grouped with the education instructional space, but require good access to staff amenities such as washrooms, lockers, and break rooms. Since many education staff may be part time (teachers, facilitators, artists, or performers), they may not need permanent desks or workstations; a shared computer and telephone for checking daily e-mails, schedules, and reports may be sufficient. Similarly, in many museums, education staff share meeting rooms and project rooms with all other staff on a first-booking basis.

Docent or Volunteer Space: Volunteers or docents are the backbone of many education programs. Typically, they don't need permanent offices, except for the volunteer coordinator, but do need access to a shared telephone and computer. On a daily basis, volunteers need a way of checking into the museum and being identified by their photo ID badge, a secure place to store their belongings (lockers) and to prepare for their tour of duty, and a place to rest, have coffee or lunch, and recoup for further endeavors.

> A volunteer lounge with an adjacent locker area with a mirror, purse lockers, and coat rack provides an important amenity that enables volunteers to do their job effectively, and shows that they are valued and respected for their contribution. Since they are not paid, socializing with each other and with museum professionals is an important part of their reward for volunteering their time and talent.

Volunteers and docents also require meeting space and training space. They may attend special lectures or films as part of their training process, and hold regular coordination meetings. Often the museum's meeting rooms, seminar rooms, and library can be made available for these needs; if not, a training room with some study carrels as well as meeting tables and chairs can be supplied.

The following table presents a sample space list for museum learning spaces in square meters and square feet, assuming certain occupancy levels.

8.8　SUMMARY OF DESIGN ISSUES

The spaces outlined in the preceding section, which typify the spaces museums require for learning programs, are diverse in use, ranging from visitors services and amenities to learning environments to back-of-house support. Each of these categories in turn contains specialized spaces with diverse functional requirements, some only fully understood by a specialist such as a theater designer. At the same time, spaces for learning have a common aim, to support and facilitate the learning process for their users, whether these are of homogeneous or differing ages and needs. Some basic design principles can

Figure 8.2. A Sample Space List for Museum Learning Spaces

Public Non-Collection Space	Occupancy	Unit per SF	SM	Base Space SF	SM	Functional Comments
AUXILIARY OR VISITOR SERVICES SPACES						
Pedestrian Walkways						Hard surface, handicapped accessible walkways
Car Drop-Off						At least one space for car to drop off VIP or handicapped visitors
Bus Drop-Off & Parking						At least one drop-off space; bus parking may be off-site
Handicapped Parking						Parking stalls for handicapped visitors' vehicles, with walkway access
Staff and Volunteer Parking						Parking stalls for staff and volunteers TBD
Lunch Patio						Covered area with benches and/or picnic tables, garbage disposal, vending machines
Group Entry Lobby	120	54	5	3,229	300	Able to hold 2-3 school classes, provide live and video orientation, for arrival and departure assembly
Education Reception & Booking Counter	4	40	4	161	15	Computerized advance booking system, may also serve as electronic box office. Windows for check-in of school and tour groups.
Schools Backpack Storage	30	1	0	32	3	Space to store backpacks, lunches, winter coats in movable bins or pull-out racks
Children's Washrooms	10	39	4			Boys and Girls, barrier-free, no doors except to stalls
Family/Handicapped Washrooms	2	43	4			User and attendant, adult handicapped changing table optional
Parent's Room	2	54	5	108	10	Room for nursing mothers, baby changing, with window to Playroom or Children's Gallery, and separate toilet room
Children's Sickroom	2	54	5	108	10	Ideally adjacent to Children's Washrooms at Activity Classrooms
Lunch/Birthday Party Room	30	32	3	969	90	Can double as an Activity Room
Vending nook	4	22	2	86	8	Snack service for schoolchildren

(Continued)

Figure 8.2. A Sample Space List for Museum Learning Spaces (Continued)

Public Non-Collection Space	Occupancy	Unit per		Base Space		Functional Comments
		SF	SM	SF	SM	
DEDICATED LEARNING SPACES						
Activity Room	30	43	4	1,292	120	Activity classroom customized for individual museum needs and specific age group, for both clean/dirty activities, sturdy surfaces, natural light preferred
Art Studio	30	43	4	1,292	120	Similar to an artist's studio, spacious, flexible setup, natural light, paint sink
Biodiversity Lab	30	43	4	1,292	120	Lab for studying live animals, insects and plants. Rearing, food growing and storage need to be adjacent. Separation from sensitive collections areas.
Multipurpose Room	60	54	5	3,229	300	Flat floor multipurpose event and informal performance space, AV and projection capabilities, potentially divisible into smaller spaces as needed.
Resource Center Reading/ Computer Access Room	30	108	10	3,229	300	Includes reference counter, reading room, online computer access to collections information and images, and scanning/printing/copying services
Group Listening/Viewing Rooms	4	22	2	88	8	Enclosed room for 2-6 users to listen/view/record music, interviews, images. Multimedia music/image terminal, wide screen monitor, recording and playback equipment TBD
Teacher's Resource Center	10	32	3	323	30	Area where teachers can check out teaching aids, kits, etc.
Seminar Room	15	22	2	323	30	Adult-style meeting and seminar space with flexible seating
Smart Lecture Hall	200	12	1	2,400	214	Smart symposium room, raked floor/amphitheater for lectures, presentations, films, broadcast recording etc.
Preschool Play Room	15	54	5	807	75	Child-friendly, safe, modular play and story area for preschoolers and parents
Hands-On Loans Boutique	5	32	3	161	15	Small boutique for displaying loan-out artifacts and specimens
Community Gallery	30	54	5	1,615	150	Gallery for display of learning program or community exhibits
Children's Gallery	50	151	14	7,535	700	Child-friendly, safe, modular plug and play gallery type for children aged 6 to 12

(Continued)

Figure 8.2. A Sample Space List for Museum Learning Spaces (Continued)

Public Non-Collection Space	Occupancy	Unit per		Base Space		Functional Comments
		SF	SM	SF	SM	
LEARNING SUPPORT SPACES						
Interpretive Collection	N/A			215	20	Storage for artifacts and specimens used in Education Programs
Photo Studio	N/A			969	90	Primarily for art and artifact photography, digitized image photography for record, database and publication requirements
Film & Video Archives	N/A			161	15	Cool storage for film/photo media
Photo Records	N/A			161	15	File area for photo records
Library/Archival Supplies	N/A			161	15	Storage for clean paper supplies for book cataloguing etc.
Photo/Image Digitizing Lab	N/A			205	19	Document photography and image scanning area
Sound Digitizing Lab	N/A			205	19	Sound recording digitization setup
IT Node	N/A			97	9	Closet space for multimedia racks etc.
Education Offices	10	97	9	969	90	Private and landscaped office cubicles
Education Offices Support	N/A			388	36	Coffee, copy, files, stationery supplies
Office Reception/Waiting	4	54	5	216	20	Reception desk and waiting area
Staff meeting space	10	16	2	161	15	For groups of 8-10 staff, meeting table and chairs
Staff Break Rooms	10	22	2	44	20	Lunch and break area with lunch tables and chairs, adjacent kitchenette
Staff Kitchenettes	2	43	4	86	8	Kitchenette adjacent to work areas and break rooms
Staff Washrooms	10	43	4	431	40	Male and Female
Staff Day Lockers	10	11	1	108	10	Male and Female, for contract and part-time staff
Volunteer Training Room	30	16	2	480	45	With bookshelves and study carrals, meeting tables and chairs
Volunteer's Purse Lockers	10	11	1	108	10	For docents and volunteers
Industrial First Aid/Emergency Room	3	54	5	161	15	Outer treatment room with inner toilet room, door wide enough for EMR stretchers
AV Equipment Storage	N/A			108	10	Storage for lights, AV carts, miscellaneous equipment
AV Work/Repair Space	N/A			108	10	Assembly, maintenance and repair area with workbench
Smart Lecture Hall Control/Projection Booth	N/A			215	20	Must support video conferencing etc.
Education Prep Room	N/A			431	40	Workroom with built-in storage, counters, utility sinks, sturdy central work table
Education Program Supplies	N/A			269	25	Non-artifact supplies in compacted system
Education Gallery Storage	N/A			377	35	Storage accessible to each gallery space for associated program supplies, carts, stools, etc.
Media Production Suite	N/A			538	50	Multimedia editing workstation for Webmaster, internal broadcast production
Chair and Table Storage	N/A			646	60	Adjacent to multipurpose room

be used to direct the design process and to assess and test the results. Spaces for museum learning need to be:

- Functional
- Flexible
- Productive
- Accessible
- Aesthetically pleasing
- Cost-effective
- Secure/Safe
- Sustainable

The aim of good design of museum learning spaces is to give people a healthful, stimulating, and safe environment in which to learn while at the same time providing the best learning environments possible for the budget.

Functionality

Functionality of learning spaces relates to size and layout of rooms for best use, but also to the relationships between spaces that promote effective daily activities.

To receive and orient students and others to the learning programs:

- Understand the flow of students from cars, buses, or the street, to the main or group entry point; cluster visitor services at the entry lobby.
- Provide for access to learning spaces after museum galleries are closed.
- Make visitor services, such as the admissions counter and toilets, highly visible and easy to locate and access for all visitors.
- Enable visitors to store personal items so they don't have to be carried.
- Provide drinking fountains and vending machines in or near the lobby area.
- Provide clear paths with wide corridors from the receiving area (lobby and visitor services) to the learning spaces and galleries.

To enhance learning for individuals, teams, and all ages:

- Integrate group-related spaces—activity rooms with their prep spaces, storage, and cleanup facilities.
- Provide support spaces and facilities (storage, utility sinks) in the learning spaces rather than at a distance.
- Connect spaces visually with colors and patterns, particularly for primary school children.

- Provide level changes and differing ceiling heights within the learning spaces—platforms and banquettes can act as low barriers, seating, or worktops. Alcoves can highlight a special topic or activity, or provide for quiet play, reflection, and reading. Provide different heights of seating and worktops for different users in the same space.

Flexibility

Flexibility is always a significant design issue in planning space for museum learning. Will the space be able to be modified when the program changes—whether the change is moderate or radical? Programs inevitably change as educators gain experience in working with specific audiences and their needs. In working with museums established at all periods from the 1870s onward, it is remarkable to see how often space (always scarce) is adapted to serve the requirements of the time. In constructing new museum space, the question should always be asked whether some flexibility has been built in to allow for future program changes; however, even the most quirky space can possibly be adapted, and its unique character may make the program that much more appealing.

To ensure flexibility and adaptability for changing programs and audiences:

- Consider how spaces may be used by different users at different times of day or year, for different purposes (e.g., daytime/evening, children's activities/adult classes).
- Consider modular or gridded spaces which can convert to other uses over time.
- Use operable walls to convert from larger to smaller spaces when required.
- Provide underfloor and dropdown power and data capability over a wide grid.
- Accommodate for future technology upgrades.

Productivity

Spaces for learning can be especially productive when they provide the physical conditions that support and promote observation, concentration, communication, and creation. You'll want to:

- Use natural as well as artificial light wherever possible. Studies[3] show a positive correlation between daylighting and student performance.
- Use lighting systems that promote visual comfort and can be adjusted from area to area.
- Provide a connection to the outdoors, with operable doors and windows in learning spaces.

- Ensure acoustical comfort.[4] Reduce or confine ambient noise within learning spaces, and make it possible for learners to hear well. Meet ANSI/ASA Standard S12.60-2002, *Acoustical Performance Criteria, Design Requirements and Guidelines for Schools.*[5]
- Ensure superior indoor air quality, which helps museum objects as well as people. Children typically are more sensitive to indoor air pollutants than adults and more likely to suffer ill effects such as allergies and asthma.
- Ensure thermal comfort. Keep temperature and humidity in the comfort zone and allow each learning space to be adjusted individually.
- Ensure cleanliness and order by providing for housekeeping and maintenance of learning spaces, and storage of supplies and projects. Users including children should have access to trash and recycling bins for basic cleanup of learning spaces.

Accessibility

Accessibility is one of the prime issues around design of museum spaces generally, and learning spaces in particular. This is due to the extreme mix of ages, and physical and mental capabilities among museum visitors, all of whom at some time may be viewed as learners. Museums have grappled with design issues ranging from ramps and widened doorways to accommodate wheelchairs, grab bars, and hoists to assist seniors and others, to issues of readability and lighting of labels and graphics, and accessibility of computer hardware and software. In terms of legislated standards for handicapped accessibility, museums strive to meet and surpass the requirements so that every visitor may have the best possible experience. The key goals can be stated as follows:

- Design spaces, furnishings, and equipment to meet the specific needs of learners and teachers with disabilities, and the needs of accompanying family members and caregivers, for physical, visual, and aural access to learning spaces and experiences.
- Consider issues of intellectual access to museum spaces and experiences in facilities design.
- Design for future flexibility, which enables spaces to be easily modified.

Museums provide almost a perfect laboratory for exploring and exemplifying the principles of open or universal accessibility, often termed *universal design*. As described by the Center for Universal Design at North Carolina State University, the intent of universal design is to simplify life for everyone by making products, communications, and the built environment more usable by as many people as possible at little or no extra cost. Universal design benefits people of all ages and abilities. Many of the design features that are user-friendly and flexible are simply good design practices, rather than requirements of a building code or accessibility standard or guideline. Universal design principles cover:

- Equitable use
- Flexibility in use
- Simple, intuitive use
- Perceptible information
- Tolerance for error
- Low physical effort
- Size and space for approach and use

In the United States, the Smithsonian Institution is a leader in promoting universal design principles in exhibit design and in general facilities design. Museums which have incorporated the principles into facilities, exhibit, and communications design in a comprehensive way include the Cincinnati Children's Museum, whose Web site offers glimpses into the accessibility offered within its exhibition and learning environments.

Aesthetics

The building's architecture and the design and decoration of individual learning spaces can significantly enhance the learning process. Keep in mind:

- The museum building's architecture can be a learning as well as an aesthetic experience and can help signal to visitors that they will have a memorable day at the museum.
- The building approach and surroundings can present sculpture, play structures, and landscaping that is beautiful and has an element of learning.
- The building entry point and the portal to the learning spaces can be welcoming, intriguing, and inviting to learners.
- An interior environment that is visually comfortable and stimulating can be created by integrating natural and artificial lighting and eliminating glare.
- To create the best overall, general lighting indoors, design for diffuse, uniform lighting in studios and activity rooms, but note that special workstations may require spotlighting or task lighting.
- Incorporating colors that stimulate or soothe, depending on the space function, can enhance learning.

Security and Safety

The safety of learners of all ages is of great importance to the museum, and visitors generally regard the museum as a safe environment in which they and their children can feel secure. At the same time, the mix of age groups in the visitor population may give rise to worries on the part of teachers and parents about unauthorized adults having access to children. General raised consciousness about security issues is prompting reconsideration of safety and security issues around learning programs. Consider using one or more of these options in the public space areas of the museum:

- Maximize visual access to corridors and to indoor and outdoor play areas, by teachers, museum staff, and caregivers.
- Use video cameras where appropriate to supervise learning spaces, outdoor access paths, and building perimeter.
- Use good outdoor lighting and alarm systems to prevent intrusion into learning spaces.
- Examine adult backpacks, luggage, and parcels entering the learning area and store outside the learning area if contents are suspect.
- Control access to learning areas and separate areas where young children may be alone (e.g., in learning area toilet rooms) from general public circulation.
- Increase occupants' sense of ownership and "territoriality" by providing comfortable, not institutional, rooms and by clearly defining the learning area boundaries.
- Control access to individual spaces with appropriate locking systems.
- Use durable, easily cleaned and nontoxic building and furnishing materials. Use nonslip surfaces on ramps, stairs, and activity floors.
- Ensure that storage units are accessible yet safe, with antitipping devices.
- Design furniture, casework, and millwork with rounded corners, no sharp edges. Furniture should be stable and appropriately sized to the age group of users.
- Place controls and operable fittings out of the reach of children.
- Provide safe egress and shelter in cases of emergency.

Cost Effectiveness

Museum educators desire quality spaces for learning, with the best possible design and finishing to withstand many years of constant and active use. Investment in quality can result in reduction in life cycle costs of maintaining and running the building, and lengthen the useful life of spaces and furnishings, but needs to be balanced with the overall capital and operational budgets.

- Select materials and systems (power, water, data) on the basis of life cycle cost analysis and flexibility in use.
- Consider the recyclability of materials.
- Specify materials and products that are easy to maintain and/or to replace (balance this with their impact on children's health and the environment).

Sustainability

Museums are institutions that are expected to have long lives and museum buildings are typically built to last. With increasing construction costs and costs to the environment from recycling dangerous building materials and construction and operating activities, museums are increasingly looking to green and sustainable solutions to building challenges. These initiatives can be incorporated into learning area design and programming:

- Use energy, water, and other resources efficiently.
- Integrate renewable energy strategies, such as passive solar design and, where appropriate, solar thermal systems and turn them into learning tools.
- Integrate high-performance mechanical and lighting systems.
- Conserve and protect natural areas. Provide barriers that protect children, plants, and wildlife.
- Incorporate materials and products derived from sustainable-yield processes and/or are manufactured locally.

NOTES

1. L. Dickson, *The Museum Makers* (Toronto: Royal Ontario Museum, 1986), p. 49.

2. D. A. Kolb, *Experiential Learning: Experience as the Source of Learning and Development* (New Jersey: Prentice-Hall, 1984).

3. http://www.edfacilities.org/rl/impact_learning.cfm#6144.

4. http://www.wbdg.org/design/acoustic.php?r=elementary.

5. http://www.access-board.gov/acoustic/index.htm.

CHAPTER 9

Interpretative Planning and the Media of Museum Learning

Hugh A. D. Spencer

The communication of meaning is common to all core functions of museums:

- We develop and maintain *collections* because they embody knowledge and experience; they are the content, implicit or explicit, of any museum learning communication from the institution.
- We conduct *research* because there are often a variety of meanings represented in the collection—and between collections. Research provides an intellectual synthesis that combines existing and mediated knowledge with original meanings found in artifacts, specimens, or works of art.
- We *interpret* these meanings because we wish to convey a thesis or the outcomes of research into our collections. We may also want to interpret our research and associated collections because we feel that the findings may be of value to potential audiences and groups in our communities. Of course, there are different values that we may be expressing—social, scientific, aesthetic, economic, even entertainment value.

It is with the last function—*interpretation*—that we usually connect the communication process within the museum. In this context we regard interpretation as the *intended and effective* communication of messages and experiences to visitors—through exhibitions and other public programs. *Interpretative planning* refers to integrated and strategic approaches to communication to achieve the communication and learning goals established by the institution.

A classic model of communication is the basis for all interpretative planning:

Figure 9.1. The Message from Sender to Receiver

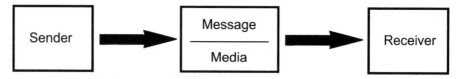

In the museum context this model can be expanded as follows:

Figure 9.2. The Message from Museum to Visitor

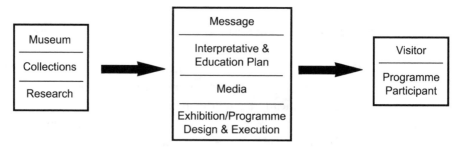

A dialogue begins, and the communication roles are reversed, when the original sender starts getting feedback in the form of questions, suggestions, ideas, opinions, and even new information from the original receiver.

Figure 9.3. The Message from Sender to Receiver, Including Feedback

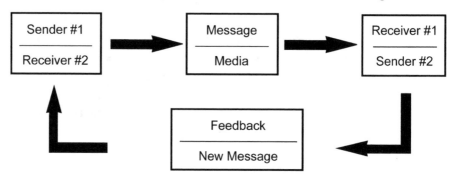

Museums have sometimes initiated this kind of exchange with their publics when they conduct evaluations of how accurately and effectively their existing or planned exhibitions and programs are communicating with visitors. Museums may conduct front-end evaluations to solicit ideas for new programs or exhibitions, or to identify areas of need among different groups in the community. Dr. Barbara Soren discusses evaluation in the following chapter, but it is also relevant to interpretative planning, especially at this front-end stage.

Evaluation played a key role in the temporary exhibition on the creative processes entitled *Go Creative* that is the subject of the case study in this chapter by Keri Ryan. The original version of the exhibition was the result of front-end research carried out by the British Council and the Hong Kong Ministry of Education, which determined that creativity needed to be viewed more highly among families and school children in the region. A second version of the exhibition in Trinidad and Tobago drew on informal *summative* evaluation of the Hong Kong show to better meet the educational needs of school children as identified by the National Institution for Higher Education and Research into Science and Technology (NIHERST).

GO CREATIVE: LEARNING ABOUT CREATIVITY FROM A LOW-COST BUT EFFECTIVE EXHIBITION
Keri Ryan

Go Creative is a simple yet powerful exhibition that offers surprising and unexpected learning opportunities to each visitor. The exhibition explores what it is to be creative, who is considered creative, and, of course, offers visitors opportunities to *Go Creative* themselves. The exhibition was initially developed by Lord Cultural Resources for the British Council in Hong Kong and subsequently modified for the National Institute for Higher Education Research in Science and Technology (NIHERST) in Trinidad and Tobago. While Hong Kong and Port of Spain in Trinidad and Tobago might seem worlds apart, both clients had a desire to inject creative thinking and innovation into their formal school curriculum, and foster a broader appreciation of the role of creativity in many aspects of daily life. Both clients felt that an entertaining, yet informative exhibition focusing on the many facets of creativity would inspire individuals within their own communities to become more creative themselves. This case study demonstrates how a small, entertaining, and informative exhibition not only gave visitors personal learning opportunities, but also resulted in communities learning and working together.

Lord Cultural Resources was initially contracted in Hong Kong to develop *Go Creative* for the British Council, who recognized that formal education in Hong Kong and mainland China is very structured and based mainly on exams and memory-based learning, thereby limiting the amount of time and opportunities that Chinese children have to be freely creative. Moreover, the British Council wanted to demonstrate that creativity is not only a concept connected to the liberal arts but also applies to math, science, and business. The British Council planned to tour the exhibition in conjunction with Hong Kong's millennium celebrations, as Hong Kong had chosen to dedicate 2000 as "the year of innovation." The team met in Hong Kong to determine how to develop such an exhibition most effectively, and what was needed to make it accessible to visitors. The greatest challenge for developing this exhibition was the short time frame; the team had only six weeks to plan and design the modest 1,500-square-foot (c. 150 sq. m.) exhibit. A second challenge was the relatively small budget allotted to the project. Both of these challenges provided the exhibition team with the opportunity to *Go Creative* themselves.

The key to developing a successful exhibition about creativity lay in engaging children and their families—especially given that the exhibition would be mounted in shopping centers in Hong Kong and mainland China.

In order to pique the interest of this target audience, "creativity" was broken into three key states:

WOW—the excitement and enthusiasm that comes from being creative, FLOW—the state of being that one enters when being creative and, finally, STUFF—the results of one's creativity.

These three states were personified in three friendly and welcoming mascots. These mascots were critical for engaging the interest of children and their families in China, who, at the time were very familiar with Anime computer game animation—especially Pokéemon. Once they felt connected to the mascots, they were ready to follow each mascot to discover the exhibition's deeper meaning.

Parts of the exhibition were developed using Edward De Bono's theory of lateral thinking and was therefore structured in such a way that concepts were introduced and explored using techniques that shifted patterns of thinking from the predictable to the unconventional. The exhibition was divided into five key areas:

What it Means to Be Creative, Who is Creative,
The Stuff of Creativity, Get in the Flow,
Go Creative.

In the first area, the mascot WOW invites visitors to debunk myths about creativity; for instance, at one point WOW asks visitors some true or false questions.

Q: Creativity is a magical skill that only a very few people have.
A: False! Creativity is pretty exciting—even inspiring sometimes—but it is much more common than most of us realize.

Q: There's no single proper, correct, or true way to be creative.
A: This is very true. There are many, many ways to be inventive; creativity can be expressed in a variety of ways.

Q: You are either creative or you aren't. That's what makes creative people so special.
A: Not really! We do know that creativity is a skill that you can build up through training and practice. The more creative things you do . . . the more creative you become!

Once visitors understand that creativity isn't a trait, like having red hair or being left-handed, they are invited to discover *Who is Creative*. At this point the WOW mascot invites visitors to question the preconception that creative people are only musicians, artists, and writers. Visitors learn that everyone can be creative, including doctors, business people, and gardeners.

Next, FLOW invites visitors to learn what it means to experience the state of being creative by hearing stories from an astronaut, a doctor, and an author. They are then invited to practice their creativity through some lateral thinking exercises. The last two areas in the exhibition explore the outputs of creativity. The third mascot STUFF shows visitors some innovative products; this part of the exhibition featured an area for the British Council to display winners of their Innovation Award. Finally, in *Go Creative*, visitors can dance with color, make music, build with Lego, and realize some of their own creative potential.

The structure of the exhibition proved successful for programming and instructing about creativity, and the impact of the exhibition reached the National Institute for Higher Education Research in Science and Technology (NIHERST) in Port of Spain, Trinidad. NIHERST researchers were developing an initiative for building creative capacity within their community. They were looking for an exhibition that would anchor this initiative in their National Science Center, and which could later travel to other Caribbean islands. Using the framework of the *Go Creative* exhibit developed for the British Council, NIHERST worked with Lord Cultural Resources to modify the exhibition in such a way that it reflected their unique community, thus ensuring that visitors in the Caribbean region would be inspired to *Go Creative*. The formerly Chinese mascots were given a Caribbean flare, videos featured successful Trinbagonians, and games highlighted inventions from the islands—for example, the steel pan drum and Agnostura Bitters. The STUFF section provided NIHERST the opportunity to showcase the winners of their annual Young Inventors Award.

While the exhibition provided a place for school children and families to learn about creativity, it also provided NIHERST with a springboard for taking this message further. The exhibition became a catalyst for a broader *Go Creative* initiative that was developed in collaboration with the Caribbean Council for Science and Technology (CCST) with sponsorship from the Organization of American States (OAS). The project aims to inspire and develop in children the skills for applying creativity to their lives. The exhibition became part of this regional project which plans to host camps to develop scientific literacy amongst children, as well as to encourage participation in the Caribbean Young Inventors competition. Countries that will participate in this project are the Bahamas, Dominica, Grenada, Antigua and Barbuda, Barbados, Guyana, Jamaica, St. Kitts and Nevis, St. Lucia, and St. Vincent and Grenadines. The *Go Creative* exhibition is being used to motivate, inspire, and teach about creativity through its travels to these countries.

In a world where arts funding is being cut, field trips are becoming less frequent, and "teaching to tests" form the basis of the standard education system, the freedom to be creative is often overlooked. The British Council in Hong Kong and NIHERST in Trinidad and Tobago both recognized the value in encouraging children to understand their own creative abilities and learn to apply these skills across all aspects of their lives. Moreover, the need to nurture creative thinkers was viewed as a key requirement in developing a thriving and successful society. What began as a small exhibition in Hong Kong which challenged visitors to reconsider their preconceived ideas about creativity has evolved into a catalyst for building creative capacity across the Caribbean. Thinking out of the box, indeed.

Incorporating the evaluation process results in the following refinement of the communication model for museum learning:

Figure 9.4. The Message from Museum to Visitor, Including Front-End and Summative Evaluations

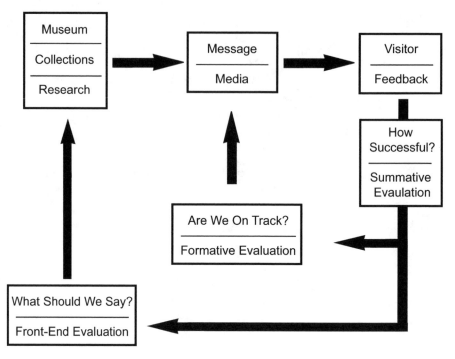

COURTESY OF LORD CULTURAL RESOURCES.

Museums employ a range of different media to convey their messages. One of the most important tasks in interpretative planning and visitor experience design is the creative and effective combination of communication objectives with means of expression. In the early stages of interpretative planning, it is advantageous to suggest more than one means of expression for each communication objective. Then as time, budget, technology, materials, personnel, and equipment affect the planning, design, and implementation process, the means of expression may vary, but the communication objectives will be retained.

Contemporary museums' means of expression can take many forms, including:

- Graphics, which should be tiered from headlines through text panels (which should never be more than sixty words per panel) to labels, which should always be placed at a height where they are visible without forcing the visitor to stoop, and which should be printed with effective contrast between the letters and the color of the support surface.
- Acoustic guides, wands, or sound cones conveying commentary, drama, birdcalls, the sounds of musical instruments, or atmospheric and environmental sounds.
- Historic or natural settings, some to look at and others which visitors can walk through.
- Dioramas, a traditional natural history museum display technique.
- Interactive exhibits, which may be physical and mechanical, or digital.
- Audiovisual and multimedia presentations of all kinds, ranging from big-screen film showings in auditoriums to individually operated computer work stations.
- Live demonstrations or performers, who may tell their stories in the third-person ("This is how a nineteenth-century blacksmith made horseshoes."), or first-person, in which the actors take on the *persona* of a historic period, interacting with each other, with the audience, or both.
- Object theaters, in which artifacts or specimens are featured with the aid of lights and live or voice-over sound interpretation, so that the objects become the "actors" narrating the museum's themes.
- Motion simulators that allow visitors to feel kinaesthetically a simulacrum of a historic, contemporary, or futuristic vehicle.

The advent of online culture and digital technologies—through computer-to-computer communication and increasingly sophisticated multimedia—has created remarkable and exciting challenges for museum interpretation and learning. The following sections of this chapter show how the digital world of the twenty-first century allows institutions and members of the public to exchange ideas in ways that are faster and more responsive than ever before. Further, the public now has access to online tools and perspectives so that users can actually shape and transform not only the messages communicated by a museum, but the very media it uses. These sections explore the evolving role of online and digital capabilities of museum education by:

- briefly considering the history of online services—to help museum professionals understand essential aspects of the nature of digital technologies and culture
- reviewing the prevalent forms of online educational services offered by museums and art galleries
- examining a few instances of museum online and digital educational services offered by specific institutions.

9.1 ONLINE EDUCATION: THE CHALLENGES OF DEFINITION

In order to plan and deploy a category of services, it is useful to have an accurate and brief idea of what those services are. This may be an obvious notion, but in the case of online education, there are some challenges to arriving at shared and clearly understood definitions.

In the early twenty-first century, the realm of "being digital" (as Nicholas Negroponte expressed it) influences almost every aspect of our lives. This includes museums and art galleries as well as institutions where we might expect a greater technological presence such as science centers, children's museums, and world's fair pavilions. Furthermore, just as being digital affects almost every aspect of society, digital services and technologies are also relevant to all of the key functions of museums and cultural institutions.

One way of looking at this effect is to think of museums as "cultural engines" that research, collect, preserve, and interpret their collections and/or subject areas in order to generate collective memories and social meanings that drive communities into the future. Digital technologies and applications "supercharge" the cultural engine of the museum by making every function of the institution more effective and efficient. Digital services and technologies are relevant to:

- Collections documentation and management
- Research
- Building functions and environmental controls
- Marketing techniques
- Exhibition and interpretation media and approaches
- Education and Public Programs

It's important to stress that the appropriate forms of being digital are useful to museums, because there are attitudes among museum professionals that in some cases impede the best use of these technologies and services. These attitudes range from utopianism to pessimism, and may be balanced by a duly considered pluralism:

Utopianism: Technological utopianism—an overriding faith in the transformative and profoundly positive impact of technology—has been a long-standing cultural and political tradition throughout the industrialized world, at least since the late nineteenth century. In the case of digital and online technologies this has taken forms such as the promise of paperless offices, the Dotcom boom and bust, as well as the supposed political impact of new virtual communities. Even a brief consideration of the fate of some of these grand notions suggests that there have been some bumps along the Information Superhighway.

The danger presented by utopian thought is that it often leads to unrealistic expectations, which can in turn (like any utopian enterprise) result in the waste of resources and, ultimately, disappointment. In turn, this means that the true potentials of digital services are not realized.

Pessimism: There is a considerable body of opinion that is highly critical of the online and digital world. Some, like the late Neil Postman, viewed the Internet and multimedia as yet one more socially corrosive manifestation of mass media while Clifford Stoll's study *Silicon Snake Oil* takes the position that much of what digital technology offers is essentially trivial and unnecessary.

Unrestrained pessimism has the same effect as utopianism: If people do not believe that something can be done, then in all likelihood it will not be done.

Pluralism: This is the most complex and dynamic attitude, and presents both the greatest risks and richest potential for online museum learning. Digital and online cultures have a prevailing grassroots character—both in their development and in the range of their applications. The genesis of the Internet itself is an example of this pluralist and grassroots character, as the original system of telephonically linked computers was initially intended as a defense resource to allow cities and military installations to stay in communication in the event of nuclear attack or natural disaster. The ARPANET system would have remained largely dormant if it had not been for the continued use of enthusiast groups who began to post nonmilitary and nonscientific information to larger and larger groups of users. The innovative use of digital technologies by enthusiasts and trendmakers continues to be a factor—even in the area of museum learning.

Another pluralist aspect of digital technology is that while its impacts and influences can be widespread it is relatively cheap and accessible to many different communities. *Today it is much cheaper, faster, and requires fewer personnel for an institution to create and operate its own Web site and multimedia programs than to set up a planetarium or large-format cinema with an accompanying destination film.*

This lower capital and creative cost means that smaller institutions or communities with less money are capable of producing sometimes very sophisticated digital products and services. There are some immediate advantages resulting from this relatively democratic access:

- There is a regular supply of fresh approaches and potential for educational programming, as long as cultural trendmakers stay engaged with this technology.
- Participation in the digital realm is open to a wide range of institutions and communities.

However, there are also difficulties in functioning in an electronic grass-roots world—particularly in determining how well an institution's level of digital standards meet appropriate standards of quality and accuracy. Also, continually changing technologies and applications may place a museum at risk of having its earlier installations made obsolete—sometimes sooner than expected.

9.2   ONLINE MUSEUM EDUCATION APPLICATIONS

The main uses of online services for learning by museums and related cultural institutions as of the early twenty-first century are:

- Web sites
- Web casts and other download programs
- Virtual museums

Museum Web Sites

By the mid-1990s many museums had developed some form of Web site service. One of the earlier versions was pioneered by the National Library of Canada in Ottawa, which in 1993 opened a Web site to provide supplementary educational materials to accompany its temporary exhibition program.

The Web site produced for the library's *Out of This World* exhibition on science fiction was a typical example of the Web sites offered by cultural institutions at this time. It was considered quite advanced because it was able to provide still graphics for exhibition art and selections from the collections, but it was still a passive text-based site where users were able to call up written descriptions of exhibition content. The online educational service took the form of an exhibition reading list and a schedule of authors' readings and public events.

As production technology has improved and become more accessible, the carrying capacity of the Internet has also grown. Web sites—including museum Web sites—are able to provide more complex, dynamic, and interactive experiences. By 2006, even smaller and regional museums are able to operate Web sites that rival broadcast media for the delivery of their content.

As the example from the Sir Alexander Galt Museum in Lethbridge, Alberta—a medium-sized regional institution—indicates, most museum and cultural institution Web sites include:

- History, mission, and mandate statements—so that visitors to the site get a clear sense of what the institution is about, the different roles it plays and how it came to be. This is often the initial "sell" point where the online user decides if this is the place he or she wants to be.

- User information—with location maps, opening hours, floor plans, program times, and admission rates (if applicable). Once users have decided that they are interested in the museum, this is the information that allows them to plan actual in-person visits.
- Highlights of the public experience at the museum—which can take the form of a virtual tour with images from the galleries, building and grounds, summaries of exhibitions and gallery topics, and an outline of the types of educational and public programming offered at the institution. Sometimes the museum combines images and content as digital experiences that can only be accessed via the Web site.
- Highlights from the museum's collections and archives. In some cases the Web site will offer tools for online inquiries and research. The presence of links to other collections, institutions, and resources is also an important research tool that museum Web sites offer.
- Information about the museum's retail store—which may include the ability to purchase items online. To a greater or lesser extent, these Web sites include information on other amenities such as cafes, playgrounds, cinemas, or party rooms.
- Electronic versions of the institution's newsletters and publications.
- Mechanisms for establishing a dialogue and relationship between the public and the institution. These connections may take the forms of:
  - Membership information
  - Donor contacts and procedures
  - Contact information for the Web site itself, the institution, and sometimes an online staff directory
  - Links—as well as aiding research, these links to other sites establish the role of the museum as a gateway and helper in the user's quest for knowledge and entertainment

Museum Web Sites and Museum Learning

From the very outset, the provision of educational services has been a priority for many museum Web sites. Overall, these services can be grouped into the following categories:

Museum Learning Programs and Events: On earlier Web sites these consisted simply of posting information to promote and provide better access to programs offered at the site of the institution or somewhere within its community. However, as the online capacity of museums has improved, their Web sites have increasingly become the vehicle for delivering the actual programs. These programs can take the form of interactive study guides, games and quizzes based on museum collections and exhibits, Web casts and remote views of natural heritage sites or deep space, and even virtual exhibitions.

Collection Study and Research Tools: Again, the earliest versions of these were often text-based programs in which users could call up written descriptions of objects. Over time these tools have evolved to better defined graphic images of objects and works of art, along with multimedia descriptions using text, sound, and insert video to show objects in use, in various contexts, or in various stages of production. Collections data online may also include links to relevant objects and disciplines either at the institution or another institution's collections.

Interactive controls allow users to manipulate an object from a variety of different perspectives, in effect picking up an object and turning it around in your virtual hand.

These types of research and learning tools—where digital manipulation of artifact images is applied—require us to establish museological standards for interpretation and information design. *While new software and electronic photography techniques allow us to study the context, means of use and production, and materials of composition, in unique and insightful ways, the degree of interactivity and animation should not change or compromise the authentic meaning of the artifact or work of art.* The growing field of museum digital photography is still determining appropriate standards and specifications to govern formats, documentation methods, and presentation criteria for high-definition and three-dimensional collection photographs.

Forums, Chat Rooms, and Web Casts

All three of these online capacities can be viewed as museum learning services, in that they create the ability for the public to contact the museum, and in turn the museum can use these means to reach out to the public. Unlike many outreach programs, these services can connect to people and institutions around the world.

Electronic bulletin boards and forums were the original basis for the growth of the Internet as a public and cultural entity. In the late 1970s and early 1980s, fans and enthusiast groups of various types—from genre literature and sports to film and even TV trivia and nostalgia enthusiasts—started posting electronic messages to each other. They exchanged information and opinions and experiences in online venues such as "The Well" where they formed what Howard Rheingold refers to as "virtual communities," that is, communities of interest, and to some extent intentional communities that do not occupy any physical space but congregate only in the machines and minds of their members.

Subject and enthusiast-based forums continue today, and museums and other cultural institutions use and sometimes even host them. These forums can range from bird watching and "ask a gardener" forums to the electronic newsletters distributed by nature centers and botanical gardens to moderated postings and specialized links to other organizations and interest groups. The American Museum of Natural History, for instance, provides regularly refreshed programs on new developments in the various science disciplines.

Some science museums and science centers have pioneered the electronic delivery of interactive electronic programming via their Web sites. Again, these online educational program services have had a relatively long history, in terms of the digital world. The 1980s marked the first continuous offering of online courses. Although these were initially developed by formal educational institutions, museums and other informal learning institutions are now increasingly able to provide them.

Like most online services at the time, programs such as Connected Education were text-based, and employed a simple but effective educational model:

- Computers with modems and telephone connections were the means for delivering near-instantaneous lectures and educational support resources.
- The Internet was also a high-speed means of submitting questions and answers as well as written assignments.
- Once the instructor had collected the assignments, the evaluations could in turn be electronically delivered to students around the world.

Museums and science centers have offered similar educational programs in the form of "ask a curator" forums or institutionally hosted chat rooms. With forums, users can e-mail in questions and ideas, so that experts can send back their answers. These questions and answers can be either e-mailed directly or posted publicly on the museum's Web site. An institution can also use its Web site as a gateway for setting up an online chat room where participants can ask questions and receive real-time answers.

Digital services are usually not sufficiently advanced that audio and video can also be downloaded via a museum's Web site. *EMPLive*—operated by the Experience Music Project in Seattle—has been a pioneer in this field, with music education programs featuring downloadable lectures and interactive music lessons.

Digital online services can also be used for research and development of new exhibitions and other learning programs. *Humanitas*, a cultural institution that is currently under development in Toronto, is using this technology to gather life history accounts and other information from the public to shape the eventual content of its public programs and gallery exhibitions.

The Exploratorium Web site, originating from San Francisco, provides access to many educational resources. One of the most advanced and enjoyable is *Iron Science Teacher*. The content of this program is videotaped on the floor of the Exploratorium's main gallery and the format is something of a parody of the popular TV cooking show, *Iron Chef*. Science teachers from the Bay Area are invited in to create insightful (and usually entertaining) science demonstrations competitively, using randomly selected materials. As with all game shows, an enthusiastic audience watches and the contestants are graded—but unlike many game shows scientific principles are explained as well.

Iron Science Teacher is a program that you can download off the Exploratorium Web site, which also offers an extensive archive of past programs. And these programs are suitable not just as on-screen entertainment on personal computers, but are resources that students in a classroom environment can use. *Iron Science Teacher* is also remarkable because it establishes the Exploratorium as an important authority and resource for science education, and simultaneously serves to market the facility as an attraction around the world.

Dedicated Downloads and Podcasts

Much of what online museum learning can do and the directions it is developing are the outcomes of technological convergence and "Negroponte Shifts" in which different technologies and systems are bundled together, and where capacities and content developed for one medium find new and sometimes unexpected uses in a different context.

The process of downloading files from Web sites—often associated with enterprises such as music distributors and film studios—has converged into new methods of text, graphic, audio, and video interpretation for museums and related cultural institutions. In this case, traditional acoustic guides, printed guides, and docent guided tours have transferred much of their content to mobile devices that visitors already own and can bring with them to the museum:

- iPods and other MP3 players
- Palm Pilots and other personal data assistant units (PDAs)
- cell phones
- digital cameras

Some visitors take technological convergence even further and carry hand-held units that combine the features of all of the systems listed above.

Again, the Experience Music Project was a pioneer in this area. MEG units were originally conceived as an advanced form of acoustic guide—appropriate in a museum dedicated to popular music where visitors would want to hear some of the music represented in the exhibitions and collections. However, MEGs also had a wireless capacity that allowed visitors to download text, graphics, and audio files from exhibits and transfer them to their home e-mail addresses. In this manner visitors could create their own personalized multimedia record of their museum visit—a personally authored digital catalogue. MEG hardware is similar in size and operation to an acoustic guide—units are about the size of an older portable CD player and are rented out to visitors as they enter the galleries.

Since EMP opened in 2000, mobile communications technology has evolved to the point where institutions do not have to distribute special hardware from their institutions—or the hardware that is distributed is even smaller and offers online access to graphics and the institution's Web site while the visitor is in the galleries. The Canadian Museum of Civilization is currently introducing smaller PDA interpretative systems that use inset LED screens to provide animated interpretation of exhibits and collections on display.

Cell phone-based interpretation is also possible in the museum environment—although to date these applications have been used mostly at historic and architectural heritage sites. Here visitors can enter codes on their cell phones to call up audio descriptions of what they are looking at.

Podcasting—which takes its name from the process of distributing audio and video files via downloads to iPods and other MP3 players—also represents a new and potentially important area of museum educational programming. Podcasting is also an example of two major trends in digital culture:

- A lower level of hardware investment—so that institutions can concentrate on content and interpretation, rather than investing in purchasing and maintaining new hardware. Visitors bring their own iPod technology to the institution.
- Grassroots pressure is also evident with podcasting. Some public galleries and museums first became aware of podcasts when they discovered that visitors were creating their own unofficial audio guides to the exhibits and making them available on personal Web sites and blogs (short for "weblogs"). The institutions had to move into this area of educational programming in order to reach their audiences in ways that were already in use and to make sure that their point of view on their own collections was being conveyed.

Virtual Museums

So-called virtual museums are bodies of information and images that exist only online. As the bandwith of our computers and the Internet itself increases, so does the sophistication and capacity of virtual museum sites, and therefore so does their educational value. Virtual museums usually take one of the following forms:

As previews of physical museums that are under development. In the mid-1990s, the Experience Music Project launched *EMPLive* which functioned as a virtual museum for several years before the actual site opened in Seattle in 2000. As a virtual museum, *EMPLive* provided views of the institution's growing collections and its ongoing research, as well as access to educational programs related to musical forms and the social history of musical expression in America.

As successors of physical institutions that have closed. The Museum of Sequential Art in Boston ceased operation in 1999. However, it reappeared as an online museum that features regularly changing and curated virtual exhibitions of this form of popular culture. This virtual museum is actively maintained, provides useful educational services, and cultivates links between artists, critics, and enthusiasts.

As gateways to virtual and physical sites. The Virtual Museum of Canada is a long-range collaborative project that combines links to both online and physical cultural resources and collections. The mission and mandate of the VMC is stated on its Web site:

> The *Virtual Museum of Canada* celebrates the stories and treasures that have come to define Canada over the centuries. Here you will find innovative multimedia content that educates, inspires, and fascinates!
>
> This groundbreaking gateway is the result of a strong partnership between Canada's vast museum community and the Department of Canadian Heritage.[1] Spearheading the enterprise is the Canadian Heritage Information Network,[2] a special operating agency of the Department of Canadian Heritage, that for thirty years has enabled the heritage community to benefit from cutting-edge information technologies.
>
> The VMC harnesses the power of the Internet to bring Canada's rich and diverse heritage into our homes, schools, and places of work. This revolutionary medium allows for perspectives and interpretations that are both original and revealing.

Thus, at one level, the VMC is a gateway for users to discover existing museums and heritage materials that may relate to specific areas of interest. In this way the VMC is a powerful multidisciplinary research and teaching tool that can combine the collections and research of institutions in new and insightful ways. For example, a teacher may use VMC links and search engine to compile a comprehensive list of ethnographic First Nations materials from the Royal Ontario Museum in Toronto, the Museum of Man and Nature in Winnipeg, or the Museum of Anthropology in British Columbia—and then take her class in to see them!

The VMC also allows for even more balanced and comprehensive searches by providing access to smaller and more remote institutions. An ethnographic search through VMC might also offer materials from different cultural centers in First Nations communities throughout Canada. Users may be in isolated situations, but through the VMC they can access images, data, and interpretation of their own and others' cultures.

Another function of gateway sites such as the VMC is to provide a forum for virtual exhibitions and educational programs that exist only online. Again, if we view the highlight of the VMC as listed on their Web site:

- More than 7 million people visit the VMC each year
- The Image Gallery features over 420,000 images
- There are more than 150 interactive games
- VMC[3] hosts over 500 *Virtual Exhibits* and *Community Memories Exhibits*

In response to the growing use of the Internet by teachers, the VMC launched the AGORA Learning Centre in the spring of 2007. This initiative is intended to provide educators and learners with an interactive online environment that offers a compilation of learning resources (text, images, video, and multimedia) and tangible outcomes, all created by Canadian institutions.

As Negraponte notes, "bytes are easier to manipulate than atoms." Therefore, projects such as virtual exhibits and community memories exhibits allow more groups and institutions to participate in the VMC or similar virtual institutions, because they are less expensive to set up, distribute, and update.

As with all digital media, the greater access and flexibility has the corresponding challenge of ensuring the accuracy and appropriateness of the content. In the case of the VMC, all content and educational programming is reviewed and refined through a wide-ranging and multidisciplinary peer review process. An evaluation of VMC programs is the subject of a case study in the following chapter by Dr. Barbara Soren.

9.3   CONCLUSION: THE CULTURAL DYNAMICS OF MUSEUM ONLINE LEARNING

Online capacity offers tremendous potential for access, and creative and comprehensive educational programming for museums. However, as the need for extensive peer review at the VMC and guidelines for the digital photography and manipulation of collections indicates, there are definite challenges in this area.

The online world is a very dynamic and fast-changing place where new technologies and new interests by users can force institutions to make changes.

It is essential that museums appreciate the nature of these pressures and respond to them in ways that support their role as sources of enduring meaning, while at the same time communicating to their communities in the most relevant and accessible means possible. The future of online museum learning is bright.

NOTES

1. http://www.pch.gc.ca.
2. http://www.chin.gc.ca.
3. http://www.virtualmuseum.ca.

CHAPTER 10

Audience-Based Measures of Success
Evaluating Museum Learning

Barbara J. Soren

The U.S. Institute of Museum and Library Services (IMLS) describes outcome-based evaluation as a systemic way to determine if a program has achieved its goals. In this type of evaluation, museum staff can ask program partners and other stakeholders, "Why are we offering this program, what do we want to accomplish, and who do we want to benefit from it?" If they want to know if their program is successful, "What will the results look like for the people we served?"[1] Knowing the museum's audiences, their needs and wants, and what programs can do to help them achieve their aims are important.

In a 2001 publication by IMLS, *Perspectives on Outcome-Based Evaluation for Libraries and Museums*, the late Stephen Weil, then Emeritus Senior Scholar for the Center of Education and Museum Studies, Smithsonian Institution, described "two distinct revolutions" in the North American museum. The first revolution during the past fifty years has been a shift in focus from being inwardly oriented on growth, care, study, and display of its collection, to becoming outwardly focused with a range of educational and other services to its visitors and its communities. The second revolution is related to public expectations that a museum experience "will demonstrably enhance the quality of individual lives and/or the well-being of some particular community."[2] For Weil, measuring outcomes are the benefits or changes for individuals or populations during or after participating in program activities.

Weil wrote more specifically about outcome-based evaluation in 2003 when he elaborated on what a museum can learn from its visitors' experiences— "both inside and outside its walls." He explained:

> In evaluating a museum's worthiness, the starting point must be the positive and intended differences that it makes in the lives of the individuals and communities that constitute its target audience. The critical issue is

not how those differences are measured but that such differences must become and remain an institution's central focus. . . . The museum that does not provide an outcome to its community is as socially irresponsible as the business that fails to show a profit. It wastes society's resources.[3]

Weil described the complexity of measuring the impact of museums on their visitors as well as the astonishing diversity of objectives that museums pursue today. This complexity requires "a vast arsenal of richer and more persuasive ways to document and/or demonstrate the myriad and beneficial outcomes"[4] that may occur for individuals and impact communities.

In 2005, Weil took this theme one more step, describing a success/failure matrix to determine the overall performance of a cultural enterprise such as a museum. He outlined four key dimensions for measuring success.

Four key dimensions that define success in museums:[5]

The Matrix	
Purpose	Resources
Effectiveness	Efficiency

Success according to Weil depends on the ability of museum staff to:

1. articulate a clear and significant purpose that is both worthwhile and responsive to an identifiable need of its target audience(s);
2. assemble the resources necessary to achieve that purpose;
3. demonstrate the possession of skills necessary to expend these resources to create and present public programs that achieve the museum's articulated purpose;
4. demonstrate possession of managerial skills necessary to create and present those public programs in as efficient manner as possible.

Weil compared these four key dimensions to a series of hurdles, which must be addressed in sequence. He argued that "care must be taken not to muddle the quantitative measures of efficiency appropriate for evaluating outputs with the qualitative estimates of effectiveness required for evaluating outcomes."[6] Measurement of success must include numbers or quantitative methods, as well as anecdotal or qualitative methods, as noted in the chapters I contributed to Gail Dexter Lord and Barry Lord's *Manual of Museum Planning* (1999) and *Manual of Museum Exhibitions* (2002).

Robert Janes, coeditor of *Looking Reality in the Eye: Museums and Social Responsibility*, was invited to give the 1st Annual Stephen E. Weil Memorial

Lecture at the Mid-Atlantic Association of Museums conference in Baltimore, Maryland, in 2005. In a series of case studies in his book, Janes and G. T. Conaty look at alternatives to current museum practice based on what people visiting museums and their Web sites might want and need.[7] Each case study describes creative and innovative ways to:

- become a socially responsible museum;
- understand that attendance flows from significance, and significance flows from providing meaning and value to one's community;
- create meaning and inspiration in exhibitions, special events, programs, and activities;
- demonstrate a commitment to idealism, intimacy, depth, and interconnectedness as tests of genuineness and quality.

Janes and Conaty define these terms as:

Idealism: Thinking about the ways things could be, and not simply accepting the way things are.

Intimacy: Providing communication and quality of contact in the physical museum and on its Web site.

Depth: Ensuring deep and enduring commitments to the maintenance of human relationships.

Interconnectedness: Making connections between families, organizations, the environment, and the whole of humanity.

In one particularly powerful case study,[8] Ruth Abrams explains how the Lower East Side Tenement Museum in New York has become a *mission-driven museum*. The museum's mission has driven:

- the type of objects exhibited, interpreted, and documented;
- the subject matter focus;
- the primary activities;
- the museum's stakeholders' beliefs and values;
- planning for target audiences for whom programming is of special interest;
- expectations for visitor experiences;
- outreach activities such as the museum's Web site.

10.1 HOW TO DEVELOP AUDIENCE-BASED MEASURES OF SUCCESS

Indicators that demonstrate the success of exhibitions and programs from an audience or visitor perspective are based on a museum's mission and/or mandate related to individuals visiting exhibitions or participating in programs, intended objectives for visitor experiences, and the results or outcomes for people who visit a physical museum or browse a museum's Web site. My article on "The Learning Cultural Organization of the Millennium: Performance Measures and Audience Response" in the *International Journal of Arts Management* (2, no. 2 [2000]: 40–49) explored each of these factors as they are examined again here, and in the case studies in this chapter. The following is an example of an Audience-Based Program Evaluation Template that I have found useful.

AUDIENCE-BASED PROGRAM EVALUATION TEMPLATE

Name of program/event:
Date of program/event/exhibition:
    Date of template completion:
    Dates of subsequent revisions:
    Person completing template and contact information:
Mission/Mandate: [museum's mission/mandate]

Part A—Preparation

Aims/Goals:
[statement of intent, midway in generality between mission/mandate and objectives that describe the purposes of the program/exhibition; for example, target audience, educational expectations]
Evaluation:
[from previous year(s) if a repeat event or refer to past exhibition surveys/evaluations]
Description of exhibition/special event/education program: [please underline which]
[a rich description of your program as if you are promoting your museum to potential funders to sponsor it, encouraging people who have not yet visited to attend, or orienting new board members, staff, or volunteers. This is the beginning of creating a brand identity with target audiences related to your museum's offerings and visitor benefits. Include date event established (if an event), general history, and information about event]
Research materials/Artifact loans:
Conservation issues:
Security:

Technology:
Target group(s):
[who you want to visit the museum, both traditional and nontraditional visitors, for this program, that is, members and current visitors, local communities (ethnic/racial groups, artists/historians, subject matter enthusiasts, novices), tourists, professionals from other communities nationally and internationally, elementary, secondary and postsecondary students and educators, touring and special interest groups, outreach and extension activities to educational and community groups]
Education and public programs:
[connections with the curriculum, involvement of education staff in exhibition or program production, hands-on activities to be incorporated into exhibition or program, special events to occur in conjunction with exhibition or program (talks, meetings, special days)]
Web presence:
Timelines:
[timelines for exhibition or program production]
Objectives for the visitor experience:
[Objectives focus on opportunities that will be provided for the visitor experiencing an exhibition or program, or intentions of museum staff designing an exhibition or program. If objectives are clearly articulated in exhibition and program planning, they should provide a basis for assessing the extent to which an exhibition or program is effective, and ways to improve; specific statements of what individuals will be able to do during their experience in an exhibition or program (e.g., behaviors, performance, problems to solve, emotions, hands-on activities). Objectives might be: to present exhibitions or demonstrations of . . . ; to demonstrate . . . for public audiences; to foster confidence in the viewer's own interpretation and reading of . . . ; to present an exhibition or other public program which offers . . . ; to benefit a broad range of age groups by.]
Outcomes after a visitor experience:
[Outcomes focus on what a visitor who interacts with objects in an exhibition or participates in a program will know or value as a result of that experience, or the result of the visitor's experience at the museum. If outcomes are clearly articulated in exhibition and program planning they should provide indicators for measuring the success of the museum's exhibition program for visitors (e.g., new appreciation, sensitivity, understanding; a strong feeling; wanting to do something, find out more; valuing an idea, topic, person, object). Outcomes may be, for

example: participated in your museum's exhibition/program; asked questions about objects or displays they experienced; contributed a written response; asked for printed material, to be on the mailing list, and/or to participate in a workshop; have increased awareness of the museum's programs.]

Activities for achieving goals, objectives, and outcomes:

Marketing and promotion:

Funding and resources:

Budget:

Facilities for program or exhibition:

Community linkages:

Location:

Leadership and staffing:

[full-time, part-time, volunteer]

Evaluation Tools/Methods/Strategies:

Program success indicators [directly linked to achieving outcomes]: [What are the signs or evidence indicating to museum staff that visitors have experienced what was expected during their visit or participation? What indications are there that individuals may use or apply knowledge gained, do something to learn more, or value their experience after they leave the museum? Generally, these indicators can serve as benchmarks to compare the success of your museum's program from year to year.]

Quantitative outputs [number of invitations sent and accepted, number of visitors attending opening, tickets sold, number of people attending special event, cars parked, number of people booking tours or special programs, seats filled in theater, requests for other exhibitions, number of group tours, sales from the gift shop]

Qualitative indicators [what was learned from the exhibition, behaviors that changed as a result of the experience, visitor comments in guest book or on comment cards, observations compiled as a result of interviews with visitors]

Part B—Evaluation/Impact

Weather:

Other community events or factors:

Total Attendance:

Estimated expenditures: **Estimated revenue**:

Actual Expenditures:

Item	Cost	Comments
	Total:	

Actual Revenues:

Item	Revenue	Comments
Gift Shop Sales		
Donations		
Admissions		

Praise/constructive criticism for the coordinator/staff/volunteers:

Critical Assessment of the Program/Event:

Please evaluate the level of staff and volunteer involvement, the success of the program/event, and make recommendations for future improvement including a recommendation not to repeat if applicable.

10.2 OBJECTIVES AND OUTCOMES FOR VISITOR EXPERIENCES

Objectives focus on opportunities that will be provided for visitors experiencing an exhibition or program in a physical museum, or browsing the museum's Web site. If objectives are clearly articulated in exhibition and program planning, they should provide a basis for assessing the extent to which an exhibition or program is effective, and ways to improve. *Objectives are specific statements of what individuals will be able to do during their experience in an exhibition or program (e.g., behaviors, performance, problems to solve, emotions, hands-on activities, and/or interactions with live interpretation).*

How can museum staff evaluate if they are achieving the objectives they have articulated for the exhibition or public program to ensure continuous improvement? They might try to evaluate visitor experience through, for example:

- Verbal feedback and written comments in a comment book on the success of the exhibition or program
- A questionnaire to determine:
  - where audiences are coming from
  - individuals' interests, expectations, and previous exposure to subject matter
  - how they heard about the museum or exhibition
  - how many times they have visited
  - what their experience was of the exhibition or program
  - what their needs are in the museum
  - what other services/interpretive aids they would like or would use in conjunction with the exhibitions to enrich their viewing experience
  - what they might do as a result of their experience
- Staff and volunteer observations of visitor response to exhibitions and programs
- An annual meeting with local teachers, educators, and related instructors who have experienced the exhibition or program to discuss outcomes of the educational program, and ways to continue to improve these services
- Meetings with other community group leaders/instructors to develop ways to identify and reach new audiences, and to strive to develop appropriate interpretive activities to meet their needs.

Outcomes focus on what a visitor who interacts with objects in an exhibition or participates in a program will know, do, or value as a result of that experience, or the result of the museum visitor's on-site or online experience. If outcomes are clearly articulated in exhibition and program planning they should provide indicators for measuring the success of the museum's exhibition program for visitors.

What are signs or evidence indicating to museum staff that visitors have experienced what was expected during their experience in an exhibition or participation in a program? What indications are there that individuals may use or apply knowledge gained, do something to learn more, or value their experience after they leave the museum? Generally, these indicators can serve as benchmarks to compare the success of a museum's learning programs from year to year. They can help staff working across departments collaborate on how the museum can better reach visitors and program participants.

Some *quantitative indicators* that can measure success include the number of:

- Invitations/handouts printed and distributed for each program (mailed, distributed to schools, on hand at the gallery, archival)
- Visitors attending exhibition openings or program debuts
- People attending auditorium lectures or gallery talks
- Visitors attending exhibitions or participating in programs
- Advanced group bookings for gallery tours annually and actual annual bookings
- Hands-on workshops annually for school groups in conjunction with tours
- Requests to circulate exhibitions originated by the museum
- The extent and quality of the media coverage of museum programming and the audiences reached through these media
- The level of support the museum receives and from whom, acknowledging the merit and value of the museum's activities (e.g., demonstrated by both increases in annual activity grants and comments from peer assessment juries).

However, to effectively evaluate exhibitions and programs and determine how successful they are, qualitative measures are equally as important as quantitative measures. Some of the *qualitative indicators* of success can include:

- A new appreciation, sensitivity, or understanding
- A strong feeling
- A valuing of an idea, topic, person, and object
- A meaningful experience related to specific physical or digital objects, the creators or owners of the objects, or different interpretations of the objects
- New self-learning or learning about others during a visit
- A curiosity to find out more (e.g., by buying a related book or object in the museum's gift store, sharing an experience with friends and family, returning to the museum, visiting the museum's Web site, donating an object to the museum, or visiting a related museum).

In two of my own case studies—one about visitor experiences at four physical museums, the other about user experiences planned for eight museum Web sites—I used some ideas from Weil, Janes, and Conaty to think about how to measure success from an audience perspective. I used a combination of qualitative and quantitative strategies to provide multiple perspectives for understanding the visitor experience. Both strategies are needed to evaluate the effectiveness of exhibitions and programs, and are useful for finding indicators of success for visitor experiences. These case studies are provided here to complete this chapter.

DEMYSTIFYING AND DESTIGMATIZING PERFORMANCE MEASURES AT FOUR ONTARIO MUSEUMS

Barbara J. Soren

During 2002–2003 a partnership of four small- to medium-sized museums representing archives, a history museum, a city collection, a historic site, and a living history site in southern Ontario, Canada, embarked on a project to implement a system of audience-based performance measures. The partners were Wellington County Museum and Archives, the City of Waterloo's Heritage Collection, Doon Heritage Crossroads, and the City of Guelph's museums. The project was financed by the Museums Assistance Program of the Department of Canadian Heritage and municipal employers. Key components of the project were to be collaboration, learning from one another, and professional training. Important outcomes were:

improved tracking of statistical information and reporting,
the development of descriptive templates for exhibitions and special events,
more skill at using performance measures in the daily work lives of staff
    and planning cycles,
demystifying and destigmatizing "performance measures."

During monthly workshops, the partners developed a master audience-based program evaluation template that blended generic performance measures categories and the Program Evaluation Form being used by staff at Guelph Museums that is included in this chapter. Staff at each museum then selected a special event, exhibition, or program and evolved a template specific to that activity. The group also looked at each museum's visitor statistics, visitor surveys, and surveys specific to exhibitions and programs, and took Microsoft Excel training workshops to improve their reporting about visitors. They decided which questions were most important to ask and provided the most meaningful information on the Program Evaluation Forms (e.g., for school, holiday, and summer programs). Finally, the group considered how staff at each partner museum could use their audience-based performance measures work as a benchmark, comparing visitor response and behaviors during 2002–2003 with 2003–2004. The following summary highlights the nature of activities at each of the partner museums and demonstrates the value of the audience-based performance measures project across the four municipal and community museums.

WELLINGTON COUNTY MUSEUM AND ARCHIVES

The Wellington County Museum and Archives wanted to implement a system of performance measures at their sites using standard templates that could be altered to fit their individual site-specific program and statistical needs. For Director Bonnie Callen the project was two-pronged. Museum staff wanted to develop templates to help program and exhibition staff better plan and evaluate what the museum offers its visiting public, and to create a more accurate and versatile database system for the statistical tracking of visitor attendance. Basically, they wanted to "wow" their board, public, and themselves with pie charts and graphs instead of the old-fashioned single column listing month-by-month totals. They knew intuitively that to measure their performance in delivering quality programs and services, they had to learn how to track and identify the makeup of the museum's clientele.

The curatorial staff at the Wellington County Museum and Archives worked with the audience-based performance measures template in the early stages of a new permanent exhibition, *First Story: The Neutrals of Wellington County*, which opened in June 2003. The curator was more than willing to utilize the form because it allowed her the opportunity to recon-

Figure 10.1. The Longhouse Gallery, Wellington County Museum and Archives.

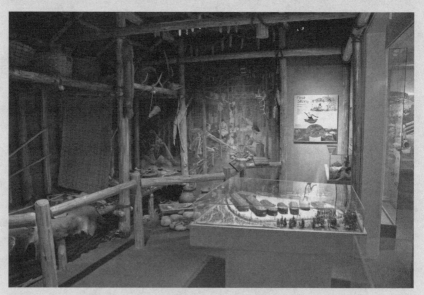

COURTESY OF WELLINGTON COUNTY MUSEUM AND ARCHIVES.

firm on paper the overall aims and goals of this exhibition, rationalizing why the theme was chosen, describing in detail her vision of the finished product, and identifying target groups and media opportunities. The form was helpful to all the curatorial design team working on this gallery. It also helped the museum activities programmer who needed to know what was being planned in order that she could begin her curriculum-based programming. Since the opening, staff has been tracking the exhibition's success by examining improvement in the various success indicators that had been projected on the audience-based Program Evaluation Form in the early stage of exhibition development.

Callen feels that exhibition and program templates have proven to be useful to her staff, improving the quality of what the museum offers its publics. From the outset, curatorial and program staff recognized the value of the performance measures project. By making a conscientious effort to keep them informed and consulting them along the way, Callen found it easy to garner and maintain their support. *The key to implementing an effective performance measures system at a museum site is to respect the input of staff because it is based on their knowledge and experience.* If all the staff is not committed, consistency in planning, evaluating, and tracking will be difficult to attain.

Another vital part of measuring performance in a museum setting is developing a consistent database system for the tracking and reporting of attendance. Off-site Excel training was an excellent way for the staff to focus on the program, ask questions relevant to their own sites, and feel confident in adopting new templates for tracking attendance. The training sessions in Excel brought about a whole new confidence and enthusiasm for the performance measures project.

CITY OF WATERLOO'S HERITAGE COLLECTION

As a "team of one," the curator of the City of Waterloo's Heritage Collection, Anne Chafe, relies on contract staff and volunteers to assist with the development of exhibitions and programs that are offered in various city-owned facilities such as the Canadian Clay and Glass Gallery.

A Business Measurement Project for the City of Waterloo was precipitated by the province's introduction of the use of performance measures for municipal services in March 2001. Those measures were designed to enhance accountability to the local taxpayer and to act as service improvement tools. Throughout this city project, Chafe found it difficult to apply the measurements for the programs offered by her colleagues to those developed by the city's heritage resources unit. The audience-based performance measures project provided the focus she was looking for in measuring the success of the city's heritage programs and exhibitions.

Chafe was particularly interested in learning how performance measurement could assist her in maximizing limited financial and staff resources in order to provide quality programs. Working in a municipal climate of accountability, she was also looking for a way to expand the view within her organization of the value of the city's heritage programs. She wanted to communicate the impact of their programs in a meaningful way, other than by attendance numbers and budget figures.

Chafe discovered that embarking on performance measurement requires an extensive commitment of time, and recognized that she could not possibly measure every program. She decided for this project to concentrate on a 1,000-square-foot exhibition, *Charlie Voelker: Architectural Designer, Alderman, and Visionary*. While the commitment of time was extensive, the benefits of conducting audience-based performance measurement for this exhibition were many, particularly given that there is only one person in this Waterloo example who is ultimately responsible for the development, installation, and promotion of an exhibition project.

Benefits included, for instance:

- Articulating the aims, objectives, and outcomes of the exhibition, which provided focus for the project and clarity of communication and thinking.
- Providing direction for determining the exhibition's content by identifying specific outcomes for the exhibition, and the relationship between the desired outcomes and the visitor experiences needed to lead to these outcomes.
- Creating a succinct description of the exhibition up front, which was a time saver in the end as the information was easily transferable for use in media, promotional, and sponsorship material.
- Identifying target groups, which assisted in the effective distribution of promotional material and directed the development of the media release content (e.g., because Chafe had identified families with children as a target group, she made sure that the media release highlighted the activities available for this audience).
- Sharing the completed form with contract staff, which ensured that they also had a clear vision of what the exhibition was attempting to achieve.

For Chafe, the most beneficial part of the process was the articulation of activities and evaluation tools for achieving goals, objectives, and outcomes. However, it also proved to be the most challenging for Chafe to follow through on, due primarily to time constraints. The planned publication and one of the two workshops could not be completed in time for the exhibition. She was also overly ambitious with the identification of her evaluation tools. The outcomes she had identified required a variety of evaluation methods. Inspired by the impressive Excel charts prepared by Guelph Museums, she had hoped to develop an exit questionnaire and similarly chart the results. As the opening date for the exhibition drew near, this kept getting pushed to the bottom of the "to do" list and was never done, leaving a hole in the evaluation process.

However, it was rewarding to see during the review and the critical assessment portion of the process that most of the objectives for the exhibition had been met. Documenting these successes in this format has proven to be a valuable tool. Chafe has been able to justify to her manager, who does not have a background in museum work, the resources (both staff and financial) needed for annual exhibitions. Working in an ever-increasingly competitive environment for public funds to provide municipal services, the performance measurement system has assisted her in securing additional contract staffing resources for exhibition activity.

Based on the success of this performance measures activity, she plans on continuing to develop performance measures for Waterloo's annual exhibitions, and to initiate their use for new programs. She also better understands that doing this requires a commitment for action and improvement and a willingness to learn from past experiences. All those who have worked or are working in one-person or similar small-staff museums can identify with her.

DOON HERITAGE CROSSROADS

Doon Heritage Crossroads, a living history museum in Kitchener, Ontario, recreating a rural village and two farms to the year 1914, is located on sixty acres of environmentally sensitive forest, marsh, and farmland. The institution also serves as the collecting and preservation facility for a regional history collection, and is owned and operated by the Regional Municipality of Waterloo.

Tom Reitz, manager/curator of Doon Heritage Crossroads, found that the Evaluating and Achieving through Performance Measures project helped museum staff discover that they have many more quantitative measures than their annual attendance figures, and that they do have some existing qualitative measures. Doon Heritage Crossroads was initially daunted by the language of the world of evaluation, because museum staff had no formal training or experience in evaluation.

Figure 10.2. Vistitors to the Dry Goods and Grocery Store at Doon Heritage Crossroads Experience the Holiday Season of 1914 during the Museum's *Country Christmas* Event held each December

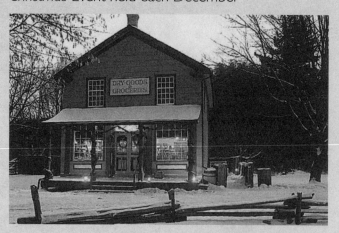

COURTESY OF DOON HERITAGE CROSSROADS.

At Doon, staff chose their *Country Christmas* event for consideration as part of the audience-based program evaluation project for several reasons. First and foremost it was opportune, as the event was one of the last of the museum's eight-month season schedule, and so fit with the evaluation project timeline. More importantly, however, *Country Christmas* was a repeat event, which in December of 2002 was about to take on a potentially new focus with a change in audience demographics.

Country Christmas is one of several seasonal events that the living history museum presents in the month of December. The living history village buildings are decorated for the Christmas season and special highlights for these event afternoons include horse-drawn wagon rides, carol singing in the village's church, and a visit by Father Christmas. Previous years' attendance at the event varied, but the staff anticipated that approximately 250 to 300 people would visit the Heritage Crossroads each Sunday.

In the fall of 2002, well in advance of the start of seasonal Christmas programming, the museum was approached by the Region of Waterloo's Home Child Care Division, which provides a flexible type of licensed care and is especially suited to families who work shifts or have irregular hours of employment. The division requested complementary passes to the museum for its clients.

Also in 2002, Doon Heritage Crossroads was writing new mission and vision statements for the village. Museum mission statements have traditionally focused on the five pillars of museum functions: to collect, educate, interpret, preserve, and research. Doon Heritage Crossroads' new mission and vision suggest a "higher" mission for the museum. The proposed vision read:

> "Doon Heritage Crossroads enriches the quality of life in the Region of Waterloo. Doon Heritage Crossroads makes better Canadian citizens by increasing knowledge of what Canada is, has been, and will be."

The proposed mission also includes a number of guiding principles. One of these principles relates to the concept of community:

> "Doon Heritage Crossroads has a unique opportunity to enrich the quality of life in our own community and lives of individuals in the many communities Doon Heritage Crossroads serves. Doon Heritage Crossroads does this by being inclusive in our programs and activities, reaching out to the community with our services and programs, serving as a center for community gatherings, and serving as a bridge between different communities and cultural groups."

The inclusion of statements in the proposed mission regarding the museum's role in the community is reflective of an emerging trend in museums not just to reflect communities in their exhibitions and programs, but also to ensure that the museum is an active, participatory institution in the life of a community. The emphasis on community is also reflected in changes to the Community Museum Standards, reintroduced in 2000 by the Ontario Ministry of Culture, the granting and policy authority for the Ontario provincial government.

It was clear that honoring the request for complimentary admission passes from the Region of Waterloo's Home Child Care program was in concert with the institution's new mission, and more specifically celebrates and affirms the museum's role in the community. Doon Heritage Crossroads saw the audience-based performance measures project as an excellent opportunity to test the new effectiveness of the proposed vision and mission, to evaluate the impact (if any) of honoring the request by Home Child Care, and to get a head start on implementing the Community Standard that would be required by the government in 2005.

The audience-based Program Evaluation Form for *Country Christmas* pointed out the success of the event and the impact of the distribution of the complementary admission passes. Staff distributed 1,300 complementary passes, and 378 of these admission passes were redeemed (29 percent of the coupons available). Although Doon Heritage Crossroads did not complete a survey of visitors attending *Country Christmas*, Reitz felt it was fair to assume that most if not all of the 378 individuals who entered the village using a complementary admission pass would not have visited otherwise. On each of the two Sundays for which passes were distributed, the total visitation was approximately doubled by complementary pass holders.

The evaluation template indicated what the staff believed was a successful win-win endeavor. The *Country Christmas* event would have occurred regardless of the distribution of complementary admission passes. By offering these passes, the museum was able to meet its newly written mission statement's guiding principles to be inclusive in their programs and reach out to the community with their services and programs.

The museum is not able to quantify beyond attendance figures the potential qualitative impact these complementary admission passes may have in the future on the lives of those who used them. Reitz believes, however, that opportunities such as these demonstrate how Doon Heritage Crossroads enriches the quality of life in the Region of Waterloo.

CITY OF GUELPH MUSEUMS

The director of Guelph Museums and his staff were versed in both the terminology and practices of performance measures, since a system was already being used for special event planning, exhibitions, and attendance tracking. Staff made some adjustments to Education Program Evaluation Forms and attendance tracking as a result of this project, but Laurence Grant, director at the time, focused on using the audience-based program evaluation template for an exhibition called *The Neighborhood Store*.

This community-based exhibition was about the history of neighborhood or corner stores from the mid-nineteenth century up to the present day, and included a section of photographs by a contemporary Guelph photographer. The exhibition spoke to the changing ethnocultural ownership of neighborhood stores and the struggle with the big chains in maintaining a viable share of the market. There was a hands-on play store for children within the exhibition.

Grant found the template very useful in thinking through the process of preparing for the exhibition. Discussions with museum staff and project partners helped him to come up with ideas that genuinely improved the final exhibition product. For the director, the form was ultimately a very

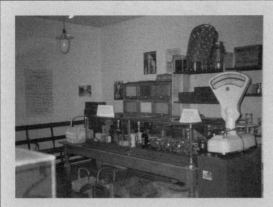

Figure 10.3. Hands-on Store in the Guelph Civic Museum exhibit *The Neighborhood Store* COURTESY OF THE GUELPH CIVIC MUSEUM.

good communications tool with curatorial and education staff, and a time saver. One "thought and planned" first and then "did," he observed. *It helped Grant ensure, for example, that education staff had an opportunity to become involved in the development of an educational use of the exhibition from the beginning and not just at the end, as is too frequently the case.*

The audience-based program evaluation template for the exhibition was in constant evolution and changed considerably during the exhibition development process and even after the exhibition had opened. Description and Research Materials sections helped to define the focus of the exhibition and sources of materials. In his experience with Guelph Museums' staff, Grant found that people have the most trouble with differentiating sections labeled Objectives and Outcomes. A Leadership and Staffing section was very important for everyone to understand their roles in this team-based project.

Staff returned to the Evaluation Tools section following the close of the exhibition. This section of the template suggests that the evaluation form can have a life far beyond its initial composition. Guelph Museums also added an Impacts section, which is very important for follow-up. The template was most useful in enabling Guelph Museums' staff to improve events and exhibitions through the Impacts section. Prior to a repeat event, they could use the past year's form to look at staff comments, and to improve board fundraising projects. It is very important to have down in words what the goals of the project are and how staff will know if it has been successful. Staff at Guelph Museums have continued to use parts of the template and to work toward the goals of this most worthwhile project.

The museum professionals in this partnership have made very important contributions to their local and regional communities, as well as provincial and national museum associations. Our monthly workshops helped the group better understand the important contributions that community museums make to their local neighborhoods. The project also demonstrated how museums can work together to develop and market meaningful programs across a region. Each museum now has a better sense of how important audience-based performance measures can be for measuring the success of their exhibitions, special events, and programs, and the staff has tools for reporting visitor responses to stakeholders and funding agencies statistically and anecdotally.

RESEARCH ON "QUALITY" IN ONLINE EXPERIENCES FOR MUSEUM USERS OF THE CANADIAN HERITAGE INFORMATION NETWORK AND THE VIRTUAL MUSEUM OF CANADA

Barbara J. Soren

"Quality" in online museum experiences depends, in part, on what motivates individuals to search for and browse a museum Web site. What engages them to explore the site more deeply? What helps them to better understand the online content after their online experience? The goals of the Canadian Heritage Information Network (CHIN) research project on *"Quality" in Online Experiences for Museum Users* (http://www.chin.gc.ca/English/Digital_Content/Research_Quality/index.html) were:

- to ensure consistency through the content and interface of the Virtual Museum of Canada (VMC) (http://www.virtualmuseum.ca/English/index_flash.html),
- to determine what factors define "quality" in online museum projects,
- and to consider how to measure this quality through a thorough analysis of existing online museum products in the VMC portal.

During semistructured telephone and in-person conversational interviews with project managers and multimedia developers, I explored successes and challenges in developing products and potential best practices for producing quality in online experiences for Virtual Museum of Canada users.

Expectations for user engagement, objectives, outcomes, and success indicators were important factors at the outset of the project. Critical factors during and after Web site development included the needs of intended and other interested audiences, and opportunities for reflection and evaluation following the launch of the product. Finally, with CHIN staff I considered how to build an exhibit that meets partners' interests and changing needs, and the factors that contribute to a project's lasting impact.

ONLINE AUDIENCE-BASED MEASURES OF SUCCESS

In consultation with project managers, I analyzed a cross-section of seven VMC virtual exhibitions and one interactive game, ranging from early exhibits created and developed in 1997 and launched in 1998, to a virtual exhibit developed in 2003 and launched in 2004.

Five of the virtual exhibits were *executively produced* with CHIN project managers directly involved in creation, development, production, and translation. Project managers worked closely with the multimedia developer and as many as ten to fifteen international partners on projects.

Haida Spirits of the Sea: http://www.virtualmuseum.ca/Exhibitions/Haida/index.html, launched in 1998, invites discovery of the Queen Charlotte Islands and the Haida Gwaii people's profound relationship with the sea.

Butterflies North and South: http://www.virtualmuseum.ca/Exhibitions/Butterflies/index.html, launched in 1999, allows users to identify butterflies and moths, teaches how to watch and attract butterflies and how to protect their habitat, and offers links to more related information.

Staying in Tune: http://www.virtualmuseum.ca/Exhibitions/Instruments/index.html, launched in 1999, enables users to discover traditional Francophone musical instruments and the people who invented the instruments.

Panoramas: The North American Landscape in Art: http://www.virtualmuseum.ca/Exhibitions/Landscapes, launched in 2001, focuses on the North American landscape in art and has four themes: evolving, social, mythic, and personal landscapes.

Perspectives: Women Artists in North America: http://www.virtualmuseum.ca/Exhibitions/Perspectives/index.html, launched in 2002, celebrates from historical, modern, and contemporary art perspectives, and across cultures and periods, the important contributions of women artists from Canada, Mexico, and the United States.

CHIN-commissioned virtual exhibits were developed with themes related to the humanities, history, ethnology, and the natural sciences. Museums that had already researched and developed ideas for an exhibition became partners on commissioned projects. The Museums Advisor from the Government of Yukon Heritage Branch was the project manager for the two commissioned virtual exhibits, launched in 2001, included in the research sample:

Explore Herschel Island!: http://www.virtualmuseum.ca/Exhibitions/Herschel/English/menu.html introduces users to an island off the Yukon North Slope in the Beaufort Sea. The island was home to ancestors of the Arctic people, and a landmark and sanctuary for those traveling and working in the Western Arctic.

Yukon Photographers: http://www.virtualmuseum.ca/Exhibitions/Goldrushphoto/02english/02intro.html features historical photographs taken just before, during, and after the Gold Rush by people visiting Yukon.

The *interactive game* included in the research was *Safe Trax*: http://www.virtualmuseum.ca/Exhibitions/Rail/english/index.html, launched in

January 2003 (on the site, the copyright is 2002) and marketed with a contest on the Sympatico portal. It aims to teach youth about train safety by engaging them in a Flash-based game that guides two imaginary youngsters through train-related territory. The multimedia developer tried to translate research and content into an experience that would be attractive for the targeted 13- to 15-year-old user.

THE INTERVIEW PROCESS

Key questions that CHIN project managers and multimedia developers considered during the semistructured conversational interviews included:

- Types of interaction that users would have with the VMC product
- Strategies for engaging online visitors
- Models or frameworks for creating, developing, and producing VMC products
- Successes related to online user experiences
- Challenges or obstacles to developing a product
- Best practices or considerations from the development and production processes of VMC products that successfully provide quality online experiences.

CHIN project managers and multimedia developers talked about the multiple, unique ways that development teams expected users to interact with their VMC products:

Share or Obtain Information: Users feel that the information on this type of site is accurate, authoritative, reliable, and comprehensive. For instance, *Haida Spirits of the Sea* helps to raise consciousness about the Haida as a living culture. *Butterflies North and South* identifies butterflies and moths found in users' backyards.

Learn and Experience: Browsing this kind of site, users have the feeling that the experience is interesting and story-like. It invites responses of "Wow!" and promotes interaction and serendipity (i.e., the user feels fortunate to have found the exhibition) when users discover new things. For example, both *Panoramas* and *Perspectives* offer content based on the user's interests, providing an element of surprise, giving options, and dynamically presenting works based on a user's choices.

Communicate: Enabling online social communication, chat groups, and discussions with a "many to many" connection typify exhibits intended to communicate. For *Staying in Tune*, during the development process, young curators shared their impressions of working with the musical instruments

Figure 10.4. Butterflies North and South

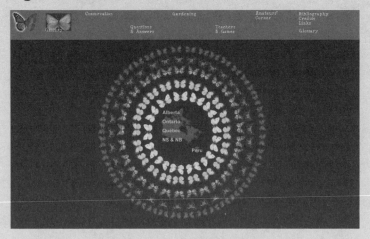

COURTESY OF CANADIAN HERITAGE INFORMATION NETWORK (CHIN).

Figure 10.5. Haida Spirits of the Sea

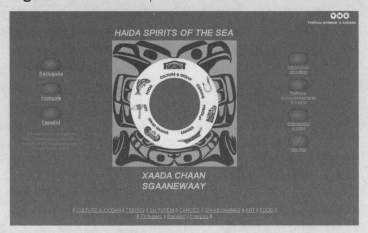

COURTESY OF CANADIAN HERITAGE INFORMATION NETWORK (CHIN).

on the site. (The example does not carry forward to the public's possibility for social communication.)

Experiment: Through experimentation users can find things that are surprising, complex, and challenging, and that promote action. While developing *Explore Herschel Island* and *Yukon Photographers*, production teams continually experimented to see what did and did not work (e.g., colors, a prologue, music and sound to evoke feeling, and improved navigation).

Figure 10.6. Yukon Photographers

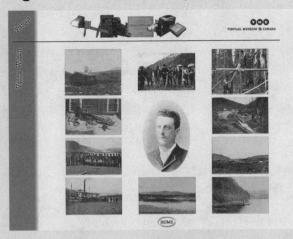

COURTESY OF CANADIAN HERITAGE INFORMATION NETWORK (CHIN).

Explore a Database: A database offers access to collection information through digital images, textual descriptions, catalogs, archives, audio, and video clips. *Panoramas* and *Perspectives* provide database collections that enable users to learn about their unique interests as they move through each exhibition.

Exchange Ideas: An online exhibition for exchanging ideas allows users to establish and create a network or a forum among users, or between museum experts and users. It allows them to discuss and share, and to build a virtual community or a means of creating links between communities. E-mail listserves with groups of people who have common interests allow the sharing of information on *Explore Herschel Island!* and *Yukon Photographers.* Also, *Panoramas* and *Perspectives* provided opportunities for partners in Canada, the United States, and Mexico to exchange ideas during the creation and development process. Partners could see what was different about each, what was common, and learn about themselves through their contact with others. Curators exchanged ideas, thereby creating new ones. Users could appreciate the environment around them and see the conceptual landscape with different eyes.

Experience-Rich Resources: An online exhibition can provide users with resources that are rich in content, images, and variety. Both *Panoramas* and *Perspectives* integrate multimedia in resource-rich exhibits and enable users to enjoy all the elements of the exhibition using noninvasive plug-ins. *Explore Herschel Island!* and *Yukon Photographers* offer rich content, images, and variety to engage users on different levels.

Critical Response and Creative Process: An online exhibition that invites response and creativity provides users with opportunities to respond critically to online content, and to participate in a creative process. For example, putting the responses of critics, art celebrities, or others on the Web and inviting the user to also become a critic gives individuals the opportunity to publish and have a voice. Providing creative, conceptual tools that let users create and post content facilitates the creative process and inspires users.

PLANS TO ENGAGE USERS AND MEASURES OF SUCCESS

Interviews provided insights as to how project managers at CHIN, multimedia developers, and partner heritage organizations planned to engage users. The interviews also made it clear why there may be more traffic for some VMC products, and why users might spend more time browsing some exhibits.

Strategies for Engaging Online Users

Interviews highlighted specific strategies that teams used for engaging online users across the eight VMC products. In discussions of these strategies, a number of complex issues surfaced, such as market analysis, usability and accessibility, expectations of users from different age segments, user-driven content, human-computer interaction, interface design, and the use of narratives and stories.

Models or Frameworks for Producing VMC Products

Different models or frameworks guided the development, production, and project management of individual VMC products:

- A more traditional model provided users with information in layers, in contrast to a more constructivist approach, which helped targeted users build meaningful experiences for themselves.
- Developing a theme, project plan, calendar, and the various objectives to be reached was critical.
- On larger international projects, partners from heritage organizations brought a wealth of input and content to the project, and were often

selected because they had already completed research related to the topic or theme for the VMC product.

The more constructivist approach is outlined in my article, "Constructing Meaning and Online Museum User Experience" in CHIN's *Creating and Managing Digital Content Tip Sheet* (2004), available online at http://www.chin.gc.ca/English/Digital_Content/Tip_Sheets/constructivism.html.

Outcomes and Success Indicators for Users and Partner Heritage Organizations

For each project, multimedia developers thought about outcomes and success indicators for users. For instance, they considered how best to interest users in the design of the online exhibition, and create new and novel experiences for users through the exhibit architecture and content structure. The harmony of working together to produce unique and powerful online products with different contents seemed to be a learning experience for partner heritage organizations. The experience of working on online products can also help curators and museum educators in the development of exhibitions and other programs for visitors to their physical museum.

Successes of Web Sites for Online Users

Interviews also enabled project managers and multimedia developers to reflect on and evaluate both successes of their Web sites for online users and challenges they encountered during the development and production process. Successful Web sites:

- Are sensitive to the needs of their users, and work from the user's perspective
- Promote good relationships with multimedia companies who work with leading edge technologies, as well as with students and interns
- Involve good working relationships with high quality museum and heritage organization partners, nationally and internationally
- Have excellent quality of content and images, different language versions, marketing to regions across Canada, and are linked to the promotion of tourism to these areas
- Provide opportunities for the building of technical capacity in Canadian museums and heritage organizations.

Challenges and Obstacles in Development and Production Processes

The challenges and obstacles encountered in the development and production processes for the sample of VMC products were:

- Developing and producing a quality site within a limited time frame
- Communication infrastructure
- Consensus-building
- Writing for the Web rather than a physical exhibition
- Incorporating the newest technologies with different Canadian, as opposed to international, accessibility standards.

Potential Best Practices in Providing Quality Online Experiences

Insights into potential best practices for developing and producing VMC products emerged from the question: When VMC products are successful in providing quality online experiences, what should be the main considerations in the development process? Based on the interview sample, the best practices that seemed most important to project managers and multimedia developers included:

- Common vision, clear goals and objectives, consistency, and a solid structure
- Topics chosen that have clear and simple, yet emotional and powerful stories
- Dedicated individuals with a love and passion for the product they are developing, and collaborative partnerships
- Adequate time and budget to develop as high a quality product as possible
- Navigation and access to provide a clear organization of information and images
- Thinking in a virtual rather than physical medium
- Products that are user-focused, useful, and used by online visitors
- Leading edge technology sympathetic to the content and messages of partners
- Production process considerations that ensure accessibility.

Finally, in order to maintain sites and follow-up with partners after the launch of a site, there should be evaluation of the process, team, user statistics, and feedback messages. Flexibility in design makes it possible to revise content based on feedback from partners and users. Measuring the success of an online project can build on learning for future collaborative projects, and help partner heritage organizations and museums and multi-media companies share lessons learned.

10.3 THE VALUE OF AUDIENCE-BASED MEASURES OF SUCCESS

At the end of the audience-based performance measures project, the group concluded that it is probably fair to assume that most museums, large and small, know that evaluation is a good thing. However, since most museum workers have little experience with evaluation, it becomes one more task to find time for among cataloguing projects, preparing tours, event planning, and writing media releases. If they have not been involved in anything more than counting bodies through the turnstiles, contemplating formal evaluation of exhibitions, programs, events, or general operation can be very intimidating.

Each museum partner articulated the following important lessons learned from the audience-based program evaluation:

- Early "buy in" from core museum staff is essential to institute performance measures at a museum site. Once staff "buy in" and audience-based performance measures templates are in place, measuring performance should be easy.
- While the time commitment required for this performance measurement system can present challenges for smaller museum operations, the effort is well worth it. With limited resources, it is important when embarking on this exercise to identify what is important to measure, attempting to measure "key things, not all things," and asking two questions: "What would museum staff like to improve?" and "How do we measure up?"
- To reap benefits from the performance measures system, it is crucial to be prepared to report and share the results in a consistent format with stakeholders, such as board, staff, members, volunteers, and funders.
- Museum staff must be prepared to take action toward improvement and to plan for future measurement activities in order for performance measurement to be a worthwhile investment of scarce resources and time.
- Audience-based performance evaluation is an effective planning tool, and is also a crucial communication tool. It enables the entire team to know what is going on in other people's heads as museum staff prepare for events or programs.

The research into quality in online museum user experiences highlighted a range of audience-based measures of success and best practices that could help to inform the development of other museum Web sites. Users are becoming increasingly sophisticated and expect that Web developers are using and exploiting the latest technologies. Successful sites should be "living, breathing repositories," as one multimedia developer interviewed for this research commented, because they evolve, changing in content and interpretation over time, giving users a reason to revisit and continue to learn from the exhibit.

The project managers in the Canadian Heritage Information Network who invited me to conduct the research on quality in online experiences for museum users provided their most generous support throughout the project, and produced a high-quality online and print publication. The print copy of the report can be ordered from http://www.chin.gc.ca/English/Publications/research_quality.html.

NOTES

1. K. Motylewski and C. Horn, *Outcome-Based Evaluation* (Washington, D.C.: The Institute of Museum and Library Services, 2002).

2. S. E. Weil, "Transformed from a Cemetery of Bric-a-Brac," in *Perspectives on Outcome-Based Evaluation for Libraries and Museums* (Washington, D.C.: The Institute of Museum and Library Services, 2001), p. 6.

3. S. E. Weil, "Beyond Big and Awesome: Outcome-Based Evaluation," *Museum News* 82, no. 6 (2003): 42–43.

4. Ibid., p.53.

5. S. E. Weil, "A Success/Failure Matrix for Museums," *Museum News* 84, no. 1 (2005): 37.

6. Ibid., p. 39.

7. R. Janes and G. T. Conaty, eds., *Looking Reality in the Eye: Museums and Social Responsibility* (Calgary: University of Calgary Press and Museums Association of Saskatchewan, 2005).

8. R. J. Abrams, "History Is as History Does: The Evolution of a Mission-Driven Museum," in R. Janes and G. T. Conaty, eds., *Looking Reality in the Eye: Museums and Social Responsibility* (Calgary: University of Calgary Press and Museums Association of Saskatchewan, 2005), pp. 19–42.

CHAPTER 11

Marketing Museum Learning

Amy Kaufman

"A successful education program depends on more than just a star lecturer or great publicity. It can only be achieved by communication and cooperation between the education and public relations departments."[1]

With fierce competition from the growing cultural sector and a variety of other leisure activities, from eating out to satellite television, museum educators are looking for the most effective and innovative ways to get the word out. Marketing museum learning is itself a part of the museum learning process, because learning in museums—indeed, all informal learning—depends first and foremost on the learner's prior interest and motivation. Good marketing informs prior interest and inspires motivation.

The first section of this chapter touches on a few current trends that will help educators to see the market for programs in a new light. The other sections provide a framework for building a comprehensive strategy to approach marketing for museum learning programs. The chapter concludes with some suggestions for implementation and tracking results.

11.1 TRENDS AFFECTING THE MARKETING OF MUSEUM LEARNING

In the early twenty-first century, four key trends are currently shaping the marketplace and are expected to inform future strategic explorations and decisions:

1. As world populations grow and change, the demographic composition is changing, highlighting the need for both multigenerational and multicultural programming.

    The United States is a prime example of a country that is undergoing major demographic shifts, as minority populations are growing rapidly and Americans are living longer than ever. The same is true of Canada and Western Europe. In China, the focus is on movement from the countryside to the cities. In many other countries interregional if not international migration is occurring. Educators must keep local patterns in mind, taking into consideration current conditions, as well as strategies to cultivate the next generation as museum learners.

2. Museums are becoming an increasingly important educational tool and are positioning themselves accordingly.

Education attainment levels are rising globally, and museums are serving more students and teachers than ever. In the 2002 *True Needs, True Partners* study conducted by the Institute of Museum and Library Services (IMLS), 70 percent of U.S. museums reported that their school programs had grown in the past five years—despite the tightened focus on curriculum in the schools noted by Dr. Brad King in chapter 5.

This trend is international. The Victoria and Albert Museum in the United Kingdom recently conducted extensive research and evaluation to determine the intersection of its audience with the "creative class" as defined by sociologist Richard Florida, and found a substantial representation of persons engaged in the knowledge and creative industries among its visitors. This research has led to an overall repositioning of the potential of museum learning. Elaine Heumann Gurian's proposals in chapter 3 point to the possible impact such repositioning might have on the way museums serve their public.

3. Museums are collaborating to maximize the impact of marketing investment.

Making Culture Count, a recent study conducted by LaPlaca Cohen, the leading cultural arts marketing firm in the United States, and *The New Yorker* magazine, showed that only 54 percent of the general population is aware that cultural institutions offer family programs and events.[2] This low awareness results from the impossible task of thousands of museums and cultural organizations competing for the public's attention and the ability of only a few to make a large enough investment to be noticed. The reorientation of museums to serve families with children described by Dr. Claudia Haas in chapter 4 still has a long way to go in the minds of the general public, even in America.

Responding to this dilemma, museums have finally begun to get smart about pooling marketing budgets for more than just the occasional event or annual festival. There is a distinct trend toward formal collaboratives and consortia that bring a far louder voice to the whole than any part would be able to achieve on its own. A few examples of these include:

Greater Philadelphia Cultural Alliance, Philadelphia: The central goal of this organization is to promote cultural organizations collectively to increase participation throughout the region. To this end, they created the Campaign for Culture, a marketing initiative that includes a master database of mailing lists compiled from participating alliance member organizations. The purpose of the list cooperative is to simplify mailing list exchanges, save time for cultural marketers and cut costs for individual organizational members. Another key benefit of the program is that users are provided with direct mail response rates and improved analysis.

Defence of the Realm, Hampshire, England: This group was established in 1985 as a major tourism marketing and development project intended to leverage Hampshire's wealth of heritage sites and museums that share the Defence of the Realm theme. The group serves over forty castles, museums, great ships, and stately homes in the area, including the Royal Marines Museum, the Royal Navy Submarine Museum, and the Royal Naval Museum, among others.

The marketing program focuses on attracting individual and group visitors and getting information about the visitors themselves back to the sites. The group produces a joint brochure, which gives details of all the sites, their forthcoming events, and a range of discount vouchers.

Many of these organizations also participate in a loyalty card program called "Follow the Drum." Visitors who pay the full admission price in one of the museums receive a card giving them a 20 percent discount on admission to all the other museums in the group.

Museums of Lower Manhattan, New York: Participation in this collaborative has allowed relatively small and unknown museums in Lower Manhattan to raise their profile and attract sponsorship. Although the collaborative was largely a response to the development and revitalization plan following the disaster of September 11, 2001, not only has collaborating facilitated grant funding, but it has also increased museum attendance by promoting the area as a neighborhood of museums, galleries, and artifacts. The positioning emphasizes that the attractions are all walking-distance apart and perfect for a one-day excursion. Special discounts and offers for kids who visit several of the district's museums have made the Museums of Lower Manhattan a tourist destination.

4. The Internet has become fully integrated into all segments of society. Generation Y has never experienced life without it.

The Internet has fundamentally changed the way potential museum learners seek and find information about the activities they will pursue. While traditional advertising vehicles are still key tools, the LaPlaca Cohen *Making Culture Count* study showed that 37 percent of America's "cultural consumers" are now getting their information about leisure activities via e-mail and the Web. Furthermore, between 2004 and 2005 the number of people purchasing tickets online rose significantly from 31 percent to 37 percent, and is expected to continue rising each year. Figures are undoubtedly already higher in Japan, Scandinavia, and a number of other Western European countries.

In addition to the above percentages that indicate rising usage, it is important to consider the impact that new technologies are having from a generational perspective. While the Internet and mobile phones are relatively new to Baby Boomers (those born between 1946 and 1964) and older Generation

X (1965–1979) users, the young adults of Generation Y (those born since 1980) have never known life without them. As a result, they will be predisposed to wholly different communication tactics. For example, *Elle* magazine has recently discontinued the publication in print, opting for an online only format because that is where its young female readers will find it.

Today's teens are digital communicators, with 57 percent of Americans aged 13 to 17 in possession of a cell phone—and probably a far higher proportion in Hong Kong, Singapore, or Japan. This group is far more likely to use the mobile phone in a variety of innovative ways, including photographs, downloaded music, and other content. They can now be seen in art museums around the world taking pictures of masterpieces on their tiny screens. Another indicative statistic comes from Europe, where the European Interactive Advertising Association (EIAA) reports that young people are spending less time watching television or listening to radio, but more time online.[3]

11.2   PROGRAM DEVELOPMENT

Before marketing efforts can begin, it is crucial to be sure that the museum has developed a successful museum learning product. This means ensuring that there is an audience for the program, and that the program offers something new, different, or better in the increasingly competitive marketplace—competitive not merely with other museums, but even more with other leisure activities.

A good strategic approach to a season of programming is to create a balanced mix that includes:

- standard popular programs (such as performances and film, family days, docent tours, forum discussions)
- programs for specialized audiences (such as conferences or colloquia, or evening events for singles)
- and a limited selection of new or experimental offerings such as extended hours, professional development courses, or other special events.

Relevance to the community and current events is critical to attract public relations exposure and sponsorship. Although a good PR person will often be able to create these connections in press releases and talking points for interviews, there is no replacement for authentic relevance to contemporary community concerns as the inspiration for program development.

Always working on new programs and watching other museums, societies, foundations, and educational institutions will often help avoid overlap and hopefully encourage collaboration where there may otherwise be competition. If another institution is planning a similar program or event, consider coproducing the program, which generally results in the introduction of new audiences to both institutions as well as reduced costs. These collaborations can result in long-term relationships or even cobranded series.

11.3 POSITIONING EDUCATION PROGRAMS WITHIN THE LARGER CONTEXT

Creating an identity and claiming a defined position in the marketplace are critical success factors, first for the institution at large, then for its ancillary activities. Consider the present image or identity of the current education department: How would visitors and various types of users describe it? How can it be differentiated from that of other museums? What is the reason to visit the museum more than once?

To compete in today's market, a destination must have a simple message or profile. A good exercise is to ask, "What is it?" or "What do they do there?" Is the answer a clear, simple phrase that will inspire someone to participate? If not, how can we make it clear? This exercise is a quick way to determine how the market may see a product or destination. It also contextualizes the importance of clear messaging when one considers that word of mouth is the most important marketing tool of leisure and cultural destinations.

"Positioning" is perception: it's the place that a brand, product, or destination occupies in the consumer's mind versus other similar products. It is based on the product's unique value to its market and how it differentiates itself from its competitors. The messages that come out of the education department (or the marketing department on behalf of the education department) must be in line with the overall message and communications strategy of the museum. In larger museums, learning programs may even be considered a distinct sub-brand of the museum, which could be considered the "mother brand." Regardless of the degree to which the relationship between the museum and its public programs is articulated, it is essential that the strategies work in tandem to reinforce each other.

11.4 DEVELOPING A MARKETING STRATEGY FOR MUSEUM LEARNING

To develop an effective strategy to compete in today's crowded marketplace, the following six questions must be answered for each program, or at least each program type:

1. What are we marketing? What makes it unique?
2. What are the marketing objectives?
3. What are the marketing challenges?

4. Are there any distinguishing principals that will inform the strategy?
5. Who are we marketing to? Who are the target audiences?
6. What marketing vehicles will we use?

The answers to these questions will provide a roadmap for carefully considered and consistently promoted programs and events.

1. What are we marketing? What makes it unique?

If this question cannot be answered clearly, create a process to determine the precise nature of what is being offered. To help address this issue, the following questions should be considered:

- What is the unique identity of this department or the programs it produces?
- How are they different from other cultural, historical, or recreational offerings?
- What message should visitors and potential visitors get?
- How are these programs relevant today?

2. What are the marketing objectives? What do we want to achieve with this program?

The marketing and/or education departments may have a variety of objectives in mind, but it is important to define them, as it will inform the approach and decision making throughout the development of the program and the articulation of its marketing strategy. Objectives may include:

- Broadening the audience to include new segments of the population (identifying whom the program will serve)
- Deepening engagement with the current audience
- Maximizing earned income
- Filling an education gap in the market (for example, is it adult education or school curriculum-related?)
- Advancing research or scholarship in the field
- Attracting sponsorship and new donors
- Engaging in and/or impacting a local or national debate

3. What are the marketing challenges?

Every museum and series of programs faces a set of challenges. Formally identifying challenges will allow strategies to be developed to overcome them and will inform thinking about overarching strategies as well. Although challenges are often unique to each institution, here are some common examples:

- *A lack of funding for major marketing initiatives* requires a more creative approach; shifting the focus away from paid advertising will be necessary. Attracting media attention to a specific story, or issuing a news release prepared for the media, can be much more cost-effective than paying for ads. Partnerships and alliances are an especially good way to maximize impact and audience with a limited budget.

- *Subject matter that may not have enough impact or uniqueness* to draw an audience may require a bit of reworking in order to ensure relevant links to the community or society at large. This may be a simple matter of giving a routine program a topical twist, or finding the human-interest story behind the contribution of a docent, the lifelong service of a teacher, or revivifying the fascination of the subject matter itself.

- *Out-of-the-way locations* could make it impossible to compete for audience with other major attractions in the area—a common problem of historic houses and heritage sites. Overcoming this obstacle will require that programming generally focus on the interests of the local community, with the potential to stage "something big" that will have a broader appeal from time to time.

- *When the visitor experience of the museum is relatively static* (as in many historic houses and heritage sites), there may seem to be little content on which to develop dynamic programming. A creative approach that links programming to current issues and events, and/or the curriculum is a way to build audience as well as a case for funding.

- *The leisure trends in the area may not include attending programs at cultural institutions.* Helpful statistics and information on consumer behavior can generally be found on Web sites of Chambers of Commerce, local tourism authorities, and economic development commissions. Unless there is a surefire audience, local behavior and attitudes should inform product development as well as marketing strategy.

- *There may be competition from unexpected places.* For example, a botanical garden may be in competition with local parks and hiking trails. Again, understanding consumer preferences and building alliances with other institutions and sites can help educators to develop desirable programs and mitigate competition.

4.   Are there any distinguishing principles that will inform the strategy?

Different programs, series, or institutions may require different approaches depending on their nature. These principles may apply to the institution as a whole. The following strategies are examples that articulate a fundamental approach to a marketing plan for a given program or series.

- Embracing the Community: An institution may choose to encourage and nurture a sustainable audience of users by seeking to meet a variety of needs in the community. Often, an institution will provide space to be used for a variety of appropriate community activities.
- Creating Partnerships and Alliances: Educators and marketers will often seek to establish partnerships and alliances through which the museum can leverage additional financial resources and tap into new audiences. This could range from media sponsorships from local newspapers in exchange for sponsorship recognition at a special event, to a month-long promotion where discounts are provided to any visitor who presents a ticket stub from a partner site.
- Prioritization of Audiences: Priority may be given to one audience over another, or an institution may aim to balance local users and schools with higher-spending niche segments of its market.

5.   Who are we marketing to? Who are the target audiences?

Identifying several potential user groups, based on the market context and any audience research findings, will inform the messages that are developed to communicate about the program as well as the media channels. This section suggests the traditional ways to segment audiences, although there are a variety of additional possibilities:

- Enthusiasts and Members: This is the institution's core audience; those who are committed to the mission of the museum and the programs it produces. Depending on the nature of programming partnerships, enthusiasts in a given subject may be introduced to the museum through coproduced programming. Thus, if there is an exhibition on transportation history this month, the antique car collectors' groups may become partners for marketing the new learning experiences on offer.
- Young Families (adults 20 to 40 years of age and their children): As Dr. Claudia Haas notes in chapter 4, cultivating a family audience through a menu of visitor experiences that offers fun and educational options in both structured and unstructured settings can contribute to increased family participation. It is important to note that families seek out fun educational activities, so free listings and word of mouth are often all that it takes to build family audiences.
- School Groups and Teachers: As Dr. Brad King notes in chapter 5, effectively linking an institution's programs to the local school curriculum can often dramatically increase the museum's school tour audience. Marketing to this segment relies far more on direct contact and cultivation than on media vehicles. Web-based materials, time for advanced planning, and

workshops and open houses to educate educators are key for this segment. Utilizing curriculum titles and subtitles as headings in the exhibition graphics wherever possible is one way to communicate the relevance clearly to teachers.

- Diverse Audiences: Many institutions that embark on programs to diversify their audiences report that typical advertising strategies do not result in audiences that are reflective of the diversity in the community at large; often there are language barriers, or visiting museums and heritage sites is not a typical leisure practice for the target groups that the museum wants to attract. Successful tactics for diversifying audiences have included reaching into the community through local leadership, clubs, or places of worship. Individual contacts are important, as are targeted communications and direct invitations to programs rather than general ads and listings. Studies at select American institutions have shown that African American and Hispanic visitors prioritize "feeling welcome" as a critical issue when selecting leisure activities. Employing a diverse staff at all levels is one way to communicate this welcome.
- General Population: The general population of area residents can be targeted through a range of local advertising, listings, and partnerships. It is important to define the meaning of the term "resident" so that media vehicles can be easily identified later in the process. For example, a New York–based institution will have to consider whether its market includes all five boroughs plus parts of New Jersey and Connecticut, and a Los Angeles–based institution may or may not consider Orange County to be part of its resident market.
- Defining the resident market depends largely on labor and leisure patterns. In order to be considered a resident, one should not be driving for more than two hours to gain access to the museum. Anyone beyond this range would be considered a day-tripper, a segment of the tourist market.
- Special Interest Groups: This is an ideal way to promote programming as it directly targets the audience that is more likely to participate in a program. Special interests can be tapped in a variety of creative ways. Some general examples include:
  - Enthusiast groups or clubs that focus on the program's subject matter
  - Retiree groups (day trip packages, elderhostel)
  - Business groups
  - Garden clubs and local societies
  - Day camps and after school programs
- Direct marketing, personal invitations, promotions, and partnerships are the most effective vehicles to reach these audiences. Cultivation and a consistent, excellent product are critical success factors in attracting repeat involvement from special interest visitors and groups.

- Generations: Although advertisers have always taken the attitudes and values of different generations into consideration in terms of messaging, the digital age has created new media vehicles such as online zines, blogging, podcasting, and text messaging. These new formats are used more by certain generations than others—Generation Y more than Baby Boomers, for example. At the same time, Boomers are the next generation to enter retirement, and will have more disposable income and leisure time, making them a prime target audience for museum going and participation in learning programs.

- Tourists: Tourists are generally considered audiences for museum learning programs primarily as potential participants in public tours. However, it is possible that a particular special event may draw from outside the resident pool. To accomplish this, a clear strategy developed well in advance is required, since tourists tend to plan their trip itineraries in advance. Generally speaking, marketing to tourists can be expensive and may be best left to the overall marketing mix of the institution. It is likely that the marketing and public relations departments have already formed relationships with tourist publications, local promotions targeted to tourists, hotel concierges, and tour operators.

6. What marketing vehicles will we use?

The nature and quality of the experience is always the best form of marketing for any attraction. However, there are other measures that educators need to take to ensure visibility in the community. This section focuses on those that could benefit institutions with limited marketing budgets.

Public Relations and Publicity: Public relations and publicity can provide a cost-effective, broad-based means of communicating with audiences. A publicity program will utilize a broad range of promotional tools from distributing news-related press releases to commissioning feature stories placed in selected media, including special interest magazines. Programming and special events offer excellent opportunities to gain media coverage.

In cases where programs connect with current events or local or national interests, publicity will come more easily. A somewhat harsh litmus test to determine relevance to the community is to ask, "So what? Why is this important today?" If the answer to this question is a strong statement that would appeal to a wide audience, it may be possible to book senior staff or leading personalities in that field on local radio and television to speak about the museum and the program.

A database of press contacts should be carefully compiled and updated regularly, which should be the job of the marketing and PR departments. This database should include lists of family activity guides, and a multilingual list of general newspapers and community newspapers in addition to more well-known publications and travel and tourism guides. Representatives from local papers (including publications in diverse languages) should be invited to tour the museum and learn what the learning programs have to offer. These strategic relationships should be carefully cultivated through personal meetings as well as invitations to programs and other special events to ensure consistent free listings and as much additional exposure as possible.

It is important to consider who is qualified to represent the museum, since every public statement helps to build—or, if handled improperly, dilute—the museum's brand. In all cases, interviewees must be provided with talking points to ensure that they stay "on message." It must be understood that they are reinforcing the overall strategy of the museum, the education department, and the particular program with which they are involved.

News releases must be handled in a similar fashion. It is imperative to use the correct style and format when submitting a news release, and of course to stay on message with the overall strategy. There are a variety of guides that can assist with formatting effective news releases.

Partnerships: Media and programming partnerships can be extremely useful, expanding opportunities and driving attendance with little monetary investment. The copromotion, cofunding, and comarketing of events, services, programs, tourism routes, and packages with organizations like chambers of commerce, compatible museums, theaters, and cultural institutions is key to leveraging a marketing budget. Developing as many strategic partnerships as possible with other local places of interest is a valuable opportunity.

Any sponsorship that the media is willing to provide will offset potential advertising costs or deliver coverage that could not be afforded otherwise. It is generally required to recognize the sponsor in published materials or on-site, or both, depending on the value of the sponsorship.

Promotions and Special Events: In advertising, a limited time offer or a new product or event is referred to as a "call to action." A common marketing challenge for museums is that there is little reason to decide to visit the permanent collection exhibition *today* or to attend *this* program tonight, when there are so many other opportunities. To combat this, tactics to motivate participation must be employed. These could include promoting programs that involve visits by celebrities, or providing discounts and other incentives such as "buy one ticket, get one free" to particular audiences. The closing dates of temporary exhibitions must be featured in advertisements—for example, "only 5 more days to see it."

Nontraditional, and often inexpensive, marketing strategies such as competitions, performances, and giveaways can have a major impact when the target market is reached. Programming and education staff can produce mass appeal events that relate to the museum's mission but attract crowds that will later generate positive word of mouth, the most influential type of advertising.

Print and Collateral Materials: Printed promotional materials are the standard way to get the word out to stimulate participation at events. It is important that all print materials be to the point and relevant to the reader, noting an array of exciting activities and providing interesting information. The target audience for these materials is likely already familiar with the museum as a visitor or a member, indicating that the messaging in these materials can be slightly more complex than it would be for those who are less familiar with the institution. Photographs should show members of the target audience—a young family, for instance—enjoying themselves in the exhibition or during the experience or activity.

Web site, Blogging, and Online Listings: A welcoming, upbeat, and user-friendly Web site assists greatly in adding value to communication with audiences. The Web site should cater for all audiences. The 2005 *Making Culture Count* study by LaPlaca Cohen and *The New Yorker* found that 43 percent of persons interested in cultural programs are now using the Internet to gather information about what to visit and what tickets to purchase. This proportion is up from 25 percent in 2004, and is expected to continue to rise each year, making online listings—and ideally online ticket sales—a critical priority.

The Web site should allow the user to sign up for an electronic mailing list and to send inquiries. It should also be linked to and from other sites that will allow potential visitors to easily find the museum's site, if not make them aware of it for the first time. Usage of these links should be tracked and monitored over time, to identify which ones are most effective.

> The Web site is also an important resource for school children, parents, and educators. Materials developed for the museum's learning programs should be downloadable in PDF form from the site, which will make the institution's information available to a wide audience with minimal costs to the organization. Dr. Barbara Soren shows how effective such online learning programs can be in one of her case studies in chapter 10.

The rise of blogging has made its way into the mainstream; a recent poll of European museum marketing professionals reveals that 42 percent claimed that they plan to implement Web blogs in the next year as part of their overall strategy.[4] Another strategy is to encourage students and other participants to blog independently about their experience. Visitors can now be seen blogging or reading others' blogged reviews of an exhibition while in the galleries—a highly interactive form of museum learning that has been developed recently.

Trade and Special Interest Marketing: Cultivating strategic relationships with tour operators, teachers, school administrators, and leaders of the special interest groups identified as relevant to the exhibition or program is one of the most important free marketing tools that an institution can employ. These relationships are likely to be held primarily by the marketing or PR department.

> The strategy with trade and special interest marketing is similar to that of media relations generally: there must be outreach and special messaging tailored to each contact. This requires a letter, phone call, invitation, and personal meeting. These connections can often be developed into long-term relationships with the opportunity for cross-promotion or even cobranded programming. Annual open houses for educators are a highly effective tool for promoting school programs.

Direct Mail/E-mail: This is a relatively inexpensive way to keep in touch with frequent visitors and members. Collecting e-mail addresses into a database, particularly from users of learning programs or from willing visitors to the Web site, is an important step, as e-mail "blasts" have already become a standard tool. Mailed or e-mailed newsletters must contain listings and ticketing information and ideally a calendar that is easy to read as well as listings by program type so that, for example, parents can quickly spot children's programming.

> Direct communication is of particular importance for schools, which should receive a mailing in the spring with materials advertising the institution as a fall field trip destination. Developing a museum/school association with a designated teacher who is a member for each school is an ideal way to ensure that the mailing goes to a teacher who cares enough to make sure that the mailing goes to the appropriate teacher in the appropriate grade, rather than hoping that a busy school principal or his or her secretary will forward it to the targeted teacher. Such associations can be developed among teachers who are currently taking their classes to the museum, with the group being invited at the beginning of each school term to learn what the museum will be offering, and to send them back to their schools with curriculum-related kits about each exhibition or program, after a pleasant evening with refreshments as well as an exciting preview of the coming season.

Advertising: Advertising media includes paid spots in newspapers, magazines, radio, television, cinemas, billboards, and the Internet. In the case of many institutions, budget constraints most likely limit advertising to local newspapers and outdoor posters. As mentioned above, it is possible to seek a media partner to sponsor ad space.

Developing a simple rack card with a program calendar to place at other attractions is also an excellent way to advertise on a budget, particularly since those who visit other attractions are more likely to come to other museums as well. It is recommended that an additional promotion, such as a "dollar off" coupon, be a part of any card that is produced to assist in tracking the success rate. (Cards can even be coded before being dropped off at other locations, to help track which organizations generate the most responses.)

Ads in local foreign language newspapers are recommended. It is expected that this ad space will have a modest cost, but this tactic has helped many institutions to diversify their audiences, especially when used in conjunction with outreach to community leaders, who may even be willing to assist with translation and redesign.

Advertising in major media is for a more general audience; large institutions that produce a multitude of programs in markets with a high percentage of cultural consumers can reap the benefits of advertising. The Metropolitan Museum of Art, for instance, takes full-page ads in the *New York Times*. For most markets and for most museum programs, however, expensive ads in major publications are generally unnecessary. This is due to a combination of two factors: the audience is limited and often already engaged with the museum, and the product is complex and therefore better communicated where there is more space for explanation. As shown above, there are far more creative ways to deploy limited marketing dollars.

11.5 IMPLEMENTING A MARKETING PROGRAM FOR MUSEUM LEARNING

Frequently Observed, but Not Recommended

Generally speaking, there are two operational models to choose from when developing and implementing the marketing strategy. In the first example, the education department assumes responsibility for marketing its own programs and may consult or coordinate with the marketing department from time to time. Although marketing may advise or even allocate budget money to pay for education's promotional activities, these activities are carried out by the education department.

As seen below, on this model marketing and publicity activities become a core part of the education department's output, while the marketing department focuses on the institution at large. This model is common, but is *not*

Figure 11.1. Marketing Activities When Carried Out by the Education Department

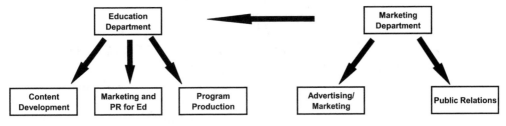

recommended; it compromises the focus of the education department, fails to draw on the knowledge of in-house marketing and PR experts, and opens the door for communications that are inefficient at best and working at cross-purposes at worst.

Preferred Relationship

The preferred model is for education and marketing to work together, each concentrating on what they know best. This model sees the education department feeding content to the marketing department. The marketing strategy will then be executed by the marketing department, which is charged with coordinating messaging, advertising, and publicity institution-wide.

All communications must include information that clearly directs potential participants on what to do: who to call for tickets, where to go to see the event, and so on. Whether an event is free or tickets are sold or reserved, additional information must be available for people who have questions or special needs. Ideally there is a box office—even if it is a back-of-house operation that operates by phone and e-mail through a booking clerk. Regular coordinated briefings with visitor services and other frontline staff is arguably the most important part of any implementation since they have the most exposure

Figure 11.2. Marketing Activities When Carried Out by the Marketing Department

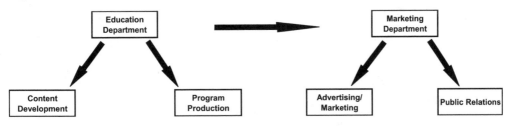

to visitors and therefore the opportunity to promote and answer questions about upcoming programs.

11.6   REPORTING AND EVALUATION OF MARKETING MUSEUM LEARNING

In this age of accountability, it is critical to measure and report accurately on attendance and revenue generated by learning programs. This data can be used to analyze successes and failures and is an essential tool for raising funds and reporting back to funders. Education officers need to create templates that are tailored to their programs, and issue reports to senior management and other departments by exhibition period, calendar quarter, or fiscal year—whatever is right for their museum.

The template below is an example that captures data by program type as well as by exhibition. It reports on a museum learning program that included a film festival, a lecture series, a conference, a series of open house evenings, and family programs related to a sequence of three exhibitions.

Once data is captured on the spreadsheet, it can be reflected in a chart, which is generally easier to read. Charts are excellent tools for showing the major points of a data set, and their visual depiction makes them more user-friendly

Figure 11.3. Sample Template to Collect Data by Type of Program and Exhibition

2006 Public Program Attendance and Revenue by Program by Exhibition

General Audience and Events				Lectures and Academic Programs				Family Programs				Total	
	Date	Atten.	Revenue		Date	Atten.	Revenue		Date	Atten.	Revenue	Atten.	Revenue
Exhibition A													
Program 1	30-Jan	121	$625	Lecture 1	4-Jan	45	$450	Open House*	12-Jan	209	$0		
Program 2	31-Jan	132	$710	Lecture 2	29-Jan	89	$760	Family Program 1	13-Feb	45	$225		
Program 3	6-Feb	260	$1,900	Lecture 3	15-Feb	123	$1,178	Family Program 2	28-Feb	25	$250		
Program 4	7-Feb	269	$1,875	Panel	25-Feb	291	$994	Family Program 3	5-Mar	56	$280		
Event	13-Feb	1200	$0	Lecture 4	13-Mar	84	$448	Family Program 4	12-Mar	20	$200		
Program 5	14-Feb	272	$2,121					Family Program 5	27-Mar	38	$570		
Program 6	27-Feb	229	$1,660										
Program 7	28-Feb	194	$1,155					*admission to this event was complimentary					
Program 8	3-Mar	78	$976										
Exhibition A Total		2,755	$11,022	Subtotal		632	$3,830	Subtotal		393	$1,525	3,780	$16,377
Exhibition B													
Program 1	22-May	258	$2,585	Lecture 1	30-May	65	$345	Open House*	29-May	150	$0		
Film Festival 1	15-Jun	200	$0	Lecture 2	6-Jun	27	$140	Family Program 1	7-Jun	18	$86		
Film Festival 2	17-Jun	200	$0	Lecture 3	13-Jun	21	$96	Family Program 2	18-Jun	12	$49		
Film Festival 3	23-Jun	200	$0	Lecture 4	20-Jun	30	$120	Family Program 3	13-Aug	25	$125		
Program 2	24-Jun	146	$1,400	Lecture 5	14-Jul	77	$270	Family Program 4	8-Sep	54	$240		
Film Festival 4	26-Jun	200	$0	Lecture 6	5-Sep	119	$510						
Film Festival 5	27-Jun	200	$0	Lecture 7	9-Sep	127	$1,550						
Program 3	2-Aug	465	$6,800										
Exhibition B Total		1,869	$10,785	Subtotal		466	$3,031	Subtotal		259	$500	2,594	$14,316
Exhibition C													
Program 1	6-Sep	299	$2,200	Lecture 1	7-Nov	93	$377	Open House*	15-Oct	235	$0		
Program 2	18-Sep	224	$1,695	Lecture 2	21-Nov	273*	$107	Family Program 1	12-Nov	65	$650		
Program 3	2-Oct	144	$1,972	Lecture 3	28-Nov	51	$290	Family Program 2	15-Nov	20	$200		
Program 4	15-Oct	271	$2,360	Lecture 4	5-Dec	191	$350	Family Program 3	10-Dec	45	$450		
Program 5	5-Nov	235	$2,115	Lecture 5	6-Dec	104	$240	Family Program 4	24-Dec	20	$200		
Program 6	9-Nov	276	$2,550	Conference Panel 1	8-Jan	200	$2,000	Family Program 5	2-Jan	72	$360		
Program 7	14-Dec	238	$2,215	Conference Panel 2	9-Jan	200	$2,000						
Event	23-Dec	215	$1,895	Conference Panel 3	10-Jan	172	$1,720	*admission to this event was complimentary					
Exhibition C Total		1,902	$17,002			1,011	$7,084			457	$1,860	3,370	$25,946
Total		6,526	$38,809	Total		2,109	$13,945	Total		1,109	$3,885	9,744	$56,639

COURTESY OF LORD CULTURAL RESOURCES.

Figure 11.4. Program Attendance by Type and Exhibition, 2006

2006 Program Attendance by Type and Exhibition

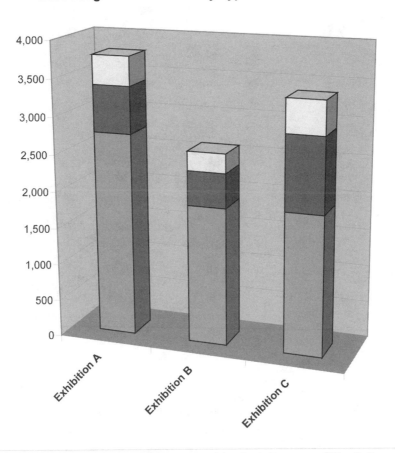

☐ General Audience and Events ■ Lectures and Academic Programs ☐ Family Programs

COURTESY OF LORD CULTURAL RESOURCES.

than a large spreadsheet. The following two charts were generated off the data in the above spreadsheet.

Evaluation and market research is the last critical piece to understanding current and potential visitors. Ideally, educators and marketers can conduct regular surveys to gather feedback on museum services, quality of experience, and preferences. This is best done with a firm that specializes in market research or a museum consultant who is trained in evaluation, although in the case of most museums, there is simply not enough additional budget for these activities. Dr. Barbara Soren in chapter 10 shows how valuable qualitative evaluation of a museum learning program can be—and this value can be realized and put to very good use by a marketing department working closely with the museum evaluation officer as well as the education department.

Figure 11.5. Program Revenue by Type, 2006

2006 Program Revenue by Type

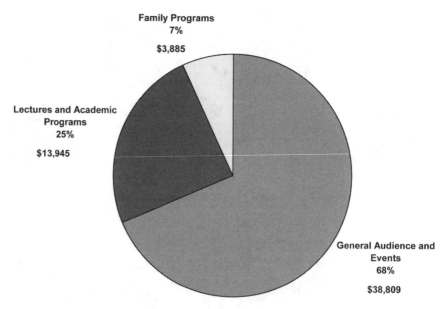

Family Programs
7%

$3,885

Lectures and Academic
Programs
25%

$13,945

General Audience and
Events
68%

$38,809

COURTESY OF LORD CULTURAL RESOURCES.

Even where money is scarce, budget constraints should not prevent the collection of at least basic data, which is key to informing program development. Most institutions have an admissions process that gives visitor services staff access to visitors. At this point, data can be collected in two key ways: through the ticketing system or cash register that should have a selection of ticket categories, and through a survey card or feedback form. The education department should collect at least:

- Postal code or neighborhood of residence
- How did the visitors learn of the museum or program?
- How many times have they been to the museum in the last year (if ever before)?
- Are the visitors members?

Following is an example of a survey card that was successfully used at Constitution Hill in Johannesburg, South Africa, the subject of Danielle Melville's case study in chapter 6. Data from these cards are plugged into a database daily by visitor services and reported to each department quarterly to inform planning:

Figure 11.6. Example of Constitution Hill Survey Card (front)

VISITOR FEEDBACK CARD

CONSTITUTION HILL

WE VALUE AND APPRECIATE YOUR COMMENTS, WHICH WE
REVIEW IN ORDER TO PROVIDE VISITORS WITH THE BEST
POSSIBLE EXPERIENCE OF CONSTITUTION HILL.

Place of residence _____

Occupation _____

Age _____

HOW DID YOU FIND OUT ABOUT CONSTITUTION HILL?

☐ Newspaper
☐ Radio
☐ TV
☐ Brochure
☐ Tour operator itinerary
☐ Friend/relative
☐ Website
☐ Other

PLEASE TELL US WHAT YOU THOUGHT OF CONSTITUTION HILL.
WHAT WAS YOUR FAVORITE/THE MOST INTERESTING THING?

_____

_____

WHAT SUGGESTIONS WOULD YOU OFFER TO HELP US IMPROVE?

_____

_____

WHAT EXHIBITIONS OR EVENTS WOULD YOU LIKE TO SEE HERE
IN THE FUTURE?

_____

_____

_____

COURTESY OF CONSTITUTION HILL.

If resources are available to conduct more comprehensive analysis, it is recommended that a researcher be retained to bring more depth by examining qualitative as well as quantitative issues. These could include:

- What type of program did you attend?
- What did you like best?
- What could have improved it?
- How likely are you to participate in another program in the next 3 months?
- How many programs have you attended in the last year?
- What programs have you attended? (Check all that apply.)

Figure 11.7. Example of Constitution Hill Survey Card (back)

PLEASE RATE THE FOLLOWING ITEMS (PLEASE TICK ONE):

	Excellent	Good	Fair	Poor
Quality of exhibits	1	2	3	4
Quality of guided tour	1	2	3	4
Value of ticket price	1	2	3	4
Signs to help you find your way	1	2	3	4
Helpfulness/courtesy of security staff	1	2	3	4
Helpfulness/courtesy of admissions staff	1	2	3	4
Cleanliness of facilities	1	2	3	4

WHAT MOTIVATED YOU TO VISIT CONSTITUTION HILL TODAY (PLEASE TICK ONE)?

	Very Much	A Little	Not Much	Not at All
Want to learn about South African history	1	2	3	4
Something to do with my kids	1	2	3	4
Interested in seeing the new development	1	2	3	4
Sight-seeing while in South Africa	1	2	3	4
Entertainment /a day out	1	2	3	4

ADDITIONAL COMMENTS:

_____

_____

_____

_____

_____

_____

_____

_____

_____

PO Box 31005   t 27 11 274 5300   info@constitutionhill.org.za
Braamfontein 2017   f 27 11 274 5302   www.constitutionhill.org.za

COURTESY OF CONSTITUTION HILL.

In addition to surveys, focus groups and in-depth interviews can be excellent tools for both program development and understanding the impact of education programs. Dr. Barbara Soren provides more information on these approaches in chapter 10.

The most important thing is to *use and share* whatever findings from data collection, research, and evaluation are available. All too often institutions collect information that reveals visitors' preferences, patterns, and satisfaction levels, yet this information goes untapped and unused. Sharing quantitative and qualitative visitor information throughout the organization can help everyone align around mission-related goals and strategies to meet them.

11.7   CONCLUSION: COOPERATION IS KEY

Marketing and evaluating museum learning programs are integral parts of those programs. By helping to make visitors better informed, more comprehensively oriented, and fully motivated for the exhibition, experience, or activity, they can make a significant contribution to the quality of the museum learning experience for all. The most fundamental condition for this success is a culture of positive cooperation between educators and museum communications, information, or publicity officers. With sufficient advance consultation and input from all players, museum learning programs can be significantly enhanced in their reach and effectiveness.

NOTES

1. B. Simon and M. Jan, *Marketing the Arts* (Paris: ICOM, 1992).

2. *The New Yorker* and LaPlaca Cohen, Making Culture Count, Research Report. Mediamark Research Interactive, 2005, vol. 3.

3. European Interactive Advertising Association, http://www.eiaa.co.uk/news/eiaa-articles-details.asp?id=66&lang=1.

4. Philip Young, Z. Ansgar, and S. Swaran, "Results of the First European Survey on Weblogs in Public Relations and Communication Management," EuroBlog 2006, available at http://www.euroblog2006.org/press/assets/EuroBlog2006_Results.pdf.

CHAPTER 12

Multiple Points of Reentry
The Challenge of Sustaining Participation in Museum Learning

MIRA GOLDFARB

Much of what we have recently learned and now assume about attracting visitors to museums—and cultural activity across the spectrum—is that diverse audiences need diverse or multiple points of entry. This line of thinking has spawned a formula of sorts for attracting first-time visitors who previously felt excluded or were uninterested in arts and cultural experiences. It has effectively removed barriers both real and perceptual. But does this approach have sustaining power, for the institutions and their multicultural communities?

A typical negative example will serve to illustrate the problem, and the challenge: an art museum presents a temporary exhibition of contemporary Chinese art; a large general museum offers one of Chinese archaeological relics; or a science center offers a traveling show of Chinese dinosaurs. In each case the institutions mount a special program aimed at encouraging residents and tourists of Chinese origin to visit the exhibition. The challenge is: how many of them ever return? How many become members? How many have a meaningful learning experience related to their motivations to come to the museum? How many will return with their families after the Chinese exhibitions have departed? Very often, the answer is very few.

This example refers to ethnic diversity, but the same opportunity and the same challenge arises among visitors who differ in age, gender, social class, economic status, learning style, and individual motivation. The challenge is often seen as a marketing or public relations problem, but at its root it is a challenge to the capabilities of museum learning programs to meet the diverse interests and motivations of the public that samples and—sometimes—returns to them.

Many museums in the United States, Canada, Great Britain, and increasingly elsewhere have embraced a multiple points of entry platform. In striving toward universal access, for example, by offering more varied programming, amenities, cost incentives, evening hours, and most notably, glossy branding and marketing strategies, they have become more available and more appealing to a broader public. But of course diversity is not only ethnic, racial, generational, or socioeconomic: we now know that people have distinct learning styles, regardless of background. Schools are increasingly adapting their curriculum and environments to accommodate and stimulate students' "multiple intelligences," and some museums are endeavoring to do the same in designing their children's programs. But how are institutions of lifelong learning accommodating the diverse needs of adults? And, perhaps even more importantly, since learning depends crucially on the visitor's reason for coming to the museum, how are they serving these adults' diverse motivations?

On the cultural landscape, museums stand out as forums of learning. A 2004 survey of cultural participation in the United States conducted by the Urban Institute and supported by the Wallace Foundation showed that the primary motivation for museum attendance was "to gain knowledge." The second and third most important factors (almost equally tied) were to experience "high quality art" and to have an "emotionally rewarding" experience. By contrast, attendees reported "socializing" as the primary motivator for all other types of cultural activities in the survey: dance, festivals, music, and theater.[1]

The Urban Institute survey also revealed that while 65 percent of museum attendees claimed that a major motivation is to gain knowledge or learn something new, only 51 percent strongly agreed that they actually had done so during their museum visit. Similarly, while 54 percent were primarily seeking "an emotional experience," only 35 percent actually found the experience emotionally rewarding. While these criteria are undeniably subjective, they are both open and categorical enough to accommodate the inherently subjective nature of personal motivation. They confirm that we have a lot to learn about how to satisfy the motivation for learning and an emotionally rewarding museum visit.

More importantly, the gaps in the survey results are sufficiently wide to merit serious attention, especially on the part of museums. Interestingly, of the five categories of cultural activity investigated (art museum or gallery, dance, arts and crafts fair or festival, music, play), *art museums satisfied audience expectations the least*, and by a significant margin. This presents a challenge and an opportunity. It persuasively suggests that the key to engaging and sustaining adult participation is in understanding motivation—which has its own sort of diversity that is unique and complex. But once museum educators and curators understand the nuances inherent in audience motivations and expectations, the challenge of creating accessible and enlightening experiences can be exciting and rewarding beyond measure. And, with thoughtful planning, such understanding and the decisions based on it need not compromise curatorial or institutional esteem.

On the educational spectrum, for adults especially, museums are places of "learning for fun."[2] They offer free choice, informal, nonregulated modes of presentation through a variety of vehicles: live, recorded, visual, audio, performance, digital, literary, interactive, social, and hands-on. Many sociologists now tell us that hierarchical indicators of cultural preference have become irrelevant and even misleading, and that a new generation of hybrid cultural consumers reject the notion of elitism in taste, seeing themselves as "omnivores" selecting from a free choice menu; hence, the classical-music lover who is more likely to enjoy more alternative musical forms than the typical rock-music lover.[3] But museums should not rest upon the assumption that offering something for everyone makes them ipso facto accessible to all.

The 2004 Urban Institute study was revolutionary in that it captured the differing motivations and experiences between types of cultural forums and events—and, critically, it identified the gaps. The findings offer compelling implications:

- *Experience is organically tied to expectation. Why* people attend and *whether* they get the experience or knowledge they are seeking reveals more valuable information than who has attended what, or even why people engage in "cultural activity" in general. Dr. Barbara Soren's emphasis on evaluation of qualitative outcomes in chapter 10 makes this point strongly.
- *Audience development strategies that are not devised with an understanding of motivation risk failure* since they may be constructed upon a false premise. John Falk and Lynn Dierking's *Learning from Museums* (2000) emphasizes the importance of understanding motivation for planning and achieving successful learning experiences in museums.

This 2004 survey published as *Motivations Matter* was built upon the major 2002 study, *Reggae to Rachmaninoff: How and Why People Participate in Arts and Culture* by Chris Walker and Stephanie Scott-Melnyk with Kay Sherwood, also commissioned by the Wallace Foundation and conducted by the Urban Institute. This study was equally dramatic in its results, since it revealed significantly higher levels of cultural participation among the more diverse populations of America (ethnic, socioeconomic, regional) by broadening the definition of cultural activity. It looked at a spectrum of urban and rural regions and concluded, among many other key findings, that overall "people are more likely to attend arts and cultural events at community locations than at specialized art venues." The study also pointed out that even though arts participation is a matter of individual motivation and inclination, individual behavior in communities ultimately creates local patterns. One pattern that many sociologists are observing is that there is a relationship between cultural participation, community cohesion, and civic engagement—in other words, civil society.[4] Museums, as forums for cultural participation and institutes of lifelong learning, can and do play a critical role in this dynamic. This is compellingly illustrated by Gail Dexter Lord in chapter 1.

The relatively recent growth of contemporary art museums and spaces in rural or smaller urban settings is interesting to consider in this context. There are satellites of established institutions, such as Tate St. Ives in southwest England or Dia Beacon in the Hudson River Valley north of New York, and independent enterprises such as the Baltic in Gateshead in northeast England, Donald Judd's Chinati Foundation and Marfa Ballroom in Texas, and SITE Santa Fe. Each faces the challenge and the opportunity of serving dedicated contemporary art audiences, a breed of pilgrimage cultural tourists whose motivations are known and understood, and at the same time large resident populations who comprise local communities—potential audiences whose motivations and barriers to participation are far less clear.

The Art Gallery of Hamilton (in Ontario, Canada) presents an instructive case study of a fine art museum in a socially diverse urban industrial community, which has diligently observed and responded to many of the needs and motivations of its entire public. As the following case study by Contemporary Art Curator Sara Knelman makes clear, the AGH has become a model of accessibility without sacrificing artistic or curatorial integrity.

MEETING DIVERSE COMMUNITY MOTIVATIONS AT THE ART GALLERY OF HAMILTON

Sara Knelman

Founded in 1914, the Art Gallery of Hamilton is the Province of Ontario's third largest public art gallery and owns one of the finest collections in the country. Its collecting strengths include Canadian and American historical, Canadian contemporary, and European historical art. The gallery recently underwent an 18-month, $18 million renovation.

In conjunction with the physical changes here, the gallery also began a process to redevelop its vision. Weakened somewhat over years of inadequate leadership and financial struggles, the gallery's physical renewal offered an opportunity for recapturing and updating its integral mandate to engage and enrich the community through art.

Under the guidance of president and chief executive officer Louise Dompierre and vice-president and COO/director of programming Shirley Madill, the gallery made strides in new directions, working with the realities facing a medium-sized public gallery in a postindustrial city in southern

Figure 12.1. Exhibition Opening Reception for *Shirley Elford: I AM*, part of the AGH Atelier Series that Investigates Work by Established Artists Who Live in or are from Hamilton

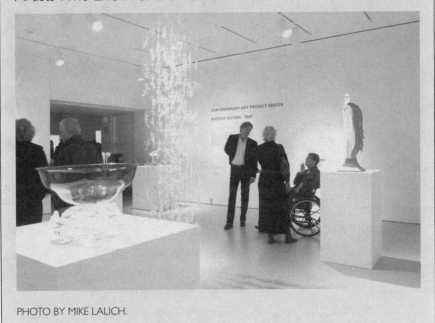

PHOTO BY MIKE LALICH.

Ontario. The new programs that grew out of their injection of life-giving energy have been too many to detail here; three particular programming developments are especially important because they reflect a new openness, inclusiveness, and responsiveness to contemporary community ideas and desires at the AGH. These programs have succeeded in generating a new relationship to our local constituents, one that continues to participate in the growth and texture of Hamilton beyond the gallery walls. The goal was, and still is:

- to treat all aspects of AGH activities in a holistic way, shaping and planning a layered program that showcases new talent as it contextualizes work in established practice;
- to make room for expression of community achievements as a means of helping to build and shape that community;
- to treat everybody who walks through the AGH door, regardless of their motivation to do so, as a potential lifelong friend to the gallery.

Three specific initiatives in pursuit of these objectives are:

- developing new membership benefits
- creating a community gallery space
- establishing the Atelier Series of exhibitions, which spotlight work by Canadian artists with roots in the area.

MEMBERSHIP

After the gallery reopened in 2005, renewing interest in membership became an imperative. There was a redoubled effort to reach past members and draw new ones, because membership is the gallery's primary way of creating a real sense of ownership among community residents. These are the people who support and populate the gallery—at the AGH, over 80 percent of members come from the greater Hamilton area, and over 75 percent from the City of Hamilton proper.

AGH membership aims to include people from all walks of life, but in the past the gallery's membership has had fewer members than the average for public galleries in cities of the size of Hamilton. The AGH continues to try to reach out to all members of the diverse communities in Hamilton. It is a continuous challenge to meet and engage with many people from the community, who are unaware, uninterested, or perhaps intimidated by the gallery. As a response, it has become a new goal to reach every visitor or user—including those in the gallery for purposes unrelated

Figure 12.2. In Conjunction with the Art Gallery of Hamilton's *The Feast: Food in Art* exhibition, Meredith Chilton, founding curator of Gardiner Museum of Ceramic Art, gives an Informative Talk on the History of Tea and Porcelain to AGH Members

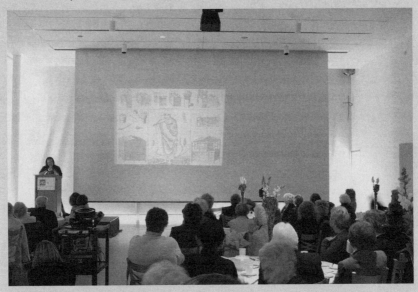

PHOTO BY MIKE LALICH.

to art. The AGH's holistic mantra therefore requires an integrated response from the gallery's departments for special events, hospitality, retail, and, of course, membership.

Of particular interest in this context, the AGH has implemented new learning programs for members. In the form of special evening lectures and a regular schedule of Tea and Tours, the AGH offers intimate access for members to exhibitions. These events are in addition to regular educational programming, and members have responded overwhelmingly to programming offered exclusively for them, enjoying privileged access to curators and artists.

A year after the reopening of the gallery building, our efforts had already met with a resounding success. By the summer of 2006 the AGH had grown its membership from 900 to 1,600, and currently projects continued expansion. It is true that membership is not a primary source of revenue to the gallery—but members are invaluable in that they are our best ambassadors to the local area and beyond. They are also that sector of our community whose motivations can best be met by the provision of an enjoyable, intelligent, and focused art museum learning program.

COMMUNITY GALLERY

The Jean and Ross Fischer "Community" Gallery developed as a direct response to community members and local artist collectives. Many people felt alienated from the gallery: community residents expressed resentment at the programming decision to focus less on the permanent collection (some of it donated directly or with funds raised by the community), and local artists didn't feel that the AGH was interested in exhibiting their work.

The Community Gallery became part of the Gallery's new vision, and has become a highly successful and much loved part of our programming. Designed to respond to community groups and art associations seeking a connection with the Gallery, it offers a way for the AGH to accommodate programming that may not be right for general gallery exhibition, but is integral to our mandate. We value our relationship to this particular community of artists. They represent a large proportion of the local art lovers whom the Gallery relies upon as loyal visitors, and also have connections to many Hamiltonians who may not otherwise visit the Gallery. Exhibitions

Figure 12.3. Exhibition Opening Reception for *Ferdinando Bilanzola: Visual Sensations*, part of a Citywide Collaborative Retrospective of the Work of the Late Hamilton Painter Ferdinando "Fred" Bilanzola

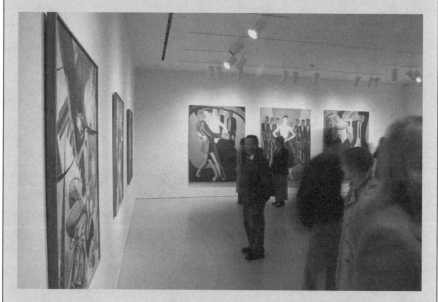

PHOTO BY MIKE LALICH.

in this space are organized and presented by individuals or groups, but benefit from arms-length curatorial input and support from our preparatory staff in order to assure they meet the highest standards of professional exhibition.

The Community Gallery began by rekindling the Gallery's previous long relationship with the Women's Art Association, who in turn gave the Gallery a significant donation to demonstrate their gratitude and cement the bond. It has grown to include regular shows from the WAA as well as from the Hamilton Region Branch of The Architectural Conservancy of Ontario, and by students and instructors at local Mohawk College. In addition, the Gallery hosts special exhibitions in partnership with local and regional projects, such as an exhibition of contemporary Colombian art that was on view in conjunction with the Hamilton YMCA's Peace Week celebrations.

During the summer of 2006, the Community Gallery played host to an exhibition of industrial photography by a local commercial photographer, Tom Bochsler. Hamilton has been called 'the Pittsburgh of Canada' and 'the Birmingham of Canada,' depending on the speaker's American or English origins. Bochsler's images from the heyday of Hamilton's steel production were mainly taken in response to commercial commissions. Their depictions of majestic machinery during that era speak to an idealized optimistic future fueled by technological developments. But they are also and above all beautiful and prideful reminders of Hamilton's industrial heritage—or, as one visitor wrote in Bochsler's guestbook: "thank you, Tom, for capturing the proud traditions in Hamilton's history and the people who made it work." The Community Gallery provides the AGH with a meaningful and appropriate way of responding to community aspirations and motivations, thereby drawing a far wider public into art museum learning experiences.

ATELIER SERIES

In addition to the programming in the Community Gallery, the AGH new vision also sought to include exhibitions by emerging contemporary artists from or living in the Hamilton area. The Atelier Series of exhibitions was developed as a way of integrating local artistic endeavors into the broader programming vision. The idea is to show recent work by contemporary artists connected to Hamilton, strategically placed within a wide artistic framework. The work is positioned in the context of both historical and international work, allowing the artists and viewers to get a sense of how certain media, techniques, themes, or cultures are expressed from different perspectives and over time.

Significantly, these exhibitions can provide new avenues for engagement with contemporary art, which is otherwise often the most challenging for many viewers. Local work offers a closer connection, serving as a grounding context for the presentation of international contemporary work. Similarly, placing it in relation to historical art offers a way of engaging visitors in contemporary art who are not normally interested in 'the new,' and a way of getting those committed to contemporary art to consider its historical context as well. This is museum learning fitted to the motivations of very different components of our market.

The Atelier series aims to give deserving local talent a presence on the national scene. This exposure can also have the effect of creating relationships between artists and collectors in the community, a means of potentially strengthening the future of the AGH collection and providing guidance and education for local collectors of contemporary art. Rather than being forced to rely exclusively on commercial venues, local artists have an opportunity to exhibit in the broader context of a public gallery, where local collectors can discover them in a more interpreted context than a private gallery would offer.

CONCLUSION

The ideas discussed here are not revolutionary. But their sensitive implementation has made them uniquely our own. They are successful not because the Gallery wishes to tick the right box or generate particular demographics—but because of a genuine desire to feed and be fed by the eyes and minds of our nearest neighbors—to tap into them as a resource, and to be an inspiring place for them in turn. While the Gallery continues to present the permanent collection and major temporary exhibitions in its mainstream galleries, these programs in membership, the Community Gallery and the Atelier series of exhibitions are ongoing methods of enhancing the museum learning experiences that we offer, and fitting them to the diverse motivations of our community.

Refocusing the audience research lens on understanding motivations is a necessary but admittedly tricky proposition. Motivations are reflections of our sensibilities and desires—textured, layered, and complex. And meeting individual expectations in a meaningful way is no easy task. Cultural consumers, whether seasoned or novice, purist or hybrid, seek and deserve rich—and enriching—experiences. Ultimately, neither the audience nor the museum will be satisfied by sound bites from a sample menu.

Providing multiple points of entry, and more importantly, reentry, does not require an institution to be all things to all people. In this new millennium, despite the onslaught of postmodernism and subsequent trends at the end of the twentieth century, the modernist mantra still resonates: *less is more*, and quality transcends. Making this meaningful for museum learning, and making it work for museum visitors, is the challenge to museum professionals today. In some cases, orientation and interpretation are sorely needed, whereas in other instances the best that the museum educator can do is get out of the way so that the individual adult museum visitors' motivations may be met. The museum that succeeds in doing both at once may fairly hope to sustain all sides of its increasingly diverse audience, and provide meaningful museum learning for everyone.

NOTES

1. The report on this survey, by Francie Ostrower, titled *Motivations Matter: Findings and Practical Implications of a National Survey of Cultural Participation*, is based on the 2004 study commissioned by the Wallace Foundation and conducted by the Urban Institute.

2. Jan Packer proposes some theoretical constructs for motivations of museum learners in "Learning for Fun: The Unique Contribution of Educational Leisure Experiences," *Curator: The Museum Journal* 49, no. 3 (July 2006). See also Bill Ivey and Steven J. Tepper, "Cultural Renaissance or Cultural Divide?" in *The Chronicle of Higher Education* (May 19, 2006).

3. This was first observed from the findings of the NEA national survey of arts participation, National Endowment for the Arts, 1998. "Survey of Public Participation in the Arts, Summary Report." *Research Division Report No. 39*. Washington, D.C.: National Endowment for the Arts.

4. This argument is furthered in Chris Walker's follow up on study published by the Urban Institute in 2003, *Arts Participation: Steps to Stronger Cultural and Community Life*.

Conclusion

BARRY LORD

In concluding, let's remember that museum learning is informal learning, and that to be effective, informal learning has to be fun. Let's remember that most of our visitors want to see the real thing, and that we have the sacred trust of giving them that—so that in some cases, as Mira Goldfarb observes in her concluding chapter, less is more and the best thing that a museum educator can do is get out of the way and allow the enjoyment and the learning to flow.

And let's remember that despite the low budgets, confined space, restricted facilities, and outmoded equipment that many of us have to work with, museum learning remains a matter between men and women, boys and girls, meeting one another, and learning as much from one another as from the objects in the room. Museum learning seems to be about objects, but is really about people.

And finally, let's remember that the lifelong learning that we have assigned to ourselves and others is a vital task in the twenty-first century. A world based on lifelong learning will be a better world. Those of us working on museum learning are at the center of a process of transformation that is fundamental to the survival and flourishing of our species. Enjoy.

Glossary

Audioguide: a portable device distributed or rented for visitors to use to listen to prerecorded narratives which provide information supplemental to text panels and labels, allowing them independence and mobility as they tour an exhibition.

Affective learning: is learning based on emotion and feeling, leading to a transformation of attitudes, interests, appreciation, beliefs, or values.

Community of origin: the people from whom either an object or a collection originated, or the social context in which an object or a collection have meaning.

Cultural tourism: visits by persons from outside the host community motivated wholly or in part by interest in the historical, artistic, scientific, or lifestyle/heritage offerings of a community, region, group, or institution.

Front-end evaluation: is used to test concepts and ideas during the initial stages of exhibition and programming development and planning (both onsite and online); the evaluation is undertaken in order to better understand intended audiences and to predict how visitors will respond to the final product.

Interpretative planning: a process concerned with projecting the quality and content of communication between a museum and its visitors, usually comprising an exhibition treatment, an interpretative plan, a script, an evaluation strategy, and an implementation schedule.

Museums of conscience: contemporary cultural institutions with or without collections that respond consciously to the issues of inclusion and relevance that have characterized museums from their beginnings by dealing with compelling topics such as racism or genocide; often but not always located at historic sites, these institutions seek to raise awareness and inspire social consciousness.

Museum schools: educational institutions that offer a range of museum-based learning initiatives, often but not always through partnerships between schools and museums.

Object theater: an enhanced presentation to a museum audience that may include displays of artifacts, specimens, works of art, replicas or other static or animated objects and/or display props, together with an audio program, a lighting program, and projected images and figures, either live or animatronic, that tell a story or explain a theme in a focused and evocative way.

Outcomes-based evaluation: a systematic way to determine if a program or exhibition has achieved its goals, after determining and defining the criteria by which success is measured; the criteria are focused on the results for those who experienced the program or exhibition.

Piaget's Stages of Cognitive Development[1]: refer to the four stages of human cognitive development identified by Jean Piaget (1896–1980), all of which should be considered when developing museum exhibits and programs (online and onsite). The four stages include:

- Sensorimotor Stage: children in this stage demonstrate their intelligence through physical motor activity without the use of symbols and possess limited knowledge that is based on physical experiences or interactions.
- Preoperational Stage: at this stage, children begin to demonstrate the use of symbols; language, memory and imagination are developed, but thinking remains illogical.
- Concrete Operations Stage: operational thinking is developed at this stage; intelligence is demonstrated through the logical and calculated use of symbols.
- Formal Operational Stage: in the final stage, symbols related to abstract concepts are used.

Summative evaluation: visitor research conducted when a physical or online exhibition or program is completed to assess whether access, communication, or other goals have been achieved, in order to determine improvements to be made in this or future projects

Transformative learning: refers to learning that occurs when individuals redefine their worldview through changes to their frames of reference by critically reflecting on their previously held assumptions and beliefs, emotions and feelings.

Universal design: a process of conceiving, developing and detailing products, communications, or the built environment to make them more usable at little or no extra cost, benefiting people of all ages and abilities. Principles of universal design include: equitable use, flexibility, simplicity, low physical effort, tolerance for error, perceptible information, and size and space for approach and use.

Visible storage: provision of public visual access to a museum collection by means of a systematic presentation of objects in storage, with open catalogs, either electronic or printed, providing interpretation in a systematic way.

Web cast: a method of communicating audio and/or video material using the Internet, analogous to television or radio broadcasts.

NOTES

1. Atherton, J. S. (2005) *Learning and Teaching: Piaget's developmental theory.* Available at http://www.learningandteaching.info/learning/piaget.htm (accessed: 13 November 2006).

Bibliography

A selected and annotated list of publications on museum learning, 2000–2006.

Ash, D. "Dialogic Inquiry of Family Groups in a Science Museum," *Journal of Research in Science Teaching* 40, no. 2 (2003): 138–62.

Ash, D. "How Families Use Questions at Dioramas: Ideas for Exhibit Design," *Curator* 41, no. 1 (2004).

Atkinson, Dennis, and Paul Dash, eds. *Social and Critical Practices in Art Education*. Stoke on Trent, UK: Trentham Books, 2005. Art educators from several countries and working with all ages write about their innovative projects with young people. Topics covered include the use of museums and galleries for teaching young children about art, and one case study describes a gallery project with disaffected teenagers.

Barr, Jean. "Dumbing Down Intellectual Culture: Frank Furedi, Lifelong Learning and Museums," *Museum and Society* 3, no. 2 (2005): 98–114. Examines the ongoing debate between those who defend wider access and social inclusion policies and practices on the part of art galleries and museums; and those who fear that this can lead to oversimplification or dumbing down of complex ideas and artworks.

Bentley, Michael L. "Community-Connected Science Education: Creating a Museum High School for Southwestern Virginia," http://www.ed.psu.edu/CI/Journals/2002aets/s1_bentley.rtf

Carr, David. *The Promise of Cultural Institutions*. Walnut Creek, CA: Altamira, 2003. Carr examines the experience of learning, particularly as it relates to visitors to cultural institutions.

Chadwick, Alan, and Annette Stannett, eds. *Museums and Adult Learning: Perspectives from Europe*. Leicester: NIACE, 2000. Addresses the creative approaches taken to encourage museum use by those who still see museums as exclusion zones. This book, published in the United Kingdom, looks to examples from other European countries on how they deal with this issue.

Chermayeff, Jane Clark, Robert J. Blandford, and Carol M. Losos. "Working at play: informal science education on museum playgrounds," *Curator* 44, no. 1 (2001): 47–59. Discusses the importance of play in informal science education, and relates this to the trend toward outdoor science playgrounds at museums.

Chew, R. "In Praise of the Small Museums," *Museum News* (2002): 36–41.

Creative Networks: Knowledge and Inspiration. "The Victoria and Albert Museum's Strategy for Learning." London: V&A, 2001. http://edward.vam.ac.uk/files/file_upload/learning_strategy.pdf (accessed 25 January 2006). The Victoria and Albert Museum's Strategy for Learning outlines the museum's role as a center for public learning.

Crowley, K., M. Callanan, H. Tenenbaum, and E. Allen. "Parents Explain More Often to Boys Than to Girls During Shared Scientific Thinking," *Psychological Science* 12, no. 3 (2001): 258–61.

DCMS. *The Learning Power of Museums: A Vision for Museum Education*. London: Department for Culture, Media and Sport. Sets out the UK government's vision of how museums and galleries can enhance the learning process. It includes a range of case studies.

Duesning, S. "Culture Matters: Informal Science Centers and Cultural Contexts," *Learning in Places: The Informal Education Reader*. Oxford, UK: Peter Lang Publishers, forthcoming.

Duncan, C., and A Wallach. "The Universal Survey Museum," *Museum Studies: An Anthology of Contexts*. Maldern, MA: Blackwell Publishing, Ltd. 2004.

Falk, John H., and Lynn D. Dierking. *Learning from Museums: Visitor Experiences and the Making of Meaning*. Walnut Creek, CA: AltaMira Press, 2000. Explains the nature and process of learning as it occurs within the museum context and provides advice on how museums can create better learning environments.

Falk, John H., ed. *Free-choice science education*. New York and London: Teachers College, Columbia University, 2001.

Falk, John H. "The Contribution of Free-choice Learning to Public Understanding of Science," *Interciencia* 27 (2002): 62–65.

Falk, John H., Carol Scott, Lynn Dierking, Leonie Rennie, and Mika Cohen Jones. "Interactives and Visitor Learning," *Curator* 47, no. 2 (2004): 171–98. Considers the nature of learning that happens when visitors use interactives—computers and other multimedia components, physical manipulatives, and simulations—in the museum setting.

Gould, Hanna. *Settings Other Than Schools: Initial Teacher Training Placements in Museums, Galleries, and Archives*. Yorkshire Museum, Libraries and Archives Council, June 2003.

Guisasola, J., M. Morentin, and K. Zusa. "School Visits to Science Museums and Learning Sciences: A Complex Relationship," *Physics Education* 40, no. 6 (2005).

Gurian, Elaine Heumann. 'Free at Last, A Case for Eliminating Admission Charges in Museums,' *Museum News* (September/October 2005). Presents the case for eliminating admission charges, allowing museums to be freely accessible.

Gurian, Elaine Heumann. 'Function Follows Form: How Mixed-Use Spaces in Museums Build Community,' *Curator* 44, no. 1 (2001): 97–113.

Gurian, Elaine Heumann. 'Threshold Fear,' *Reshaping Museum Space: Architecture, Design, Exhibitions*. London: Routledge, 2005.

Hein, George E. "John Dewey and Museum Education," *Curator* 47, no. 4 (2004): 413–427. Discussion of John Dewey is usually focused on his educational theory. In this article, Hein discusses Dewey's writings on the subject of museums.

Hein, Hilde. *The Museum in Transition: A Philosophical Perspective*. Washington, D.C.: Smithsonian Institution Press, 2000. As museums strive to become more responsive to the interests of a diverse public, Hein warns us that glorifying the museum experience at the expense of objects deflects the museum's educative, ethical, and aesthetic roles.

Hirsch, Joanne, ed. *Transforming Practice: Selections from the* Journal of Museum Education, *1992–1999*. Washington, D.C.: Museum Education Roundtable, 2000. A collection of articles from Museum Education Roundtable's *Journal of Museum Education*. The articles consider the changing theoretical basis of museology.

Hooper-Greenhill, E., and T. Moussouri. *Researching Learning in Museums and Galleries: A Bibliographic Review*. Leicester: RCMG, 2002.

Hooper-Greenhill, Eilean. "Learning from Culture: The Importance of the Museums and Galleries Education Program (Phase I) in England," *Curator* 47, no. 4 (2004): 428–49. A discussion of the British government initiative, The Museums and Galleries Education Program, including an assessment of its impact.

Hooper-Greenhill, Eilean, and Jocelyn Dodd. *Museum and Gallery Education and the Area Museum Councils of England: Evaluating the Education Challenge Fund*. London: Research Centre for Museums and Galleries, University of Leicester, 2001.

Hooper-Greenhill, Eilean, Jocelyn Dodd et al. *Inspiration, Identity, Learning: The Value of Museums*. London: Department for Culture, Media and Sport, 2004. This publication is based on the impact of DCMS/DfES Strategic Commissioning of the 2003–2004 National/Regional Museum Education Partnerships.

Institute of Museum and Library Services. "True Needs, True Partners: Museums Serving Schools." http://www.imls.gov/pdf/m-ssurvey.pdf (accessed 2005).

Ivey, Bill, and Steven J. Tepper. "Cultural Renaissance or Cultural Divide?" *The Chronicle of Higher Education* (19 May 2006).

Johnson, Bradley. "Understanding the 'Generation Wireless' Demographic: The Nearly Bionic Relationship of Teenagers and their Cellphones," *Digger News*. http://www.diggernews.com/NC/0/274.html (accessed 2006).

Kavanagh, Gaynor. *Dream Spaces: Memory and the Museum*. London: Leicester University Press, 2000. A study of memory and the museum, exploring what the author calls the "dream space," the nonrational and reflective experience of encountering material and ourselves within the museum.

LaPlaca Cohen and *The New Yorker*. *Making Culture Count, Research Report*. Mediamark Research Interactive, vol. 3, 2005.

Leinhardt, Gaea et. al. *Learning Conversations in Museums.* Mahwah, NJ: Lawrence Erlbaum, 2002. Discusses how museum conversations can reflect and change a visitor's viewpoint, discipline-specific knowledge, and engagement with the institution. It also examines what knowledge people retain over long and short periods of time.

Lin, Chyong-Ling. *Adopting Marketing Strategies in Museums.* Doctoral dissertation, University of South Dakota (UMI No. 3007069), 2001.

Lindauer, Margaret A. "From Salad Bars to Vivid Stories: Four Game Plans for Developing 'Educationally Successful' Exhibitions,'" *Museum Management and Curatorship* 20, no. 1 (2005): 41–55. This paper addresses the challenge among exhibition development team members to agree upon a shared game plan, and recommends the use of curriculum theories as a tool for overcoming this challenge.

Mezirow, Jack et al. *Learning as Transformation.* San Francisco: Jossey-Bass, 2000. A collection of essays examining adult education theory, which serves to assist cultural institutions in better addressing the adult audience and encouraging lifelong learning.

Osborne, M., J. Gallacher, and B. Crossan, eds. *Researching Widening Access to Lifelong Learning: Issues and Approaches in International Research.* London: Routledge Falmer, 2004. An exploration of how research into increasing access to lifelong learning can most effectively be conducted and the different forms it can take, as well as its significance and value for education policy.

Ostrower, Francie. *Motivations Matter: Findings and Practical Implications of a National Survey of Cultural Participation,* The Urban Institute with the Wallace Foundation, 2004.

Packer, Jan. "Learning for Fun: The Unique Contribution of Educational Leisure Experiences," *Curator: The Museum Journal* 49, no. 3 (July 2006). Proposes some theoretical constructs for motivations of museum learners.

Paris, S. G., ed. *Perspectives on Object-centered Learning in Museums.* Mahwah, NJ, Lawrence Erlbaum Associates, 2002.

Phillips, M. *Museum-schools: Hybrid Spaces for Accessing Learning.* San Francisco, CA: Center for Informal Learning and Schools, 2006.

Piscitelli, B., and D. Anderson. "Young Children's Learning in Museum Settings," *Visitor Studies Today* 3, no. 3 (2000).

Puchner, Laurel, Robyn Rapoport, and Suzanne Gaskins. "Learning in Children's Museums: Is it Really Happening?" *Curator* 44, no. 3 (2001): 237–59. This study looks at the kinds of observable learning that occurs in museums while children are interacting with exhibits at a children's museum, and suggests that learning is more likely to occur with adult interaction than without.

Ramirez, J. "New York Museum Opens Vaults to Public," *Associated Press,* 23 January 2001.

Rentschler, Ruth. "Museum and Performing Arts Marketing: The Age of Discovery," *Journal of Arts Management, Law, and Society* 32, nos. 7–8 (2002).

Sachatello-Sawyer, Bonnie. *Adult Museum Programs: Designing Meaningful Experiences*. Walnut Creek, CA: AltaMira Press, 2002. This book provides twelve basic steps a museum educator can use to design meaningful experiences for adult programs.

Silverman, L. H. "The Therapeutic Potential of Museums as Pathways to Inclusion," *Museums, Society, Inequality*. London and New York: Routledge, 2002.

Soren, B. J. "The Learning Cultural Organization of the Millennium: Performance Measures and Audience Response," *International Journal of Arts Management* 2, no. 2 (2000): 40–49.

Soren, B. J. *Constructing Meaning and Online Museum User Experience*. Creating and Managing Digital Content Tip Sheet, Canadian Heritage Information Network (CHIN), 2004: http://www.chin.gc.ca/English/Digital_Content/ Tip_Sheets/constructivism.html.

Soren, B. J. *Quality in Online Experience for Museum Users*. Ottawa, ON: Canadian Heritage Information Network (CHIN), 2004: http://www.rcip.gc.ca/ Francais/Contenu_Numerique/Recherche_Qualite/index.html; http://www.chin.gc.ca/English/Digital_Content/Research_Quality/index.html.

Soren, B. J. "Best Practices in Creating Quality Online Experiences for Museum Users (with Canadian Heritage Information Network)," *Museum Management and Curatorship* 20, no. 2 (2005): 131–48.

Talboys, Graeme K. *Museum Educator's Handbook,* 2d ed. Aldershot, UK and Burlington, VT: Ashgate, 2005. A guide to setting up and running education services in all types of museums, including very small ones.

Thompson, Jane. *Bread and Roses: Arts, Culture and Lifelong Learning,* Leicester: NIACE, 2002. Explores the relationship between arts and culture and lifelong learning, especially in overcoming social exclusion.

True Needs, True Partners: Museums Serving Schools: 2002 Survey Highlights. Washington, D.C.: Institute of Museum and Library Services, 2002.

Vom Lehn, D., C. Heath, and J. Hindmarsh. "Exhibiting Interaction: Conduct and Collaboration in Museums and Galleries," *Symbolic Interation* 24, no. 2 (2001): 189–216.

Walker, Chris. *Arts Participation: Steps to Stronger Cultural and Community Life*. Washington, D.C.: The Urban Institute, 2003

Wedde, I. *Making Ends Meet: Essays and Talks 1992–2004*. Wellington, NZ: Victoria University Press, 2005.

Williams, George. "Multi-generational marketing for non-profits," *Community Ties: An E-Newsletter from Planned Legacy*, 2002: http://www.plannedlegacy .com/newsletter/fall2002/generationalmarketing.html.

Index